MARIS
& MANTLE

Books by Tony Castro

Chicano Power: The Emergence of Mexican America

Mickey Mantle: America's Prodigal Son

The Prince of South Waco: American Dreams and Great Expectations

DiMag & Mick: Sibling Rivals, Yankee Blood Brothers

Looking for Hemingway: The Lost Generation and A Final Rite of Passage

Gehrig & The Babe: The Friendship and The Feud

Mantle: The Best There Ever Was

MARIS & MANTLE

Two Yankees, Baseball Immortality, and the Age of Camelot

Tony Castro

TRIUMPH
BOOKS

Library of Congress Cataloguing in Publication Data available upon request.

This book is available in quantity at special discounts for your group or organization. For further information, contact:

Triumph Books LLC
814 North Franklin Street
Chicago, Illinois 60610
(312) 337-0747
www.triumphbooks.com

Printed in U.S.A.
ISBN: 978-1-63727-174-2
Design by Patricia Frey

For Renee
and
Jeter

"Like the Arthurian years at Camelot, the Sixties constituted a breakthrough, a fleeting moment of glory, a time when a significant little chunk of humanity briefly realized its moral potential and flirted with its neurological destiny, a collective spiritual awakening that flared brilliantly until the barbaric and mediocre impulses of the species drew tight once more the curtains of darkness."

—TOM ROBBINS

Contents

Prologue

*"I don't want to be Babe Ruth. He was a great
ballplayer. I'm not trying to replace him. The
record is there and damn right I want to
break it, but that isn't replacing Babe Ruth."*

—ROGER MARIS

PRESIDENTIAL HISTORIAN ARTHUR SCHLESINGER JR. ONCE ASTONISHED
a Harvard University symposium on the age of Kennedy with the
stunning observation that the early 1960s in America were possibly
defined as much by baseball superstars Roger Maris and Mickey
Mantle as they were by president John F. Kennedy himself. It was
unexpected praise for Maris and Mantle from the trusted confidant
and biographer of the 35th president of the United States that elicited
questioning glances and some laughs from a mystified audience
of graduate students, professors, and fellow intellectuals. Was this
brilliant, popular Harvard professor, who was known for his trademark
bow ties, serious, or was he simply inserting a bit of levity into an
otherwise staid, scholarly reappraisal of the time of JFK?

Even the academics in the crowd who were acquainted with
Schlesinger and shared his love of baseball didn't know. Few of them

were even aware that this son of the influential historian Arthur M. Schlesinger Sr., and now a leading historian of American presidents himself had once obsessed over the same dream that tantalizes most boys throughout the country. "When I am a man I wish to be a fast-ball player," seven-year-old Schlesinger wrote in one of his earliest letters. "I would like to be a fast-ball player because I am interested in fast-ball, because it is a good sport and because it is fun."

Young Arthur was passionate about the game. Attending Red Sox games at Fenway Park and Braves game at the South End Grounds, talking baseball, and mourning the loss of Babe Ruth to the Yankees was how he and his father bonded, developing a close relationship that led to books and history. Ever the sentimentalist for his local teams, Schlesinger years later would often complain that, "pro baseball died the day the Braves moved out of Boston." Ultimately, Schlesinger stepped into his father's shoes as a leading American historian interested in big personalities, liberal politics, and a democratic world view—an egalitarian crusader who would remark that we suffer today from "too much *pluribus* and not enough *unum*." Thus, to Schlesinger, presidents and ballplayers were really part of the same national fabric, the nation and its pastime, especially that period when the age of Camelot met the age of Mantle and Maris.

"It was an age when anything seemed possible—made to seem possible by men who dared to dream and achieve what was thought to be impossible—and the men who best symbolized this new age were John F. Kennedy, a president no one expected could be president, and Roger Maris and Mickey Mantle, two teammates who, in chasing the immortal Babe Ruth, brought him back to life," Schlesinger told the symposium. "It was an age of innocence in America we may never see again."

In the first two years of the new decade, Maris and Mantle established themselves as the peacetime heroes of America's romance with boldness, its celebration of power, a nation's Arthurian self-confidence in strength during a time when we last thought might did make right. In the age of Kennedy, their heroics cast them as figures through which an America profoundly affected by nuclear fear, by a dizzying plethora of atomic panaceas and proposals, and by endless speculation on the social and ethical implications of the new world's reality, reconciled the conscious and unconscious aspects of the national psyche. In his inaugural address that was at once soaring and solemn, Kennedy had summoned Americans to harness realism to idealism, patriotism to service, and national interest to universal aspiration. This was the time and place, he said, insisting, "I do not believe that any of us would exchange places with any other people or any other generation."

Almost immediately, Mantle and Maris emerged as exemplars of their time. In 1961, the two New York Yankee sluggers brought baseball to the forefront of American pop culture for possibly the last time, as its place as the country's national pastime would soon be overtaken by the National Football League. "If this tale were fiction, the contest between the duo renowned as the M&M Boys might seem too contrived," presidential historian Michael Beschloss would observe half a century later. "In the summer of 1961, the Yankees' Roger Maris and Mickey Mantle competed to break the home run record of a Yankee predecessor, the most famous baseball player of them all, Babe Ruth—60 homers during the 1927 season. For later generations, the two men established an abiding lesson in civility and friendship. Resisting some fans and reporters who were determined to pit these two very different Yankees against each other, the irrepressible, sometimes loutish Mantle, from Commerce,

[Oklahoma], and Maris—the headstrong, introverted Croatian-American from Hibbing, [Minnesota], and Fargo, [North Dakota]—managed to keep their rivalry under control."

It's possible that Americans will never again be as focused on any sporting accomplishment as we were that year. Has there ever been another season in sports that has spawned so many reminiscences, so much commentary, so much myth and legend? Perhaps it was the innocence of that period. In a sense, Maris and Mantle were tailor-made heroes for America in the age of Camelot. In them, the country saw more proof that there were no worldly boundaries and that nothing seemed beyond the reach of American power, or of Americans' ability. The American Century was at its pinnacle. U.S. wealth and prosperity were unrivaled. Hollywood, rock music, blue jeans, and hamburgers carried American pop culture, tastes, and values to the far corners of the world. This was the New Frontier. Roger Maris had broken the Babe's record. America would soon be going to the moon. It was an innocence, which would soon have the hubris in that sentiment exposed.

There would still be moments when all seemed right. The early years of the new decade marked the beginning of a new, if brief, period in the country—the Kennedy years. President John F. Kennedy was an avid fan of his hometown Boston Red Sox, but even he couldn't ignore the specialness of the Yankees. As spring training camps opened in 1962, the country's young president wanted to cheer up his father, Joseph P. Kennedy, who was recovering in Palm Beach from a stroke he had suffered in late 1961. President Kennedy dispatched a couple Secret Service agents to nearby West Palm Beach, where the Yankees were playing an exhibition game, and asked Mickey Mantle, Yogi Berra, Whitey Ford, and Tony Kubek if they would kindly pay a visit to the elder Kennedy. The four Yankees obliged and spent part of an

afternoon with the Kennedy family patriarch talking baseball among themselves as the president's father listened attentively. The stroke had left Joe Kennedy without his speech, but Ford recalled that "you could tell he was interested in what we had to say and grateful for our visit." While in office, President Kennedy saw Mantle play in person only once, in the 1962 All-Star Game at D.C. Stadium where he threw out the first pitch, shook hands with many of the players, including Mickey, and said to Stan Musial, "A couple of years ago, they told me I was too young to be president and you were too old to be playing baseball. But we fooled them."

Kennedy lamented that Maris had not been among the Yankees who had visited the family's Florida compound. But perhaps the new president did not understand that the still fairly new Yankee slugger wasn't one who thought house calls were part of his job. Whitey Ford would joke that year that he was going to form his own presidential cabinet made up of ballplayers. Maris, he said, would be named Secretary of Grievances. Kennedy, though, was insistent. Several weeks later, he invited Roger to the White House when the Yankees opened their first series that season against the Senators in Washington on Friday, April 27. Having just returned to the White House from his Florida vacation, Kennedy presided over a meeting of the National Security Council with vice president Lyndon Johnson, attorney general Robert Kennedy, secretary of state Dean Rusk, and secretary of defense Robert McNamara among the attendees. As he waited in an outer office, Roger watched as many of the president's inner circle, the best and the brightest of the JFK administration, streamed out of the Oval Office.

"Roger told me it was the best on-deck experience of his life," Mantle later recalled. "I said, 'Well, pardner, that's how I felt being on-deck behind you last season!'"

As he entered the Oval Office, Maris was handed a baseball by the president, who asked for an autograph. It would be a historic signed baseball all its own, bearing the signatures of President Kennedy and Roger Maris, that was later auctioned at the National Multiple Sclerosis Society's annual fundraising drive. Maris and Kennedy talked briefly as they posed for photographs, with the president offering both his personal congratulations and an apology. He had hoped to make that night's ballgame at D.C. Stadium but had to join secretary of state Rusk in a helicopter ride to meet British prime minister Harold Macmillan at Andrews Air Force Base. Macmillan and Kennedy were scheduled to attend the White House Correspondents and News Photographers dinner that evening.

"I wish I could be there to see you hit one tonight," the president told Maris. "Hit one for my father, will you?"

"I'll do my best, Mr. President," Maris said.

In the sixth inning that night, Roger belted a two-out, solo home run off Senators right-handed reliever Ray Rippelmeyer, who was pitching in what would be his only season in the majors. Upon hearing of this that night at the White House Correspondents dinner, a tuxedoed JFK boasted to Kenneth O'Donnell, his special assistant and appointments secretary, "Kenny, d'ya heah that? Maris promised to hit one out for his president, and he did exactly that! Who needs Babe Ruth?"

But, a star that burns so bright perhaps only burns for half as long. The Roger Maris of 1962 was not the Roger Maris of 1961. He had set an impossible bar for himself, even as he hit 33 home runs and drove in 100 runs, leading the Yankees, even with Mantle often injured, to another American League pennant and one more World Series championship. But it would be the last World Series title in a magnificent post–World War II run for the New York Yankees, who had won 10 championships since 1947 and been in all but two fall classics in those 16 years. They would not win another title until 1977.

So sudden a fall from such a rapid rise in Camelot. The booing never let up on Roger, and the news media crucified him.

"What we have here is a cautionary tale for a media age," the late author and historian David Halberstam observed in revisiting Maris' Yankee years. "A good portrait of a decent, honest, square man determined to be himself, and unable to match in heroic words and luminescent personality what a hungry and attentive fan base wanted to go with his heroic deeds. In other ways, he was doomed to disappoint a newly created media world."

Roger's troubles there near the peak of his career seemed to reflect the increasing calamities in a global world flipped upside down in this new atomic age. Kennedy kicked off his presidency with the Bay of Pigs debacle in Cuba and showdowns with Fidel Castro and Nikita Khrushchev, a wall now divided Berlin, literary lion Ernest Hemingway committed suicide in Idaho, and a race war threatened to erupt in the segregated South. It was getting harder to believe that all would turn out all right. Life wasn't exactly something you could count on with loaded dice or a stacked deck of cards. There was a ballplayer's confidence, like believing he was going to get a hit every time he walked to the plate, and there was the reality of knowing that was impossible. What was it that Mark Twain said about faith in *Pudd'nhead Wilson's New Calendar*? "There are those who scoff at the schoolboy, calling him frivolous and shallow. Yet it was the schoolboy who said, 'Faith is believing what you know ain't so.'"

By the mid-1960s, the new president had been assassinated, the Yankee dynasty was dead, and Roger Maris, the Yankee who had broken Babe Ruth's 34-year-old single-season home run record, was no longer playing in New York. By the end of the decade, Americans were being forced to accept limits to U.S. power and to acknowledge that their reach had exceeded their grasp. With apologies to Robert Browning, that troublesome realization was not what they believed a heaven was for.

1

1959: The Devaluation of Mick

*"Throughout most of my life, I was a
hero to many people. I was as big as
Elvis. But what no one ever understood
is that it never meant squat to me."*
—MICKEY MANTLE

THROUGHOUT THE EARLY WINTER AFTER THE 1959 SEASON, MICKEY
Mantle brooded more than he usually did with the restlessness of the
baseball off-season. By then, he and wife, Merlyn, were quietly settled
in their new home in the Preston Hollow section of North Dallas.
Their three boys—Mickey Jr., six; David, four; and Billy, two—were
young and healthy, and Merlyn was pregnant and expecting in March.

Only a year earlier, a moving van pulled up in front of a low-
slung ranch home at the corner of Watson Circle and Jamestown,
interrupting a Kool-Aid party on the intersection. The neighborhood
kids knew about the new residents. The story had been all over the
news. Mickey Mantle, the biggest sports star in America, was moving
to Dallas. The pride of Commerce, Oklahoma, and the New York
Yankees was relocating his young family to Dallas so he could oversee
his new bowling alley in Exchange Park nearby. Mickey Mantle had

the world by the tail. Or so it seemed to anyone looking on from the outside.

But Mickey fretted. And worried. His 31 home runs in the previous season were his fewest since 1954. His 75 runs batted in and his .285 batting average were his worst since his 1951 rookie season. His 126 strikeouts were the most of his nine-year career. Was it any wonder that the Yankees slipped to third place, 15 games behind the pennant-winning Chicago White Sox? Over Mantle's first eight seasons, the Yankees had been in seven World Series, winning five. Then came 1959. Mickey spent much of the winter trying to figure out what had gone wrong and shouldering a star's share of the Yankees' horrendous 1959 season.

Self-doubt was eating away at Mantle. Just three years earlier he had been baseball's first Triple Crown winner in a generation, winning the first of back-to-back MVP awards—and on the cusp of realizing all the rookie predictions and expectations of greatness on the scale of Babe Ruth. He was the game's biggest name, and soon to become its highest-paid player. He was a pop culture hero to millions of youngsters, as popular on television as *I Love Lucy*, and the object of Teresa Brewer's hit song "I Love Mickey." But few knew just how insecure he was and how far his self-confidence had fallen. So low, in fact, that he had begun to wonder if his career was now, suddenly and surprisingly, on the decline.

"I have this god-awful fear that I'm done, finished, that my strength's been sapped out of me," he confided to *Dallas Times Herald* columnist Blackie Sherrod that winter. "I don't know if I can ever return to the player I was."

Mantle also made a similar confession to his longtime New York girlfriend and lover Holly Brooke shortly after Thanksgiving. He had begged her to come to Dallas, where he housed her in the presidential suite of the Adolphus Hotel, within steps of the Neiman Marcus flagship department store so she could go shopping.

"Mickey felt he had nowhere to turn for help," Holly recalled years later. "He honestly was afraid that his career was over or certainly now just going downhill."

Mantle's fear of impending doom had been reinforced by the actions of Yankees general manager George Weiss. Mickey was convinced that Weiss had it in for him, dating back to contract negotiations after his 1956 season. This was at a time before the players organized into an effective labor union. Until then, players on their own negotiated year-to-year deals with their teams' management without the involvement of agents bargaining on their behalf. This practice was in effect until 1968, when the newly recognized players union negotiated the first collective bargaining agreement with the team owners, which began the dramatic change in ballplayers' salaries and led to free agency. In 1956, Mantle won the Triple Crown, leading the American League with a .353 average, 52 homers, and 130 runs batted in. It was one of the greatest seasons in baseball history.

"I wanted to double my salary from the $32,000 I made in 1956," he recalled. "But when I asked Weiss for $65,000, he told me I was too young to make that kind of money. Then he threatened to show my wife reports from private detectives he had gumshoe me and Billy Martin. He threatened to trade me to Cleveland for Herb Score and Rocky Colavito."

Yankee co-owner Del Webb finally intervened and agreed to pay Mantle $60,000 for the 1957 season.

"Weiss never forgot," Mantle said. "After the 1957 season, he tried to cut me $5,000."

Weiss, who had built the Yankees' fabled minor league system, had the reputation of being the power behind the strongest throne in baseball. But critics blamed him and his tightfisted manner in dealing with players for being among the reasons for the Yankees downfall in the 1960s. Those critics accused Weiss of gradually weakening the team by his resistance to big-cash bonuses for promising players. The way he handled contract negotiations with Mantle was indicative, especially how Weiss tried to diminish Mickey's 1957 season. Mantle hit .365 with 34 homers while driving in 94 runs. He also had a career high of 146 walks, with only 75 strikeouts and an on-base percentage of .512, a mark unsurpassed in the more than six decades since then. Little did Weiss, or even Mickey, realize that those and his other statistics for that season would generate greater meaning in years to come. Proponents of sabermetrics and new analytics in the game would later argue that Mantle's 1957 season was "probably the greatest single season by any player in baseball's modern era."

To his credit, Mantle stood his ground in bargaining with Weiss and eventually signed for $72,000 for 1958, a $12,000 raise. Mickey helped lead the Yankees back to a World Series championship, batting .304 with 42 homers and 97 runs batted in. Weiss, though, opened their 1959 negotiations by offering Mickey a contract for only $65,000, a $7,000 pay cut. Mantle, who had demanded $85,000, eventually accepted a $2,000 cut to $70,000. So when the Yankees failed to win the pennant in 1959, Weiss wasted little time in moving to slash Mantle's salary again. That winter, Mickey received Weiss' first offer for his 1960 contract—and a staggering $17,000 pay cut.

"Mickey was upset, but it wasn't just about the money in dollars and cents," said Holly Brooke. "It was what the money meant, the valuation and, with the pay cut, the devaluation of Mickey and his self-worth. And with Mickey, as sensitive and insecure as he could be, it cut him to the quick. I don't think—no, I know for certain, that he wasn't looking forward to the 1960 season."

All that changed a few days after Holly Brooke's visit. On December 11, 1959, to be exact. On that day, the Yankees made a monumental seven-player trade with the Kansas City Athletics that would change the immediate fortunes of the Yankees and make a historic impact on a long-cherished record in the game. Mickey heard the news from Whitey Ford, who called to tell him about it.

"'Slick, they're saying it's bigger than the Billy [Martin] trade,'" Mantle recalled Ford telling him. "'[Norm] Siebern, [Hank] Bauer, [Marv] Throneberry, and [Don] Larsen. They're gone.'"

"To Kansas City? Well, fuck me, Georgie," said Mantle, alluding to Weiss. "Kansas City ain't got anyone we can use."

"'Actually, Slick, they do. Or they did,'" said Ford. "'Remember the outfielder they got from Cleveland? The outfielder with that nice left-handed swing you liked?'"

"That's right. Maris? We're fucking getting Maris?" Mantle couldn't believe it.

"'Yep. Along with a couple of nobodies.'" The other two players in the deal, first baseman Kent Hadley and shortstop Joe DeMaestri, were soon out of the majors. "'Basically, it's our four for Maris.'"

"Fuck, yeah, he's an All-Star." Mantle took a deep breath and relaxed. For the first time since the end of the season, the sense of impending doom he'd been feeling disappeared. He knew Roger Maris. He knew his game. He was an outstanding defensive outfielder with a powerful throwing arm and the kind of foot speed that Mickey used to have. Offensively, Maris had untapped potential and one of the most beautiful left-handed swings Mickey had ever seen. It was a short, compact swing, much different than Mantle's long swing from both sides of the plate.

Mickey had first seen the swing—and Maris—early in the 1957 season, when the Yankees played a two-game series against the Indians in Cleveland. It was Roger's rookie season, and it would be a year of tragedy and disarray. The Indians' longtime manager Al López had resigned at the end of the 1956 season and shortly afterward became the skipper of the Chicago White Sox. His departure was a bitter humiliation for the team.

In six seasons managing the Indians, López's teams amassed a record of 570 wins and 354 losses, a .617 winning percentage that would stand as the best in franchise history. His 1954 Indians won a then–American League record 111 games and broke the Yankees' five-year pennant run. It might have become one of the all-time great seasons, had Cleveland not been swept by Willie Mays and the New York Giants, one of the biggest upsets in World Series history.

Still, it was the high point of that era for the Indians, who finished second to the Yankees in 1955 and 1956. Cleveland fans wanted a championship and were merciless in how they took out their frustration against star players. When All-Star third baseman Al Rosen slumped late in the year while playing injured, Indians fans let him have it, bombarding him with boos and jeers. It came as a disappointment for Rosen, who had been the 1953 American League MVP. That season he led the league in home runs with 43, runs batted in with 145, and batted .336, barely losing the batting title by just over one percentage point to Mickey Vernon of the Washington Senators—and, with it, missing out on the Triple Crown—on the last day of the season.

Three years later, Cleveland fans didn't care. Incensed, the normally mild-mannered López alone defended his player, accusing Tribe fans of "bush-league tactics," and saying they were undeserving of a championship team. López also became disheartened that the Indians management failed to support Rosen against the fans' mistreatment. Instead, team general manager Hank Greenberg, the former Detroit Tigers slugger, was even quoted as saying that Rosen was going to be traded. Rosen's back and leg injuries were serious enough that he retired after the season. He was only 32. López, though, was so infuriated with the mistreatment of his third baseman that he resigned on the season's last day.

On May 7, 1957, the Yankees opened a two-game set against an Indians team about to sink into mediocrity it had not known since before World War II. But the Tribe's front office, who were so dispassionate about their former star Al Rosen, were now enthusiastically rebuilding around two of the team's most promising prospects, along with Al López's replacement, Kerby Farrell, who had led the minor league Indianapolis Indians to the 1956 Junior World Series championship. One of those prospects was rookie Roger Maris, who had been part of Farrell's Indianapolis team and was promoted to become the Indians' starting center fielder.

Maris made his major league debut against the Chicago White Sox on April 16. In five at-bats, he had three hits. Two days later, Roger hit the first home run of his career, a grand slam off Tigers pitcher Jack Crimian at Briggs Stadium in Detroit.

The other promising youngster in the Indians' plans was southpaw Herb Score, a pitching phenom with a blazing fastball and dazzling curve seemingly already propelling him to Cooperstown. He had been signed to a $60,000 bonus right out of high school in 1952 by Cy Slapnicka, the scout who had brought the Hall of Fame pitcher Bob Feller to the Indians. The scout even boasted that, "Herb Score is the left-handed version of Feller." Score won the American League's Rookie of the Year Award in 1955, when he had a 16–10 record, 2.85 earned run average, and 245 strikeouts, tops in the major leagues and a record for a rookie that would stand for 29 years.

In 1956, he won 20 games with a 2.53 ERA and was again the strikeout leader with 263 punchouts. So impressed were opponents that in spring training of 1957 the Boston Red Sox offered the Indians $1 million for Score—an extraordinary sum for the time. Cleveland general manager Hank Greenberg quickly rejected the offer, saying that Score "may become the greatest pitcher in the game's history." Hall of Famer Tris Speaker agreed. After watching Score pitch in late April, he told the *Cleveland Plain Dealer's* Gordon Cobbledick that the young hurler would be one of the game's greats "if nothing happens to him."

On May 7, 1957, the cruel hand of fate intervened.

It was a Tuesday night game, with a small crowd of 18,386 fans barely in their seats at Municipal Stadium, excited about seeing how the Indians' young two-time All-Star would handle the defending World Series champions. The Yankees were leading the league with a 12–5 record and riding a six-game winning streak. The Indians were 8–8, with two of those victories coming on the arm of Herb Score, who was a month shy of his 24th birthday. Score was 2–1 in the young season with a 2.04 ERA, having struck out 10 or more batters in three of his starts. Hank Bauer led off the game for the Yankees in the top of the first inning by grounding out to third baseman Al Smith. As Gil McDougald dug into the batters box, third-place hitter Mickey Mantle stepped into the on-deck circle. He was closely watching Score, who had given him trouble in the two previous seasons.

"Herb Score is the toughest pitcher I've faced," Mantle was to say. "I just can't hit him."

Years later, when he was a broadcaster of the Indians' games, Score would tell me in an interview that he had a different recollection of his battles against Mantle. "In his Triple Crown season," he said, "Mickey hit two of those home runs off me."

Those had been home runs on June 16 and July 14 of 1956 and Score said he was aware he would be pitching to Mantle in the first inning of May 7. "I knew he was on deck," he said. "Pretty hard to miss."

But then, on only his 12th pitch of the game, Score unleashed a 2-2 fastball that McDougald lined back to the mound. Before Score could raise his glove, the baseball struck him between the nose and right eye. Score fell to the ground at the same moment that the ball ricocheted to the third baseman. He easily threw out McDougald, who had almost stopped running, just as players from both teams rushed to the pitcher's aid. The public-address quickly called for a doctor to come down to the field, where players from both teams stood around stunned by the scene. Indians first baseman Vic Wertz had run to the mound after taking the throw for the putout on McDougald. When he saw Score's bloodied face as he writhed in pain, Wertz stopped in his tracks.

"It was like somebody had died," Mantle told me during a series of conversations after his retirement.

Score never lost consciousness but had severe hemorrhaging in the eye and a swollen retina, as well as a broken nose. He was carried off the field and spent three weeks at Lakeside Hospital. The next morning, the baseball world was shocked. The hottest young pitcher in the game was in a dark hospital room, the right side of his face grotesquely swollen, his right eye hemorrhaging. A day later, he could barely distinguish light from darkness.

"I didn't see the ball until it was a foot or two from my face," Score said afterward. "Then I saw too much of it. I never did lose consciousness even as I fell to the ground. I knew I was on the ground and I could feel the blood. Then people seemed to come at me from all sides."

A teary-eyed Gil McDougald was devastated, guilt-torn, and threatened to quit baseball if Score lost an eye or could never play again. The Yankees lost the two-game set, trying to make sense of the senselessness of a freak injury. Whitey Ford, who had pitched the previous Saturday, sat in the dugout and talked about anything except pitching and its dangers. When Roger Maris came to bat, he and Mantle dissected the rookie's beautiful swing.

"He's a dead-pull hitter," Mantle said.

"Batters with a short swing like that," said Ford, "are hard to fool."

About then, Maris unloaded on a home run off rookie right-hander Al Cicotte. It was a shot to right field.

"Like I said, a dead-pull hitter," Mantle said. "Man, would he have a field day if he played with a short [right-field] porch like at the Stadium."

"Yeah, well, good luck," said Ford. "The Indians will never let him go."

2

The New Yankee

"I don't know if I want to go to New York. They'll have to pay me a lot more money because I like it here in Kansas City."
—ROGER MARIS

ROGER MARIS WAS NOT THE MAN AMERICA'S SPORTSWRITERS MADE HIM out to be: a man so broken by the pressures of a child's game that, at the height of his career, he shrank into a shell of himself, his hair falling out, chain-smoking Camels in the clubhouse, and wishing he were alone somewhere in the Arabian Desert. It was reported he couldn't take the intense scrutiny, the daily questioning, and the close-ups of celebrity. He chafed at how everything he said or did was magnified for public consumption.

Late in the 1961 season, *Sports Illustrated* published a cover story reporting: "During the previous month, as he pursued the magic mark of 60, Maris lived under suffocating, unrelenting pressure—pressure such as no ballplayer has ever had to endure, not even Babe Ruth himself." Sports is nothing if it's not about pressure, an aspect of human existence measuring the degree to which one can feel overwhelmed or unable to cope as a result of stress that is unmanageable. But there is no barometer or thermometer to measure it. There are no new analytics or sabermetrics to offer a comparative gauge. There is no denying that Maris was under constant stress and suffocating, unrelenting pressure as he pursued Babe Ruth's single-season home run mark. Any athlete would have been, just as they would have likely reacted with the same orneriness that Maris used in his uniquely curt answers to reporters. But Maris coming close to breaking, or even beginning to unravel at his emotional seams, from the pressure of the moment?

That kind of superficiality shows just how little the sportswriters chronicling the exploits of Roger Maris truly knew the man—or how they just failed to understand that it was that very pressure that had historically brought out the best of Roger Maris in personal circumstances far greater than the chase of a home run record. As author David Halberstam was to note years later in an ESPN Page 2 reminiscence of 1961, Roger rising to tremendous stress was "very much in character with a certain contrariness that was an important part of Maris' makeup."

And Maris' makeup was extraordinary, coming from a place often overlooked in America. The place where Roger Maris came from could be called "the land of the unmeltable White ethnics," the often forgotten immigrants whom author and philosopher Michael Novak sentimentally praised for asserting their own legitimate superculture in his controversial 1972 book, *The Rise of The Unmeltable Ethnics: The New Political Force of the Seventies*. How much they may have contributed to the construction of the republic may be debatable, but their distinct ethnic presence is undeniable.

In the first part of the century, members of Maris' ancestral family made their own immigrant journey from Eastern Europe into America's Midwest. Roger's parents, Rudolph S. "Rudy" Maras (later changed to Maris) and Ann Corrine "Connie" (née Perkovich), were of

Croatian heritage and had been born in Minnesota. There, in Hibbing, Minnesota, Roger Eugene Maras was born on September 10, 1934, a year after his older brother, Rudolph.

The parents had a turbulent marriage that was no secret either in Hibbing or in Grand Forks, North Dakota, where the family moved in 1938. Their marital conflicts, that apparently included open affairs on the part of the boys' beautiful mother, became the fodder for gossip that humiliated both Roger and his brother in their teens as the family moved to Fargo, North Dakota, in 1946. In 1948, both Maras boys were playing basketball and football at Fargo High. Being Roman Catholics, they transferred to Bishop Shanley High School in Fargo in 1950.

The gossip and the talk turned an already moody, sometimes sullen young Roger Maris into an even bigger introvert. Friends from that time remember a kid who was often angry and, like his brother Rudy, who was known as "Buddy," a chip off the old block. Their father, Rudy, had toiled as a miner and engineer on the Great Northern Railway, though his big reputation was as a hothead. There were stories of Rudy beating up men he suspected of having had an affair with his wife. He was arrested on at least one occasion and spent some time in jail. There was even one story that his boss at the railroad in Minnesota, thinking that a change of scenery might improve Rudy's marriage, arranged the job that took the family to North Dakota.

But the trouble in the marriage continued. On top of that there was no love lost between Connie and members of Rudy's family. It might have been because of the rumors. But there was also talk that Rudy's Croatian family didn't accept Connie because she may have been Serbian, not Croatian. Conflict between Croatians and Serbians goes back in history to another part of the world but, sadly, immigrated to America along with customs and culture.

So was Connie Maras at odds with parts of her husband's family because she may not have been 100 percent Croatian, or was it more personal? The only thing certain is that the Maras family talked about her publicly often and in the unkindest of ways.

Cousin Nick Maras:

"There was a bad story about her. My father says she was really into the booze, and she became totally loose. He says, 'I know this was true because I was right there when this was going on.' He told me that [Connie and Rudy] started having trouble and she started drinking and carousing and stuff like that, and it looked like they were going to split up. He can't say if she started it or if Rudy was drinking too much or had gone astray."

Cousin Bill Maras:

"[Rudy] knew that his wife was messing around and that was the reason they had to leave. According to my dad, Big Nick, Connie was really upset to be going, and that's the reason she later changed the family's name from Maras. She did it just to piss off Rudy and everyone else with that name. If there was any bad blood between our families, it had to do with Connie."

For Roger, any suspicions or gossip about his mother was both mortifying and angering. He loved her without reservation, and loved his father, too. Both Roger and Buddy had followed in his footsteps as ballplayers. Rudy had played semi-pro baseball in his youth, and he could hold his own with his sons when they were boys and into their teens. Although Little League baseball had originated in 1939, it wasn't widely popularized until the 1950s. Maris said he and his brother were too old to play Little League by the time it was organized in Fargo. The only youth baseball program they were able to participate in as kids was American Legion ball, in which they both excelled.

From that time until he left high school, Rudy Maris was the superior athlete. But an incident happened when Roger was a sophomore. Although both were outstanding football players, a new coach at Fargo Central High benched Roger and demoted Rudy to the junior varsity. Roger especially took it personally. "Either I play or I'm going somewhere else," he demanded in a meeting with the coach, who didn't budge. It reinforced the feeling that had already planted its seed in Roger's psyche: it was him and his brother against the world.

Perhaps it is no wonder that Roger's hero in the early and mid-1950s was Ted Williams, whose troubled relationship with the Boston fans and media covering the Red Sox was already legendary. In young Roger Maras, Williams had a perfect disciple. "I have never been the type of person to let anyone give me the business," Roger wrote in his memoir. "I felt Bud and I were getting the short end of the stick and decided to do something about it."

High school transfers, who became common half a century later, were almost unheard of in those days. But the Maras boys knew Sid Cichy, the head coach at Fargo's small Catholic high school Sacred Heart Academy, from American legion baseball. Cichy would remain at the school for more than 30 years and establish a reputation as one of the greatest high school coaches in North Dakota history, compiling a record of 231–38 and 15 state championships.

In his first season, Cichy was already known as an innovative coach, and he sensed the two Maras youngsters would be special additions to Sacred Heart (which would change its name to Bishop Shanley that fall). He wasn't wrong. In their first season, the Maras boys helped lead the Deacons to a 7–1 record and Shanley was voted by United Press International as "the best high school football team in the state." The Associated Press named Roger, a junior, to the All-State team and

Cichy North Dakota's Coach of the Year. But in Fargo there was a furor over the boys' transfer, as Roger recalled:

"Bud and I were responsible for splitting the town in half when we switched schools. We were surprised to learn that a lot of people resented our shifting schools… We had left the Fargo High basketball and track teams a little shorthanded, and that made some people mad. We didn't let the feelings of the people bother us. Bud and I were only doing what we thought was in our best interests."

There have been some old friends of Roger who have insisted that, though there may initially have been some bad feelings toward him and his brother, the situation never amounted to the anti-Maras hostility Roger made it out to be. In re-examining Roger's life, this is a common thread that runs through his personal narrative—an incessant paranoia that the world, or someone in it, is out to get him and the need to fashion, if not a new identity, then at least something different than the real one.

There would be the name change that would come later, and there would be things like the insistence that he had been born in Fargo, North Dakota, when, of course, his birth certificate proved his birthplace was Hibbing, Minnesota. Fargo or Hibbing. Why not Grand Forks, North Dakota, where Roger lived until he was 10? Roger had played guard and co-captained his Washington Elementary School basketball team to a city championship in Grand Forks. His uncle, Jerry March, told stories of Roger waiting for the Empire Builder train that would stop in Grand Forks, and of his little nephew hustling newspapers and magazines to people on the train. "But he was so small then that he didn't know how to make change," said March, who later moved to Los Gatos, California, where he died in 2019. "When people gave him money for the paper or magazine, he would just pull out a handful of coins and hold it out to the buyer. He looked so confused, but the people usually let him keep the change."

Yet it was Fargo where Roger would stake his heart. Was it the neighborly interest and concern of the residents of Fargo in that flat Red River community of the snowy Great Plains that would win over Roger? Or maybe it was partly the pride that comes from knowing you have what it takes to endure the coldest winters in the country, when temperatures often drop to 15 below zero, with an unwelcoming wind shearing off another 20 degrees.

So by the age of 15, Roger had already made a name for himself in Fargo, where he and Bud led their American Legion team to the 1950 North Dakota state title. Batting .367, he was named the league's MVP while attracting the attention of major league scouts. Cleveland Indians scout Frank Fahey saw Roger in an American Legion tournament and sent a report to team officials. "Roger weighed one hundred fifty pounds and stood five eight," Fahey is quoted in Harry Rosenfeld's biography *Roger Maris*: *A Title to Fame*. "My opinion at the time was that he would be a major leaguer if he filled out. He could run and throw and had lots of power."

By 1951, having grown to six feet and 185 pounds, Roger had other major league scouts looking at him, though not as seriously as the Indians. The Brooklyn Dodgers and Chicago Cubs had an interest. The Cubs even invited him to a tryout camp, where it was decided he was "too small" to make it to the major leagues. Maras wasn't discouraged, as he had again excelled on his American Legion team, batting .350 and leading in almost every offensive category. But football had taken over much of Roger's attention, and even a losing 3–5 season for the Deacons couldn't diminish the talent he showed.

His most memorable high school football game may have been a game against Devils Lake. "Roger set a national record in that game for the most non-scrimmage yards in a game," recalled George "Skeeter" Ziegler, who played for Devils Lake. "He was able to return two kickoffs, one punt, and one intercepted pass, all for touchdowns." That night, Roger returned the game's opening kickoff 89 yards for a touchdown, ran back the second-half kickoff 90 yards for a TD, returned a punt 45 yards for a third touchdown, and scored on a 25-yard pass interception. "I was the kicker, the punter, and the passer," said Ziegler. "Therefore, I must have set some kind of record also!" Add to Roger's tally another 32-yard scoring run, an extra point, and a total of 280 yards on five touches of the ball.

At the end of the season, he was named to the All-State team again, and Oklahoma—riding a 47-game winning streak under the immortal coach Bud Wilkinson—wanted Roger to play halfback for the Sooners. Only Shanley coach Sid Cichy would have regrets about the season. "It was one of the two losing seasons that I had in 30 years at Shanley," he said, "and it happened with probably the best athlete I ever had."

Roger's brother, Rudy Jr., was in his freshman year at Santa Clara College, an all-male Jesuit Catholic School, in Northern California. He had accepted a baseball scholarship there, hoping to use it as a springboard to a professional deal. Santa Clara was also in the back of Roger's mind as a place where he could join up with his brother again. Although Roger had long deferred to Buddy as the better athlete, his own accomplishments in the last two years said otherwise. Observers and friends believed the younger brother had overtaken the older, but they knew the source of Roger's uncertainty: their father Rudy Sr., who always insisted that Rudy Jr. was the superior athlete.

Bobby Vee, the teen idol of the 1960s whose hits included "Take Good Care of My Baby," which in the summer of 1961 went to No. 1 on *Billboard* magazine's U.S. pop chart, grew up in Fargo as Robert Velline. He later recalled stories his father would tell of Rudy Maras coming into the café and bar where he worked. "Roger Maras' father would have lunch at the counter and talk to my dad, who liked him," Vee remembered. "I'm sure Rudy Sr. was proud of Roger, but he always talked of what a great talent Rudy Jr. was."

In 1951, during Roger's senior year at Shanley and Rudy's freshman year at Santa Clara, before Rudy Jr. ever had a chance to suit up for the Broncos' baseball team, the question of which of Rudy Maras Sr.'s two sons was the better athlete was made moot by harsh reality, as Rudy Maras Jr. was stricken with polio.

The 1952 polio epidemic was the worst outbreak in the nation's history. Of the 57,628 cases of polio reported that year, 3,145 died and 21,269 were left with mild to disabling paralysis. At its peak in the 1940s and 1950s, polio would paralyze or kill over half a million people worldwide every year. Rudy was one of the fortunate victims, suffering a mild case from which he recovered over time. He was bedridden at home for a while, and his dreams of a professional athletic career were now gone. Rudy eventually enrolled at North Dakota Agricultural College, which became North Dakota State University.

There's a sad, old saying among Roman Catholics that Catholics can be made to feel guilty about anything, and this certainly applied to Roger. The father he admired openly dismissed his athletic ability as inferior to his brother, and now that brother had been sidelined from ever fulfilling their father's belief. The kid who would one day break Babe Ruth's record and could stand up to his former Fargo High coach couldn't find it in him to confront to his father and mother on what was most important to him. *The Fifth Commandment.* Honor thy father and thy mother. His faith and his family had him in its clutch.

Roger never spoke honestly about what happened next in that year after his brother contracted polio. His mother came between him and his budding romance with Patricia Ann Carvell, the hometown girl he had met at a basketball game at the St. Anthony of Padua Church gymnasium. They were introduced by one of Roger's Shanley football teammates, Gene Johnson. "I still can go to St. Anthony's and point out the precise spot," Johnson remembered decades later. "Roger noticed two girls on the other side of the gymnasium. 'Do you know those two?' he asked. 'Yes,' I told Roger. 'One is Pat Carvell. The other is Jeanie Williams.'"

"There was only one girl for Roger," Coach Cichy would recall. "He was very dedicated to Patsy from day one."

Why Connie Maras disapproved of the pretty Catholic girl was anyone's guess. Patricia's father, who died when she was nine, had been a pharmacist in Fargo. They had three grown sons, and their two young daughters lived with their mother, Grace, after Al Carvell's death.

Roger and Pat didn't marry for four years after he had graduated from high school, on October 13, 1956, in a small, double-ring ceremony at St. Anthony of Padua Church. Roger had just finished his final season in the minors with the Indianapolis Indians of the Triple-A league American Association. Roger was 22, Patricia 21; and Patricia's mother may have shared Connie Maris' misgivings, according to Sister Bertha Hill, of the Order of the Presentation Sisters and a member of the Shanley High faculty who knew both families. Grace Carvell, she recalled, "was not too anxious for the marriage at that time, although she did like Roger. Perhaps she saw hard times ahead." Of course, within months, Roger would be earning a major league salary plus the $10,000 bonus for making it to the Cleveland Indians.

But it took almost five years to get there. Roger did accept that scholarship to Oklahoma and spent all of about 10 days on campus in Norman before deciding he was in the wrong place. The story of Roger taking a long bus ride to Norman and becoming miffed when there was no OU representative there to greet him was just a tale that fit nicely into the common perception of Maris being a difficult person to please. He never set the record straight. Feeling out of place, missing his girlfriend, and being homesick are a more likely explanation. Maris was still a few days shy of 18 when he arrived on the Oklahoma campus.

But Roger's near miss as a Sooner did give him and Mickey Mantle something to talk about when they teamed up. Mantle had also been recruited by Oklahoma, and some even wondered about what if the M&M boys had played in Bud Wilkinson's backfield together. Even if both had played for the Sooners, it's unlikely they would have played together. Mantle would have been a senior for the 1952 football season. At the time, freshmen were ineligible to play on college varsity football teams, which means that Maris, in his first year at Oklahoma, would have only been able to play on the freshman team.

Instead, Roger returned home and signed a contract with the Cleveland Indians to play professional baseball. Biographers have reported it was not the contract he had turned down earlier, possibly as much as $15,000. An actual signed contract has never surfaced, and Roger was always cagey when talking about money. Indians general manager Hank Greenberg also refused to be specific about the amount involved, having been quoted as saying his initial offer was either $8,000 or $9,000. When, after Maras returned home and called Greenberg renewing his interest, the Hall of Fame slugger knew the youngster's options had narrowed to one. He dispatched Cy Slapnicka, the Indians legendary scout, and Jack O'Connor, general manager of Cleveland's Fargo-Moorhead minor league affiliate, to Roger's home. Roger signed with the Indians for a $5,000 bonus and the stipulation of an additional $10,000 if he made the major league roster.

In the spring of 1953, Roger Maras began his professional career playing for the Fargo-Moorhead Twins, Cleveland's Class C Northern

League affiliate. In the early 1950s, minor league baseball still had six levels of competition, with Class D the lowest, and AAA the highest. Hank Greenberg and other Cleveland executives wanted Maras to start with their Class D team at Daytona Beach, Florida, where there would be less pressure on him. But Maras refused to go to Daytona, insisting that he would either play for Cleveland at Fargo or not at all. For Roger, wanting to stay so close to home that year was personal, but it had nothing to do with being homesick or wanting to look after his polio-stricken brother. The reason had to do with his girlfriend.

Patricia was about to finish high school, and he wanted to be there during that special time in her life, especially her senior prom and graduation ceremonies. More importantly, Roger feared he had lost her. They had broken up, and Patricia had even begun dating another boy. Roger, though, didn't want to be completely out of sight for the four months or so of an entire minor league baseball season. But as Patricia would later explain: "I think we started dating in my sophomore year. And the next year, when I was a junior, we were going together. And it was a foregone conclusion that we would some day marry, even though we never really discussed it. Things like that just sort of happened then."

Roger had given Patricia the gold football ring he had earned when Shanley had won it high school championship. It was their "promise" ring, a symbol of their love and their commitment. But after one of their squabbles, Patricia had been so upset that she'd given the ring back. Bob Wood, one of Roger's friends from Shanley, had been with him as they walked home later that night. He recalled that Roger was so upset that he took the ring and threw it into the cold night air, with it landing somewhere in the grass. "Who needs it now?" Roger had screamed in frustration. Minutes later, having calmed down, he knew he'd made a terrible mistake.

"Let's go back and find it," he told Woods. "Patsy is going to want it."

Those who knew Patricia usually called her Pat. But Roger and others close to her often called her "Patsy."

"There we were on our hands and knees in the dark, looking for a ring in thick grass," Woods later recalled. "We did find it. Finally."

So there was no way Roger was going to be too far away from his Patsy in that important first professional baseball season after he finished Shanley. What eventually tilted the Indians' decision to allow Maras to play in Fargo in 1953? Most likely it was the exceptional spring training camp he had in Florida where he more than held his own with other young minor league players. They included the highly prized Rocky Colavito, who was also competing for the future right-field position with the Indians. The team reluctantly gave in to Maras' demands. Roger paid the Indians back by batting .325 with nine home runs, driving in 80 runs, and being voted Rookie of the Year. Fargo-Moorhead also won its first pennant in two decades. Maras' surprise season and fellow outfielder Frank Gravino's 52 home runs helped carry the Twins to the Northern League championship with an 86–39 record.

It would be the beginning of Roger's four years in the minors, an apprenticeship that helped shape him into a future major leaguer and develop some friendships that would last through his playing career. The most prominent of those friends was pitcher Dan Osinski, who would be his roommate in three of those minor league seasons. Osinski would go on to pitch in the majors for eight seasons. That included pitching for the Boston Red Sox in 1966 and 1967, and being a member of the Red Sox team that faced the St. Louis Cardinals in the 1967 World Series. Those Cardinals included his former roommate, Maris, who by then had been dealt by the Yankees to St. Louis in

1966. Osinski pitched in two of the seven games of the Series, which the Cardinals won.

By then, the Osinski-Maris friendship was a bond that had been built on the mixture of triumph, defeat, and utter surprise that come to all major leaguers. Osinski, for instance, once told Roger the story of his own tryout with the St. Louis Browns, who were not impressed. Preparing to leave for a return bus trip back home to Chicago, Osinski was stopped outside the field by Indians scout Wally Laskowski, who had seen his tryout performance and had a completely opposite opinion from the Browns. The Cleveland scout signed him to a major league contract, and he was sent to play in the Indians farm system, where he met Maras. They roomed together from Maras' first spring training in 1953 on, and Osinski got to know him perhaps better than anyone in those years.

Osinski recalled that perhaps the only negative of Roger's first season as a professional ballplayer was the disrespect that he felt he got on the road. It was almost as if opposing teams knew how ultra-sensitive he was about almost anything, but especially about something as personal as his name. These were the minor leagues of the 1950s, where homerism was second nature. On the road, some of the home teams' public address announcers, tying to rile up the visiting team's promising rookie, took to introducing him before his at-bats as "Roger Mare-ASS," or worse.

"They would also call him 'Roger Mary-ASS,'" remembered Osinski. "He just hated them making fun of him."

3

Becoming Maris

*"Roger was bullheaded enough to go home
rather than go along with something
he didn't agree with. He didn't like being
jerked around. He just wanted to play
where he knew he could play."*

—JERRY MEHLISCH, TEAMMATE

THE SLUGGER'S PARENTS QUARRELED A LOT, OFTEN WANTED TO KILL one another, and certainly had no use for their marriage, likely staying together only because divorce was forbidden by their Roman Catholic faith. They were the children of immigrants from Eastern Europe, trying to find their way to the better life in the new country their own folks had dreamed about. The father worked a variety of jobs and kept moving his family around. The mother was often bored at home and was rumored to sometimes hang out at saloons. They often feuded not only with each other but also with members of their extended clans.

Pray, shall we, for Rudy S. Maras Sr. and Anne Corrine Perkovich, the parents of Roger Maris?

Yes, pray for them, too. But the parents referenced here were George Herman Ruth, Sr. and Katherine Schamberger, the father and mother of Babe Ruth.

The similarities of the home family lives of the two Yankee sluggers whose fates as home run record breakers 34 years apart are eerily stunning. Maris, like Ruth, was a product of the American immigrant story. Rudy and Connie Maras, like George and Katherine Ruth, wanted that elusive jewel of happiness and security that had entranced their grandparents about life in the new world. But something happened to throw off-kilter their dreams and hopes into an unexpected cruel, seemingly thankless, unhappy paycheck-to-paycheck existence that confronts and tests all marriages and relationships. Call it life. It struck the Ruths and the Marases like a fastball in the ribs.

A child's family life can influence the youngster's development and well-being beyond his parents' immediate understanding. Did Babe Ruth become baseball's most beloved extrovert because of his uncontrolled upbringing in which his parents sent him to be raised in an orphanage? Did Roger Maris become the game's most famous and controversial introvert as a self-defense response to early and continuing family trauma at home? Each became baseball's home run king, but how they handled the record-breaking glory and fame was dramatically different. One became one of America's most beloved sports heroes; the other one of the country's most misunderstood and unappreciated sports personalities.

"As a ballplayer, I would be delighted to hit 61 home runs again," Maris would say after breaking Babe Ruth's single-season record of 60 home runs in 1961. "As an individual, I doubt if I could possibly go through it again."

How did Roger Maris wind up where he found himself in the late summer months of 1961, when almost every question posed to him by the news media was met not as an inquiry but as an attack on his character? How had the American sports media that was following the assault on Ruth's record taken on the appearance of England's dreaded Fleet Street tabloids?

Roger Maris grew up resenting the gossip and innuendos about his mother, and he also grew up resenting his mother for creating the gossip and innuendos. He grew up resenting his father for not being what his mother wanted him to be, and he grew up wishing he didn't feel this way about his parents. But he did. There were times he thought that it was his fault: that if he could do something wonderful, it would make his parents fall in love with one another again and end all the bickering and fighting. In that sense, he was no different than other children of parents who have given up trying to hide their differences from their most dear loved ones.

By the time he was a young man, Roger understood that his parents being happy with one another was a futile prayer that would never be answered. Worse, their unhappiness threatened to spill over into his future. His mother didn't approve of his girlfriend, and she made no secret of telling people. Roger once overheard Connie telling a friend that her son "dates the biggest slut in town." It was mean and not true, but the point was to hurt a son she knew would soon be leaving her for a young woman who she feared would be everything she couldn't be to the children she would bear for Roger. Most mothers would love such a woman for their son, but Connie Maras wasn't most mothers.

It was a time when mental health was still in the dark ages in much of America. So, sadly, she would never have the benefit of therapy or treatment. Based on her symptoms, Connie Maras likely suffered from a narcissistic personality disorder that may have been at the root of her issues with the extended Maras family, as well as with her sisters, with whom she also had problems. Sons of narcissistic mothers can suffer damage to their autonomy, self-worth, and future relationships. Narcissists lack empathy and the ability to nurture their children. They don't see them as individuals, but as extensions of themselves. They feel entitled and insist on getting their way and exact compliance through control, manipulation, guilt, and shame. Interviews with Maras family members and others are filled with anecdotes of how Connie's behavior and actions often fit these descriptions.

After his 1953 season with Fargo-Moorhead, Roger knew it was time to move on, even if the Indians wanted him to spend another season with the Twins. Maras and Cleveland's front office were at loggerheads again over where he should be the next season. He would agree to go to the Tribe's Class B minor league team at Keokuk, Iowa, for the 1954 season, which would be fortuitous for him. For that he can thank Hank Greenberg.

Before he was the Indians general manager, Greenberg had been one of baseball's greatest sluggers of the pre-steroids age. He was the American League's home run leader four times, and his 58 home runs for the Detroit Tigers in 1938 equaled Jimmie Foxx's 1932 number for the most in one season by anyone other than Babe Ruth. Greenberg helped carry the Tigers to World Series championships in 1935 and 1945, and he had a batting average over .300 in eight seasons. His 183 RBI in 1937 is still the third most in a single season in baseball history.

Greenberg was also the first Jewish superstar in American team sports, preceding Sandy Koufax by a generation. The great Dodgers left-hander of the 1960s made his name a national symbol for Jewish pride when he refused to pitch Game 1 of the 1965 World Series because it fell on Yom Kippur, the holiest holiday in Judaism. But 31 years earlier Greenberg had done the same. In the homestretch of the 1934 pennant race, he announced that he would not play on Rosh

Hashanah, the Jewish New Year that fell that year on September 10, or on Yom Kippur, September 19.

The Tigers hadn't won the pennant since 1909, so naturally fans grumbled. Greenberg was not particularly observant religiously. But after serious soul-searching and discussions with his rabbi, he agreed to play on Rosh Hashanah. Greenberg hit a pair of home runs as the Tigers beat the Red Sox, 2–1. But he stuck with his decision not to play on Yom Kippur in a game the Tigers lost to the Yankees, 5–2. Detroit media and fans criticized his decision, but what mattered most to Greenberg was that he received a standing ovation from congregants at the Shaarey Zedek synagogue when he arrived for Day of Atonement services. The Tigers still went on to win the American League pennant before losing to the St. Louis Cardinals' "Gashouse Gang," who won in seven games for their third championship in nine years.

Greenberg saw more potential in Roger as a pull-hitting long-ball threat than a line-drive gap hitter, especially for a future in Cleveland, with its inviting 320-foot distance down the right-field foul line. Yankee Stadium's even shorter right-field porch wasn't even a thought at the time. But Greenberg's mind was working. In Keokuk, the Indians had manager Jo Jo White.

White had been Greenberg's roommate on a Tigers squad that won back-to-back American League pennants in 1934 and 1935, as well as the 1935 World Series. He became so popular in that period that he appeared on Wheaties boxes and played golf in the off-season in Florida with stars Mickey Cochrane, Dizzy Dean, and Babe Ruth. Although he had not been a home run hitter himself, White developed a post-playing-career reputation as a knowledgeable hitting instructor.

Greenberg believed he was the coach with the temperament who could handle the often stubborn, temperamental Maras through a swing change. White himself had been a left-handed hitter, which might help in working with Roger. "I liked Roger right away—I liked his nerve, the way the way he'd run into fences for you, the way he slid," White told the *New York Post's* Leonard Shecter in 1961. "He'd rip that bag and the man right along with it. He had what it takes to be a ballplayer—great desire. It stuck out all over him. I knew damn well he could be a big leaguer."

Under White's tutelage, Roger became a power hitter in a memorable season. He belted 32 home runs, drove in 111, and batted .315. He also stole 25 bases, five more than future American League stolen base leader Luis Aparicio, who was playing for the Chicago White Sox's minor league team in Waterloo, Iowa.

Maras played for White again in 1955, a season he began in Tulsa, the Indians Class AA affiliate, where he was a bad fit under its manager, Dutch Meyer. Maras and Meyer evidently didn't like one another and, according to some stories, had a falling out when the manager tried to help Roger break out of a slump with a series of drills that the young slugger refused to do.

"He kept trying to change everything I did," Maras said of his manager. "According to him, I couldn't do anything right. I was really getting fouled up." When Meyer benched Maras, Roger appealed to Indians executives, who sided with their potential star outfielder. Maras was moved to the Indians' Class A team in Reading, Pennsylvania. Meyer was soon fired. And why not? His handling of Roger had been disastrous. He had hit only a single home run in his time in Tulsa. In Reading, it was the Maras of old: 19 home runs, 78 RBI, and a .289 batting average, with 24 stolen bases and 18 drag-bunt singles. Reading finished in first place, with Roger as the poster boy of Jo Jo White's coaching and managing.

"He was one of the great influences I had in baseball," Maris said of White years later. "I can't imagine a young fellow breaking into baseball being in better hands."

The end of the 1955 season marked a change in Roger. He turned 21 that September, and he was now of age to do what he wanted. When he bought his new car, a DeSoto convertible, with his bonus money, he was underage and had to have his mother Connie sign the state registration papers. It had been a bad idea. One day, while he was visiting Patricia, Roger stepped outside to discover the DeSoto missing. When he called police to report it stolen, he learned that Connie Maras, the car's legal owner, had had it towed to her home. Possessive, bizarre, neurotic. Call it what you will. Roger was at his wits' end.

Was Rudy Maras Sr. any better as a role model? Roger had had enough. What is it they say about victory or success? That they have a thousand fathers? The same seems true about the story of how the Maras name became Maris. The story has changed often in the retelling. But maybe it is one of the few things that the immediate family can agree upon: whether it was Connie's ultimate way of getting back at the Maras family or just Roger finally tiring at the taunting puns on Mare-ASS, they all got on board. That fall, the family of Rudolph S. Maras Sr. legally changed their Croatian name to Maris.

Holding the newly christened Roger Maris together at this moment—and for much of his future life—was the woman he would marry within the year. Patricia Carvell would give Roger six children. She would become the Maris family matriarch when Roger passed prematurely at the age of 51 in 1985. She would be the bedrock for the Marises as they came into incredible wealth well after Roger's death, financial security that was beyond anything he could have imagined, but still the result of what his fame from baseball could bring. So in

1955, while she may have intimidated the Maras brood, Connie Maris was no match for young Pat's love and emerging inner strength that would fortify Roger at home and on the road in the coming years.

Patricia and Roger married October 13, 1956, at St. Anthony's Church in Fargo, in a small wedding attended by family, friends, and former classmates. One of those was Dick Savageau, who remembered that the only negative note may have been what he detected in Roger's mother.

"That's what I'd surmised," he said. "But there could have been some things in the family that went on. You know, if Connie says, 'I don't know why Roger would marry Pat,' well, obviously Pat would not be very happy with her. At the wedding, I was talking to Connie and Pat told her, 'You didn't need to say that to Dick.' There was something between them. Pat's very pleasant, but she can be tough."

4

Becoming Mantle

"I'll tell you what I know about
courage. My father was the most
courageous man I ever knew."
—MICKEY MANTLE

THAT MICKEY MANTLE WAS BORN AT ALL IS A MINOR MIRACLE, OR perhaps just the good fortune of fate giving biology a helping hand. Who hasn't wondered at some time how different life might have been, being born to a different mother or another father? Years later, after the Hall of Fame career and the New York fast life and long after he had become accustomed to the role of being Mickey Mantle, Mickey occasionally would chuckle with a hint of curiosity at the thought that he might easily have been his aunt's child. For before his father, Elvin Clark Mantle, had his eye on the woman who would give birth to Mickey, he had had designs on the woman's younger sister, a neighbor in the mining town of Spavinaw in Mayes County, Oklahoma.

Elvin, the first of four children, who from his crib days had been known as Mutt, was in his mid-teens. Lovell Richardson, the woman who would one day be Mickey Mantle's mother, was a grown woman 10 years older than Mutt and, at the time, married to her first husband,

William Theodore Davis, a farm boy from nearby Craig County with whom she ran off at the age of 17. She bore two children by William Davis, Theodore and Anna Bea, before divorcing.

Later, she explained her marital breakup to Mickey by simply stating, "We had a bad misunderstanding." Lovell Richardson, a tall, slender woman with gray eyes and reddish-blond hair, returned to her parents' home, where she met Mutt one day when he came to court her sister. Months later, at the age of 17, Mutt Mantle married Lovell in a civil ceremony.

Mickey Charles Mantle was born October 20, 1931, in an unpainted two-room house on a dirt road outside Spavinaw, Oklahoma, a town of a few hundred people about 35 miles southwest of Commerce in the flatland northeast corner of the state, which was also the hub of the Oklahoma mining district. Spavinaw was in the heart of Cherokee Indian country and part of the legendary Dust Bowl, the Oklahoma plains where red dirt blanketed everything when the wind blew. The Missouri state line is just 10 miles east, and Kansas is five miles to the north. On the day they finished the last section of Route 66 at the Kansas-Oklahoma state line, Cherokees came down from their reservation to watch, squatting along the highway, wrapped in blankets, to glumly witness the passing of an era.

The world in which Mickey Mantle was born and experienced his childhood is so closely linked in our minds with America's worst economic depression that it has become almost impossible to view it historically as anything other than cheerless. A period of drab and desperate existence, spiritually void and mired in hopelessness, the '30s for most people evokes the stolid and stunned faces of tenant farmers immortalized by Pulitzer Prize–winning author James Agee and photographer Walker Evans in *Let Us Now Praise Famous Men.*

In the country as a whole, except for the hordes of forgotten poor of the 1930s, this era of economic debacle was also filled with more major political, social, and intellectual developments than the nation had ever known. In Oklahoma, however, the '30s reflected the uprooted, impoverished existence of a Steinbeck novel. Baseball, already ingrained as the national pastime, was both a diversion and a summertime remedy. To raise funds to help the unemployed in the Depression, in September 1931, the Yankees, Giants, and Dodgers played a series of benefit games that raised more than $100,000. In a pregame fungo-hitting contest, Babe Ruth, normally a left-handed hitter, batted right and drove a ball 421 feet into the center-field stands.

The 1930s were hard times in the Oklahoma plains. In Spavinaw, many of the Mantles' neighbors who were unable to make a living moved out to California, far away from what would become an ecological and human disaster that took place in the southwestern Great Plains region. It was caused by misuse of land and years of sustained drought. During the years when there was adequate rainfall, the land produced bountiful crops. But as the droughts of the early 1930s deepened, the farmers kept plowing and planting and nothing would grow. The ground cover that held the soil in place was gone. The Plains winds whipped across the fields raising billowing clouds of dust to the skies. The skies could darken for days, and even the most well-sealed homes could have a thick layer of dust on the furniture. In some places, the dust would drift like snow, covering farmsteads. At the same time, the country was experiencing the Great Depression, the worst economic slump ever in U.S. history, and one that spread to the entire industrialized world. The Depression began in late 1929 and lasted for about a decade.

It was into this America, scandalously troubled economically but holding on to a moral purpose of unwavering optimism, that Mickey

Mantle was born. As in the life of every man, the intricacies of his nature can be traced back to where he came from and to those who shaped him. For Mantle, it all started and ended with his father, a teenager when Mickey was born but ultimately the most influential person in his life.

Mutt Mantle held the same dreams for his first son that other fathers have had for their children since the beginning of time. With Mutt, however, it is fair to say his dreams for Mickey were obsessive. "The feeling between Mutt Mantle and his son," Merlyn Mantle once said, "was more than love. Mick was his work of art, just as much as if his father had created him out of clay. He spent every minute he could with him, coaching, teaching, shaping him, and pointing him toward the destiny he knew was out there. Baseball consumed Mickey. He talked, when he talked, of little else. It was the number one priority in his life and, in a way, always would be."

Mutt Mantle found the 1931 season a fortuitous one. Months before Mickey was born, Mutt had decided that his son would be named after one of the princes of his beloved game. "If my child is a boy," Mutt told his friends, "he's going to be a baseball player. I'm naming him Mickey—after Mickey Cochrane." The catcher and spark of the Philadelphia Athletics' championship teams of 1929 and 1930, Mickey Cochrane had a .345 batting average for those three years. He later would lead the Detroit Tigers to two pennants and a World Series championship in 1935. In 1947, he and A's battery mate Lefty Grove would be elected to Baseball's Hall of Fame. But in 1931, as he helped the Athletics win the American League title, Cochrane also caught Grove's historic 31-win season.

On October 10, 10 days before Mickey was born, Mutt Mantle got the best of both worlds. His favorite player, who had hit .349 that season, made it to the World Series, but his favorite team, the St. Louis

Cardinals, won the championship, defeating the A's, in the seventh game of the series. On the day Mickey was born, Cochrane was still playing baseball, part of an All-Star squad on a barnstorming trip to Hawaii and Japan. On that day, too, Frankie Frisch, the Cardinals' fiery leader and another of Mutt's heroes, after hitting .311 and a league-leading 28 stolen bases, was named MVP of the National League.

"Mama says Dad showed me a baseball before I was 12 hours old and it almost broke his heart when I paid more attention to the bottle," Mickey would say years later. "Baseball, that's all he lived for. He used to say that it seemed to him like he just died in the winter, until the time when baseball came around again. Dad insisted on my being taught the positions on the baseball field before the ABCs. He was that crazy about baseball… I was probably the only baby in history whose first lullaby was the radio broadcast of a ball game. One night, Mama says I woke up during the seventh-inning stretch. She pleaded with Dad to please cut off that contraption and let me sleep. 'You got Mickey wrong, hon,' Dad said. 'I don't blame him for screaming. He knew the situation called for a bunt instead of hitting away.'"

Mutt named his son Mickey Charles Mantle, after both Cochrane and his own father. He apparently was unaware that Cochrane's given name was actually Gordon Stanley and that "Mickey" was an informal name that had been derived from the nickname "Black Mike" that Cochrane had been given at Boston University for his competitiveness on the football team. Mutt, though, was not one who was too concerned about the exactness of names. Mickey spelled his father's name "Elvin," but Mutt Mantle's Oklahoma driver's license spelled his first name "Elvan," and it was spelled "Elven" on his headstone at the Grand Army of the Republic Cemetery between Miami and Commerce, where he was buried after his death in 1952. It was also spelled "Elven" on the birth certificate of Mickey's youngest brother,

Larry. "I'm not sure how he spelled his name," daughter Barbara later said. "The only way I ever saw him sign anything was 'E.C. Mantle.'"

From his father, Mickey inherited something far more important than a name: an incredible, almost mythic physical strength that one day would produce his prodigious home run power. Mutt Mantle was a lead and zinc miner who had played semi-professional baseball, and his father, Charles Mantle, had played baseball on a mining company team. Mickey was to later look back on his father's baseball talents with a son's wishful memory, saying he believed Mutt could have been a fine professional baseball player if he had been given the chance. But it turned out to be the mines that were in Mutt Mantle's blood. Mutt worked in the lead and zinc mines of the area but had also worked as a tenant farmer both before Mickey was born and later when Mickey was in his teens.

For his entire life, Mickey was to lament the life that fate had placed on his father. "I always wished my dad could be somebody other than a miner," a regretful Mickey would reminisce. "I knew it was killing him. He was underground eight hours a day. Every time he took a breath, the dust and dampness went into his lungs. Coughed up gobs of phlegm and never saw a doctor. What for? He'd only be told it was "miner's disease." He realized that if he didn't get cancer, he'd die of tuberculosis. Many did before the age of 40. 'So what the hell? Live while you can,' he'd say and light another cigarette. A confirmed chain-smoker, I hardly remember him without one stuck in the corner of his mouth."

Mickey Mantle's parents, Mutt and Lovell, were raised in a town of dissimilar personalities and cultures, so it is no surprise that they, too, were a study in contrasts. Those two different personalities were to equally polarize young Mickey's own self-image and emotional development.

"My father was a quiet man, but he could freeze you with a look," Mickey said once. "He never told me he loved me. But he showed that he did by all the hours he spent with me, all the hopes he invested in me. He saw his role as pushing me, always keeping my mind on getting better. I worked hard at doing that because I wanted to please him. He would drape an arm around me and give me a hug... I adored my dad and was just like him in many ways—I was shy and found it hard to show my emotions. I couldn't open up to people, and they mistook my shyness for rudeness."

Sadly, the way he was molded by two unemotional parents would influence the way Mickey himself would model his relationships with his own sons. "He had been brought up a certain way," Mickey Jr. said of his father, "and if he couldn't deal with his feelings, he buried them. He paid a high cost for packing away the affection that was so close to his surface. For most of our lives, when we greeted each other after a separation of weeks or months, we would shake hands. It wasn't just him. Everybody in his family, my uncles, his cousins, kept the same distance."

For Mutt Mantle, that emotional detachment had been a method of self-survival. As a young man, Mutt had been forced to grow up quickly and dropped out of school to take a job grading county roads. Not long after marrying Lovell and having Mickey, however, Mutt lost the grading job and thought seriously about taking his young family to California. Instead he became a tenant farmer, working 80 acres of land but seeing little in return.

Lovell, meanwhile, was busy raising her own two children as well as Mickey and she was pregnant with the second of the five children she would have by Mutt. Lovell was a devoted wife to her second husband. What bonded them together was that both came from a long line of Oklahoma people, five generations of Americans with family bloodlines of English, Dutch, and German stock. At one point, there was unfounded speculation, in part spurred by Mickey's pride in the American Indian heritage of his beloved Oklahoma, that his mother was part Native American.

What is undeniable is that Mutt fell in love with a woman not only significantly older, but also more distant personally than even he himself was, and with a greater difficulty in showing her emotions than he had. For young Mickey, the impact may have even been greater. Lovell, the daughter of a carpenter, was reticent even with her loved ones and Mickey would later say that his mother "didn't lavish affection on us either… when Mom wanted to show her love, she fixed a big meal." However, one of the few times that Lovell did show some emotion, she overdid it. Once, when Mickey's twin brothers Ray and Roy were playing high school football and a fight broke out, Lovell ended up on the field slapping the opposing players on their helmets with her purse. Still, it was not until later, at her 80th birthday party in Oklahoma City, that she was to tell Mickey and the family why she had married Mutt: he was tall, handsome, and a real gentleman under the rough exterior.

Merlyn Mantle's recollection of her mother-in-law seemed to capture the essence of Mickey's mom best: "Lovell was not a warm or openly affectionate woman, but she was a tireless and protective mother. She had seven children, two by a first marriage, and I never saw anyone do as much laundry. She did it by hand, on a washboard in the back yard, and hung it on row after row of clotheslines to dry. They lived in the country and didn't yet have electricity."

As poor as they were at the time, however, Mickey always looked back with pride at how his parents persevered without reaching out for charity or even credit. "We were about the only family in Commerce that didn't buy groceries on credit," he remembered. "We only bought what we needed, and my dad paid cash. The grocer appreciated it so much that he let us kids pick out a free bag of candy."

The Mantles did not have much of a traditional spiritual life, surprising considering they lived in a community of God-fearing neighbors in the heart of the Bible Belt. Commerce had four churches. Mickey later said he had been in all of them at one time or another, "yet nobody in my family took religion seriously. I suppose it was my dad's influence. He used to say, 'Religion doesn't necessarily make you good. As long as your heart is in the right place and you don't hurt anyone, I think you'll go to heaven—if there is one.' Mom felt the same way. She backed him no matter what he believed."

If Lovell Mantle was not a God-fearing woman in a traditionally God-fearing community, she did have her own fears for her children— the biggest of which was a local area known as the "Alkali." This was a flat stretch of plain in Commerce where the lead-mine shafts had been sunk and then left abandoned, and where tall piles of exhausted ore stood like miniature pyramids. The plain of the "Alkali" was used for sandlot baseball games where a ball that got past the outfielders often rolled undisturbed for several hundred feet. Mickey would later joke that playing there as a boy with the endless outfield was what had convinced him to be an infielder. Mickey, however, wasn't even supposed to be playing ball on the makeshift "Alkali" baseball field. His mother had strict rules forbidding him to play there. According to Mickey, his mother "would haul me home and really warm my britches" on the few occasions when she caught him disobeying her. The reason for Lovell's concern was the caved-in old mine shafts, which were closed off only by sagging fences that were regularly climbed over or cut through by curious youngsters. She had grown up with stories about children who had fallen into the cave-ins and died in the black holes and worried, like other mothers, of such a disaster taking one of her own.

Lovell Mantle, though, also had a dark side to her, something that wasn't talked about until years later. While there is no documentation to suggest that she was an abusive mother, Mickey later would reluctantly talk about whippings he had been given by his mother. Years later, too, Mickey would see some of his mother's dark side in her treatment of little David Mantle, who would describe his grandmother as "always mean to me." David also remembered his grandmother with sadness. "She used to chase me around and hit me with a broomstick," he said. "Maybe it was because I was so hyper. One day I was sitting on a stool in her kitchen, and I did something a kid would do. Dad told me she just backhanded me and knocked me off the stool. After that, he never let her watch me anymore because it really hurt him that she would give me that kind of swat. He said she used to whip him, too, something he didn't like to admit. She was still Dad's mother, and I respected her, but I didn't have the love for her that I did for Mom's folks."

That coldness that could sometimes border on cruelty was just one of many ways in which Lovell and Mutt were so dissimilar. Whereas he was occasionally carefree, rugged, athletic, but overly demanding of Mickey, she tended to be a loner, if not lonely, emotional on occasion, and subservient to her younger husband in his wishes on how Mickey would be raised. Yet Mutt, despite his unquestioned love for his oldest son, was far from possessing the emotional maturity ordinarily necessary for being the dominant parent in a family.

Mutt was not even 10 when his mother had died of pneumonia, just a week after giving birth to her fourth child, Emmett. Charles Mantle would struggle to raise his three oldest children, while an aunt and uncle raised the baby. As the oldest child, Mutt became in charge of brother Eugene and sister, Thelma, while Charles put in long hours as a butcher in Spavinaw. Mutt's own childhood effectively was sacrificed to help his father raise the family. Raising your own family, however, can present an altogether different challenge, and it can be strongly argued that Mutt fell into the same trap that has ensnared fathers throughout history. In raising Mickey the way he did, obsessed from the cradle with his son becoming a professional baseball player, Mutt imposed upon him the pressure of not only fulfilling his own dashed dreams but also a level of expectation of almost immortal achievement.

Year later, fans and friends were often touched to hear Mickey lament that he had not been the same kind of father to his own oldest son. "If my father had been his father," Mickey said on more than one occasion, "Mickey Jr. would have been a big leaguer." To which, Mickey Jr. voiced some serious reservations. "I'm not so sure," he said. "More likely, if Dad had cooped me up in the back yard for three or four hours every day, playing catch and pitching to me, I would have run away from home."

Mickey's wife, Merlyn, would be convinced that Mutt's overbearing fathering unchecked by Lovell's own detached manner left Mickey emotionally and psychologically traumatized and unable to turn even to his loved ones for help:

"The early pressure on Mickey to play ball and his self-imposed drive to play it better than anyone caused real emotional problems for him. A lot of the conflicts in him later had their roots in those years. Mick wet his bed until he was 16 years old. I would hope that this would not be taken as demeaning him. But it is important, I think in understanding what he went through, and how much he wanted to please his dad. This is what the pressure of wanting that approval did to him. He told me that he knew from the time he was five years old that he wanted to be a ballplayer, and how he could never face his father if he didn't make it to the major leagues. Interestingly, the bed-wetting stopped when the Yankees sent him to Independence, Missouri, for his first season in Class D. He had to solve the problems before any of his teammates found out. He could not abide anyone making fun of him. He stopped by asserting his own pure willpower, because the pressure didn't end then, or with the Yankees. It never ended. I know exactly how much he ached for his dad's approval… His father had this wonderful but obsessive dream for Mickey, and only for Mickey. He was anointed from the cradle. When his dad would pitch to him for hours, out of a hundred pitches, Mick would be in terror of missing one and looking bad, and having his father frown or criticize."

Mantle would later talk about the bed-wetting on a 1970 appearance on *The Dick Cavett Show* on which songwriter Paul Simon was also a guest. It was Simon, in a nostalgic expression of longing for the innocence and simplicity of an earlier and happier time, who had written in the lyrics for a popular song of the 1960s, "Where have you gone, Joe DiMaggio? A nation turns its lonely eyes to you." In that talk show, Simon was dumbstruck by the revelation of another of his heroes and expressed the shock of millions: "Mickey Mantle wet his bed?!"

Sportswriter Phil Berger would observe of Mantle's relationship with his father: "Anything short of success would be an affront to Mutt, and the thought of disappointing his father weighed heavily on him. The wetting of his sheets was an early and vivid indication of the burden under which young Mickey toiled, and the pressure it exerted on him."

However, there was one childhood trauma that Mickey never spoke about publicly. Around the age of four or five years old, his half-sister Anna Bea and some of her teenage friends sexually molested him. He was humiliated in such a demeaning manner that he could never bring himself to tell anyone. Only much later, in the year before his death, would Mickey be able to confide to Merlyn the sexual molestation he had suffered. Anna Bea would toy with him sexually, pulling down his pants and fondling his penis, often as her girlfriends watched and giggled, howling their laughter and derision at the times when he would get a tiny erection. The molestation and the teasing continued for several years, until Anna Bea moved out of the house, but the traumatic scarring would last a lifetime. Merlyn suspected that it was the source of his unhealthy relationships with women—a large part of the reason he never respected women, his affairs, his one-night stands, the crude and vulgar language he used around women when he drank.

Mutt would never know of the molestation. Like other abused children, Mickey felt shame and guilt over what had happened. Beginning in childhood, he would go to great lengths not to disappoint his father. Mickey himself would later say of his childhood relationship with his father: "No boy, I think, ever loved his father more than I did… I would do nearly anything to keep my father happy… He never had to raise his hand to me to make me obey, for I needed only a sharp look and a word from him and the knowledge that I had displeased him to make me go and do better… I knew from the time I was small that every small victory I won, and every solid hit I made or prize I was awarded, brought real joy to my father's heart."

5
Creation

"My dad taught me to switch-hit. He and my grandfather, who was left-handed, pitched to me every day after school in the back yard. I batted lefty against my dad and righty against my granddad."

—MICKEY MANTLE

STORIES OF THE YOUNG MICKEY Mantle learning to switch-hit and being pitched to for hours on end every afternoon by his father and grandfather became as much a part of the Mantle lore as the young Arthur pulling Excalibur from the stone is central to the legend of Camelot. In 1934, when Mickey was three years old, Mutt took a job as a shoveler at the Eagle-Picher Zinc and Lead Co. and moved his family from Spavinaw to Commerce, near Interstate 44, which connects Tulsa and Joplin, Missouri.

Commerce was a small town of fewer than 3,000 people, where the main street was only seven blocks long. This was a town so small it was once called simply North Miami because it was only four miles north of Miami, Oklahoma, in Ottawa County. But in 1914, lead and zinc mines were booming, so business people thought Commerce would be a better fit. The same year the Mantles moved to Commerce, on April 6, 1934, the notorious outlaws Bonnie and Clyde got stuck in the mud on the road between Commerce and Miami. At gunpoint, they forced a trucker to pull them out. A passing motorist happened to notice a bullet hole in Bonnie and Clyde's car's windshield and called the police. In the ensuing shootout, the Commerce police chief was taken hostage and the constable was killed.

Life was a lot calmer at 319 South Quincy Street, a four-room clapboard house that became home to the Mantles for the next 10 years. Mutt, by this time, had become a ground boss in the Eagle-Picher lead and zinc mines, earning $75 a week, extremely good pay in the 1940s in Oklahoma or anywhere else in the country. Mutt, however, was supporting not only his growing five children and a wife but his father, Charlie, as well. The house on Quincy Street would become the one that Mickey would most associate with his youth. It was situated some hundred yards off the highway on a gravel road leading down to the house from the family mailbox. Often Mickey would wait at the mailbox for his father to come home from the mines, and they would walk together down the road to their house talking about baseball. From the time Mickey had been in his crib, Mutt had made sure his son had a baseball cap nearby. Lovell Mantle had used material from some of her husband's old baseball pants and shirts to fashion miniature uniforms for her son. Here, on Quincy Street on the edge of town, sometimes in uniform and sometimes without, young Mickey began honing his swing with a tin shed for a backstop.

"You take this bat," Mickey remembered his father telling him, "and you try to hit the balls we throw to you. We won't throw them hard, so don't worry about getting hit. Anyway, these tennis balls won't hurt you."

Mickey took the bat and swung it enthusiastically right-handed. Mickey was a natural right-hander.

"Now there's one other thing I want to tell you," Mutt explained to his son. "When I throw the ball, you go ahead and swing the way you're doing it now. But when Grandpa Charley throws the ball, I want you to turn around and swing the other way. Understand?" Mutt pitched left-handed. Charley Mantle pitched right-handed. In conventional baseball wisdom, right-handed hitters generally have greater success against left-handers and left handed hitters greater success against right-handed pitchers. A right-handed pitcher's curveball will break away from a right-handed hitter, usually making him harder to hit against, and vice-versa. Mutt calculated that switch-hitters—hitters who could hit both right-handed and left-handed—were a valuable commodity in professional baseball.

In 1938, about the time Mickey's switch-hitting lessons began, there were only 11 switch-hitters on the rosters of major league teams. In 1951, there would be only 10 major league switch-hitters, counting Cleveland Indians pitcher Early Wynn. But by 1971, in the generation of players influenced by Mantle, major league rosters would have 41 switch-hitters. So in the front yard of 319 Quincy Street, at the age when other children were playing cowboys and Indians, Mickey Mantle began learning the art that would one day make him the greatest switch hitter in the history of the game.

"Mickey didn't like it at all in the beginning," Lovell Mantle recalled, "but I know now that he is glad he listened to his father."

At first, Mickey found it extremely difficult to switch-hit, especially to hit left-handed. But the practice continued, day after day, starting around four o'clock in the afternoon, as soon as Mutt returned home from his day at the mines and continuing until nightfall. It was not unusual during the summer, when there was no school, for Mickey to put in as many as five hours a day taking batting practice with his father and grandfather pitching. "Once I learned to hit a ball with a bat," said Mickey, looking back, "I needed none of my father's urging to play the game. Knowing that it pleased my father to see me do well at the game only made it twice as much fun to me."

Soon Mutt and Charlie began throwing harder and tossing the incredible curves that can be thrown with a tennis ball. However, when Mickey turned six, real baseballs replaced the tennis balls. To sharpen Mickey's interest in the game, Mutt and Charley devised a set of Quincy Street ground rules. A line drive was a single. A ball hit off the side of the house became a double. A ball off the roof was ruled a triple. A ball hit over the house or into the adjoining lot was a home run. Mickey, who often listened to radio broadcasts of St. Louis Cardinals games with his father, imagined himself to be a slugger with the Cardinals' legendary Gashouse Gang.

This was Mickey's childhood, in which his two closest friends and playmates were his father and grandfather. Mickey's first real friend his own age was LeRoy Bennett, who lived up the street on Quincy. His other close childhood pal was Nick Ferguson, who lived on Vine Street, about eight blocks away. But each afternoon, as the time neared that Mutt returned home, Mickey's mother could often be heard yelling out "Mickey Charles!" Neighbors even used to joke: "When Mutt comes home from the mines, Mickey has to stop playing and start practicing."

Mickey himself would look back on the long ritual of hitting drills with fond memories: "The practice paid off. By the time I was in the second grade, I was hitting them pretty good from the right side. But Dad also wanted me to bat lefty, which I hated. When it got dark and supper was ready, Dad would turn me around, from righty to lefty. 'Your belly can wait,' he'd say. Then he'd start pitching again. He believed that any kid could develop into a switch hitter if you taught him early enough."

In the middle of the Depression, baseball was the only way Mutt saw for Mickey to escape the cycle that had gripped him, as it had most young men from similar backgrounds in northeast Oklahoma: a near-poverty existence and a lifetime of being chained to either the mines or farms of the area. This was a time in America in which, unlike a generation later, the only two sports through which youngsters could seriously dream of rising out of meager circumstances were baseball and boxing.

Mutt's second brother, Eugene, had shown some signs of pugilistic promise and was nicknamed "Tunney" after world heavyweight champion Gene Tunney. Eugene once put out a man's eye, though with a shovel, not with his fists. A fight had broken out at a dance in Spavinaw in which Mutt, Eugene, and other Mantle family members found themselves outnumbered. In defending himself, Eugene apparently picked up a shovel and struck one of his assailants. The Mantle men would always boast of never having lost a fight, including that one. Baseball, however, was the real passion for all the Mantle men. Many of them spent their weekends playing on semi-pro teams in Mayes County. Even after Mutt moved to Commerce, he returned to Spavinaw every weekend to play with the local team.

Baseball was also a bond between Mickey's father and mother. Over the years, Lovell Mantle developed a love of her own for the game. Mantle friend Nick Ferguson remembered visiting and seeing Mickey's mother doing her housework while listening to radio broadcasts of St. Louis Cardinals games. With Mutt away at work during the day, Lovell would jot down notes about the games in a kind of makeshift scorecard that she would later use to recount the games for Mutt, the family, and friends over dinner. "She'd tell you how this happened and that happened—she had it right in front of her," Ferguson told one early biographer, "and she made it sound exciting, too. And everybody had to know what went on. They'd keep asking for more and more, and she'd just keep telling them like she had actually been at the game herself."

Just how knowledgeable Lovell Mantle was about baseball, however, is debatable. Mantle was to later describe his mother as having been a fan, though hardly with the baseball knowledge and insight of his father. Nick Ferguson, on the other hand, has been quoted as claiming that Lovell Mantle—and not Mutt—had been the parent with the true "inside" perspective on the game, especially in what she would reportedly tell Mickey about his own play. "She'd never raise her voice," Ferguson said in one interview. "You'd barely hear her. But she'd sort of whisper to Mickey about what he had done in games she saw. She'd say, 'You know, in that situation, if you bunted, you woulda done this or that. If you backed a little bit at second, you'd have more room to take a ball. Or on this hitter or that hitter, you should maybe move over a little more.' She knew the game, and she could always get him to think about what he was doing."

Mantle himself remembers that his mother was most demonstrative as a basketball fan when he was playing on the Commerce High basketball team. "Mom used to rant and rave at those games," said Mantle. "If she objected to a referee's decision, you could hear her voice travel across the gym: 'Where are your glasses, you bum!' Believe me, if the referee called anything against Commerce, she'd cuss him out like a sailor. It unnerved my father. He'd cover his head with his hands and sit a few rows behind her to get away from the shouting."

Although his name became associated with Commerce and he became known as the "Commerce Comet," Mickey himself later became typically unsentimental about his adopted hometown. He would go so far as to tell friends in his later years that, as a youth, he had always felt like an outsider there. There were things in Mickey's childhood, things he would never reveal until many years later, that made an unhappy childhood, and there was a level of dysfunction in the family that planted the seeds for addictive personalities throughout most of the family.

Alcoholism ran through much of Lovell Mantle's side of the family. Her brothers were all alcoholics. It was a problem that also later afflicted Lovell's two children by her first husband. Mickey's half-sister Anna Bea married young, left home, worked as a barmaid, and died in her twenties. "Hers," said Merlyn Mantle, "was a short, sad life." Theodore, Mickey's half-brother, was also an alcoholic, though with a heart of gold. When he was discharged from the army, Theodore used most of his discharge pay to help Mickey buy Merlyn's wedding ring.

Mickey later would describe his father as "a light drinker who bought a half-pint on Saturday and sipped it for days. He would have whipped my fanny if he caught me taking a drink… Every night when he came home from working eight hours at the Eagle-Picher Zinc and Lead [mine], he'd head for the icebox and take a swig of whiskey. Dad would get drunk once in a while, like when he went to a barn dance and he might have five or six drinks. Hell, for me five or six drinks wouldn't have been a full cocktail party!"

Mickey's pal Nick Ferguson, however, suggests that Mutt's drinking may have been more than what Mantle has indicated in his autobiographies and interviews. "I'm sure he didn't chase around with women," Ferguson said in one interview, "but Mutt drank, and he used to take Mick and us kids into the bars with him when we weren't even old enough to drink." What is known for certain about Mutt Mantle is that he did have one known addiction. He was a chain smoker. Mickey excused it as something all the miners did, miners who "didn't see how nicotine could do any more damage to their lungs than the dust they inhaled every day." As a Yankee, Mickey would later endorse Camel cigarettes. Every week he was provided with a free carton of Camels, which he mailed home to his father who would exchange the carton at a Commerce store for his favorite brand, Lucky Strike. With Mickey the hottest name in baseball, the Commerce grocer would often boast to his customers, "See these Camels? They came straight from Mickey."

Even as an adult, however, Commerce did not hold the fondest of memories. In 1956, during the Christmas after his greatest season, when he won baseball's Triple Crown, Mickey and Merlyn were visiting family when Mickey decided to go visit some old pals at Mendenhall's bar on Main Street. The only problem was that he was supposed to be babysitting Mickey Jr., who was then three, and he took him along to Mendenhall's with him. A fight broke out when Mickey tried defending the bartender against a drunk. Sitting on a bar watching his father roll around on the floor, Mickey Jr. picked up his father's beer and took his first swig, just as his grandfather, Giles Johnson, came in the door looking for them. The grandfather scooped Mickey Jr. off the bar into his arms and, on his way out, kicked his famous son-in-law in the side of the head, warning him: "Don't ever let me catch you with this kid in here again."

In later life, Mickey looked back on Commerce with many reasons to have mixed feelings about his life there. Former Commerce postmaster Bill Brumley would remember that when the Civic Pride Committee tried to start a Mantle museum in Commerce in the 1980s, Mantle's lawyer had threatened a lawsuit. Some townspeople harbored hard feelings against Mantle even after his death at the way he had often slighted Commerce, among them mayor Jack Young, a 74-year-old local native.

"Mickey Mantle didn't even show up when they dedicated Mickey Mantle Boulevard," he said. "People got down on him for stuff like that."

However, there also were others, especially among the younger generation in Commerce, for whom Mantle remained a source of local pride and admiration. To this date, Mickey is the biggest thing that ever happened to Commerce, Oklahoma. In 1993, two local men, Brian Brassfield and Todd McClain, buddies since Little League, bought Mantle's boyhood home. Over they next few years, they used their savings to begin restoration of the dilapidated house in hopes of turning it into a Mickey Mantle museum. Said Brassfield: "We've even talked about the tin barn and letting kids bat against it, just like he did." They envisioned life-size bronze statues of a young Mantle and his father, posed as hitter and pitcher the way they did every afternoon from the time he started school.

If he could, Mickey might tell them about another day, when he was 10 and playing as an undersized catcher with 12-year-olds on the Douthat team in the peewee division of the Gabby Street League. Overmatched against an outstanding right-handed pitcher, Mickey had struck out three times batting left-handed. Discouraged and frustrated, Mickey decided on his own to try batting against the overpowering pitcher from his natural right hand side. However, as soon as Mickey took his stance in the right-handed batter's box, a deep, booming voice stopped the game.

"Go on home!" Mutt Mantle shouted from the far edge of the baseball field. "Go on home! And don't you ever put on that baseball uniform until you switch-hit like I taught you."

Feeling punished and humiliated, Mickey hurried home. That night, after dinner, Mickey apologized to his father and promised not to do that again.

"He never drove me to play baseball, for no one ever had to do that," Mickey would later write in *The Education of a Baseball Player*, his 1967 autobiography. "But he worked hard to help me improve and he gave me good advice to follow and played with me when he had the chance. It wasn't the thought of riches or fame that drove me. I didn't think about those things. I had no desire to leave home or to get very far from Commerce and the towns around us. What did keep me driving hard, from the time that I was 10, to hit the ball better and farther, was first of all my own love for the game and then my love for my father. I knew from the time I was small that every small victory I won, and every solid hit I made or prize I was awarded, brought real joy to my father's heart."

6
The Natural

*"A ballplayer has to be kept hungry to become
a big leaguer. That's why no boy from a rich
family has ever made the big leagues."*
—JOE DIMAGGIO

WHEN MICKEY MANTLE ARRIVED AT SPRING TRAINING IN 1951, THE
Yankee players and reporters covering the team were amazed not only
at the incredible talent they saw on display but also at how cheaply
the team had gotten him. Only a year earlier, the camp had been
abuzz at another prize prospect, Jackie Jensen, who many thought
might eventually become Joe DiMaggio's successor in center field.
Jensen, an All-American in two sports at the University of California,
was a college golden boy with a national reputation. He had pitched
and hit his Golden Bears team to the 1947 College World Series
championship. Then he had led his football team to a perfect 10–0
season in 1948 (before losing in the Rose Bowl), finishing fourth in
the Heisman Trophy balloting. He had given up his senior year to sign
a $40,000 contract that made him a baseball bonus baby. As such,
under baseball rules, Jensen had to be kept on the major league roster,
though he had proven to be a disappointment in 1950.

If Jackie Jensen, who looked like he would be a bust, at least for the Yankees, could command 40 grand, the thinking was, what kind of bonus did the ballclub have to put out to sign a phenom like Mickey Mantle? When other ballplayers and the writer heard that Mantle had been signed for a mere $1,500 bonus, most thought they had misheard. For Mickey Mantle, the kid Stengel and others were already raving about? For the next Ruth and DiMaggio? Fifteen hundred dollars? Not 15 thousand? Joe DiMaggio, for one, found it hard to believe.

"I thought they were joking, to be honest," DiMaggio would say. "I couldn't believe it. I figure he either was a rich kid who didn't need the money or some kid off the farm that had no idea of what he was worth. Oh, my, what he had to learn. And can you imagine, if I'd had another few years, what kind of bargaining unit we could have been? We would have owned a big chunk of the Yankees."

Tom Greenwade would later say that signing Mantle had been the crown jewel of his scouting career. Signing Mickey Mantle, in fact, was a well-designed plan that had been in the works for the better part of two years. Greenwade had first laid eyes on Mantle in 1948 when he went to scout a teammate of Mickey's on the Whiz Kids team on which he was playing while still in high school. Of course, a baseball scout needs to be a consummate poker player, rarely letting on his true feelings about a prospect. It was to Greenwade's advantage to downplay Mickey's potential as a future professional player when he spoke to Mutt Mantle, who used this as motivational fodder for his son. Mickey, consequently, came to believe what Greenwade had said to his father—that he had not been overly impressed in his first view of what would ultimately become his prize signing. Mickey was still slight of build and was known as "Little Mickey" by some of his teammates. Mantle, however, had hit two home runs the first day Greenwade saw him, one from each side of the plate.

"When I first saw him," Greenwade eventually admitted, "I knew he was going to be one of the all-time greats." Still, on another occasion, Greenwade would say: "The first time I saw Mantle I knew how [Yankee scout] Paul Krichell felt when he first saw Lou Gehrig. He knew that as a scout he'd never have another moment like it."

Moreover, glimpses of Mickey's prodigious power were already in evidence. The Whiz Kids' home field in nearby Baxter Springs, Kansas, that manager and coach Barney Barnett had personally built, including a $3,500 expenditure for lights for night games, was bordered in right and center field by the Spring River, that was some 400 feet to dead center field from home plate and some 500 feet from home to right field.

As a 16-year-old in 1948, Mantle was routinely hitting balls near those distances. In one game in late summer, with 250 to 300 people looking on, Mickey hit three home runs—two right-handed and one left-handed—that wound up in the Spring River. In the frenzy that erupted in the crowd, someone in the bleachers behind home plate passed a hat around to reward their slugger. After the game, Mickey was presented with $53 in small change that soon became a small headache for the Mantles. Someone reported the incident to the Oklahoma State Athletic Commission, which regulated high school sports. That commission determined that since Mickey had accepted the money, he had lost his amateur status and could not compete in high school sports at Commerce High his senior year. Mutt challenged the ruling, going to Oklahoma City personally to make the appeal. The ruling was reversed and Mickey's amateur status reinstated on the condition that he return the money. Mantle would later say he returned the money, which he had already spent, by working at odd jobs so that he could repay the $53. It is uncertain, however, whether that actually happened, since that fall Mickey was busy playing football after school. According to at least one version, Mickey repaid Barnett with a $53 check that was never cashed.

Mickey's power at that age, along with his foot speed, gives further credibility to the story that Greenwade, in fact, had been so impressed when he first saw Mantle that he wanted to sign him on the spot, before learning he was only a 16-year-old high school student. Greenwade's own admission of having reacted to first seeing Mantle the way the scout who signed Gehrig undoubtedly felt, suggests that Greenwade must have been torn, at the least, in having found his prize jewel at a time when big signing bonuses were becoming part of the business of the sport.

Thomas Edison Greenwade had more than a passing knowledge of Barney Barnett and his Whiz Kids team. The Whiz Kids were a highly competitive semi-pro team with the best players from Kansas, Oklahoma, and Missouri. The team played in the Ban Johnson League that operated in the tri-state area and had produced several major leaguers. At 16 years of age, Mickey was the youngest player and an obvious phenom. The team was composed mostly of 18-year-olds and played a schedule against other Ban Johnson League teams made up of players 18–21 years of age, and on which players younger than 18 were a rarity. "On the Whiz Kids, Mickey was ahead of his years," said Ivan Shouse, Mantle's childhood friend. "Everyone knew it. He was a boy playing with men, and he was better than all of them."

The signing of Mantle for only $1,500 is all the more incredible when you consider that around the same time, in Broken Bow, Oklahoma, another young phenom—Jim Baumer, a promising power-hitting shortstop who was half a year older than Mickey—was signing with the Chicago White Sox for a $50,000 bonus. Baumer would go directly to the majors, then become a journeyman minor leaguer for the entire 1950s before playing briefly with the Cincinnati Reds in 1961.

Eventually Baumer himself became a scout whose signings included Hall of Famer Robin Yount. In an interview, Baumer boasted of how on his high school graduation night his parents' living room had been filled with scouts, including Greenwade—who seemed confident he had Mickey Mantle safely in his pocket.

"That amount is a pittance even by the standards of that day," says Kevin Kerrane, author of the classic *Dollar Sign on the Muscle: The World of Baseball Scouting*, of the Mantle signing for $1,500. "It's amazing when you think that he was signed for so little."

The signing of Mickey Mantle was actually far more complex and involved than even Mantle fully realized, although over time he came to understand that all had not been as the Yankees and Greenwade made it out to be. Signing Mickey, in fact, would be a steal, not only in the incredibly unfair deal the Yankees made with the Mantles, but also in that the Yankees appear to have violated baseball's rules against dealing with youngsters still in high school.

In the spring of 1949, Cleveland Indians scout Hugh Alexander had heard from a friend about an outstanding teenage baseball player in Commerce, Oklahoma. Meticulous about checking out tips, Alexander noted the name on a piece of paper. He had become a baseball scout at age 20 in 1937, and the first player he signed was pitcher Allie Reynolds, who won 182 games over 13 seasons with the Indians and the Yankees. Known as Uncle Hughie, Alexander became one of baseball's best known scouts and went on to sign dozens of future major leaguers in a career that spanned six decades and countless miles on the back roads of America. A few weeks after getting the tip on Mantle, he drove from his home in Oklahoma City to Commerce and went directly to the local high school. When Alexander inquired about the promising prospect named Mickey Mantle, the school principal Bentley Baker did something curiously out of character for a small-town educator. He lied. He told Alexander that the school did not have a baseball team and that the young man he was interested in had been hurt playing football and had developed arthritis in his legs. "It's hard enough to make the majors if you're healthy and when I got back to my car I took the piece of paper and threw it away," Alexander said of the incident. "I can still see it blowing across the parking lot."

The signing of Mickey Mantle was always recounted, even by Mantle himself, with a twist of homespun heroic adventure. On the night of his graduation, the school principal excused Mickey from commencement exercises so that he could play baseball in front of a New York Yankee scout who signed him immediately after the game. According to Mickey, it was Tom Greenwade who "got me excused from the commencement exercises."

Hugh Alexander would later suggest, and the facts certainly would support, that the Yankees effectively monopolized what should have been a healthy competitive bidding for Mickey, with the help of his high school principal who, for reasons he took to his grave, was scaring off Greenwade's scouting competitors. The shrewd and resourceful Greenwade, a former Internal Revenue Service tax collector, had obviously ingratiated himself with Mickey's principal as much as he had with his father.

Mantle insisted throughout his lifetime that Greenwade signed him on May 16, 1949, the night of his graduation, in Greenwade's 1949 Chrysler, having arranged with Principal Baker for Mickey to be excused from his commencement exercises to play a game with his prized travel team, the Whiz Kids. Mantle said that after the game Greenwade approached his father to tell him things didn't look promising for his son because of his size and his erratic play at shortstop—but that hc was willing to gamble by offering a contract for a modest signing bonus.

Greenwade was lying, but Mutt Mantle did not dare call Greenwade on his lie. Mutt was anxious to get his son a professional baseball contract and too inexperienced to do justice to any negotiations on Mickey's behalf. When Mickey had turned 16, Mutt had gone so far as to take him to St. Louis trying to get him a tryout with the Browns, who had shown no interest. Mutt was disappointed, failing to understand that Mickey was still too young to impress the scouts as he soon would. Mickey was also just starting to pack on muscle and weight.

In his senior year in high school, however, other scouts began showing an interest but were possibly more mindful of the major league's high school tampering rule. Runt Marr, a Cardinals scout who was well-known in the area, visited the Mantle home one day to express interest in Mickey and asked that he not sign with anyone else until St. Louis could make an offer. Mantle said that he gave up hope that the Cardinals would make an offer after days passed without hearing from their representative. The Mantles, however, apparently didn't fully understand that major league teams were prohibited from even making contact with Mickey until he had graduated, much less making a signing offer.

Mutt's impatience about getting his son signed to a professional contract is troubling unless one understands that Mutt Mantle had been molded by the Great Depression. Although he was filled with optimism about Mickey's potential, a cold wind sometimes blew through the back of his mind—the knowledge that the world could collapse. Even as Mutt managed to overcome obstacles, the 1930s of his young adulthood whistled thinly through his memory. Those bleak years gave him an ambience of expectation about life and its pitfalls. Not too surprisingly, the Mantles used almost all of Mickey's signing bonus to pay off the mortgage on the family home. It is understandable how Mutt may have been extremely anxious to get Mickey playing professional baseball as soon as possible that summer; nevertheless, Mutt's decision to have Mickey sign so soon after becoming eligible to even talk to the pros appears to have been ill-advised at best.

At the time, Mickey was one of the area's most talented amateur athletes. The University of Oklahoma tried to recruit him for its football program. Bill Moseley, who quarterbacked Mickey's high school football team at Commerce, received a college football scholarship when they graduated and went on to play at Pittsburg State Teachers College in Kansas.

Undoubtedly, Mutt could have used the college football offers as negotiating leverage with the Yankees. As Al Campanis, the late Dodger baseball executive and himself a former scout, would later say in reflecting on Mantle's signing: "[Baseball's] rule against signing someone before he graduates from high school doesn't mean that on the day you graduate you have to sign a contract. That just marks the start of the race. Mantle was just coming into his own then. The only reasons I can see for him signing so quick would be if there'd been a big bonus—and there wasn't—or if there'd been a contract that put him on the major league team roster—and there wasn't that either. Mantle could've played [amateur] ball that summer and built up his value the more he was seen and scouted. There's no telling what he could've signed for."

In fact, the Yankees had authorized Greenwade to pay up to $25,000, if he needed to. Yankee GM George Weiss later told friends that he had authorized Greenwade to offer that much—the same bonus Bill Skowron would receive—to sign Mantle and the Baumer youngster in nearby Broken Bow. Once Baumer signed with another team, Greenwade had all the money to use on Mantle. Weiss, a brilliant businessman who had been with the Yankees since 1932, had been the architect of the organization's farm system, which he had shrewdly built by signing a lot of Depression-era players cheaply and often making incredible profits when he sold some of them to other teams. After one of those deals, then-Yankee GM Ed Barrow asked Weiss: "George, doesn't your conscience bother you?"

After the war, Weiss was trying to rebuild his sagging Yankees with whatever it took, including signing bonuses to promising players. The 1947 Yankees had won the pennant and the World Series, but the 1948 Yankees faded to third place. The 1949 Yankees had started the season inauspiciously after losing Joe DiMaggio in the spring to an unexpected second operation to remove bone spurs from his right heel. The Yankees had entered the bonus baby market, and Greenwade was aware that he had a blank check to sign a prospect like Mantle.

If anything, Greenwade appears to have been baffled that, unlike Baumer's father, Mutt had not even so much as hinted at what kind of signing deal he wanted for Mickey. Mutt, in fact, seemed to be more concerned with where his son would be assigned after turning professional. He was insistent on Mickey playing somewhere close to home that summer, preferably at the Yankees' Class D team at Independence, Kansas, 75 miles from Commerce. Greenwade had also gotten Mutt to promise that he would give him the chance to match any offers. Greenwade, though, knew what no other scout in the area knew—that Mantle wasn't the damaged prospect with bum legs that Hugh Alexander and other scouts were being told he was by Mickey's own high school principal.

Ultimately, the signing of Mickey Mantle would became part of Americana and heroic fable, fitting of a *Saturday Evening Post* cover by Norman Rockwell. As author David Halberstam would later put it: "The myth of Tom Greenwade, the greatest scout of his age, blended with Mantle's myth to create a classic illustration of the American

Dream: For every American of talent, no matter how poor or simple his or her background, there is always a Tom Greenwade out there searching to discover that person and help him or her find a rightful place among the stars."

For Tom Greenwade, Mickey Mantle would become the showpiece in the parade of 1950s and 1960s Yankee stars and mainstays that he signed, among them Mantle friend and roommate Hank Bauer, as well as Ralph Terry and Bobby Murcer. Greenwade had scoured America's heartland looking for his prized signing who would validate his life as a scout and the Yankees' decision to hire him. Mantle's signing would also forever cement Greenwade's place with the Yankees and in baseball. Greenwade would remain with the organization for 40 years, retiring in 1985, a year before his death.

Throughout his life, Greenwade would deny violating the high school tampering rule. Although he admitted to being worried of other scouts moving in on Mickey, he claimed to have waited patiently until the Sunday after Mickey's graduation from high school before offering him a contract that was ironed out in 15 minutes of negotiations between himself and Mutt. Mickey was signed for a total of $1,500— $400 for the remainder of the season with the Independence, Missouri, team of the Kansas-Oklahoma-Missouri League, and a $1,100 bonus. Altogether, Mickey would sign for a 10th of the money Elston Howard received from the Yankees a year later.

But then, the life of the baseball scout, neither then nor later, was hardly a gentleman's game. According to Kerrane, all was fair in fighting other scouts for the signature of a promising prospect. The passage of money under the table was not unheard of, especially when it came to attempting to keep competing scouts away from a prized player. Occasionally, said Kerrane, there were suspicions and allegations of scouts and their teams circumventing the rules on bonus babies. A player signed to a high bonus such as Jim Baumer was required under baseball's rules to be placed on the major league team for a period of time, which would create havoc with the team's 25-player roster. To get around this, some teams were suspected of paying part of the bonus to a new signee under the table in cash, leaving the roster of the major league team unaffected.

Of course, the job of a scout was made considerably easier when the family of a prized prospect like Mickey jumped at the first offer, and even then mismanaged the negotiations.

"I asked Mutt what they wanted to sign?" Greenwade said he told Mickey's father.

"Well, you'll have to give him as much as he'd make around here all summer, working in the mine and playing ball on Sunday," said Mutt, effectively missing an opportunity to ask for top dollar and instead asking for parity for working the mines and playing local semi-pro baseball. "His pay in the mine is 87½ cents an hour, and he can get 15 dollars on a Sunday playing ball."

"We wrote down how much he could make working with his father up in the mines in Picher and how much he'd be making playing semipro weekends in Spavinaw on the same team as his father," Greenwade told the *New York Herald Tribune*'s Harold Rosenthal a decade later. "Then we added up how much he'd make in three months in the minors and subtracted that from the first figure. It came to $1,150. That's what I could get for him to sign."

In another life, Greenwade with that flat, ridge-runner accent that made him sound so convincing, might also have been a used-car salesman because he kept manipulating the numbers. Finally, at one point he threw out to Mutt a monthly salary of $140 that Mickey would earn playing Joplin for almost three months for the rest of that summer.

"That's around four hundred dollars," he told Mutt. "Suppose we make up the difference and give you $1,100? That's about $1,500, right?"

The result would be one of the biggest signing coups ever made by a professional sports team and, unfortunately for the Mantles, a horrendous negotiating blunder that would cost the family tens of thousands of dollars. But this was to be only the first of numerous business deals during his career and after retirement in which Mickey would wind up on the short end of the stick.

"It was not until the signing was announced in the paper and I read Tom Greenwade's prediction that I would probably set records with the Yankees, equaling Ruth's and DiMaggio's, that I began to wonder if my father and I had been outslicked," Mickey said years later. "Greenwade, by his account, had just been going through Oklahoma on his way to look over a real prospect, when he stopped to talk to us. I never did find out who that real prospect was."

In his autobiography, *The Mick*, Mantle recognized that it had all been a negotiating ploy by Greenwade. "When I read the announcement about my signing," wrote Mickey, "it quoted Greenwade as saying I would probably set records with the Yankees. Stuff like that. He did tell me later that I was the best prospect he had ever seen."

7

In the Mold of Mantle

*"When I first came to Yankee Stadium, I used
to feel like the ghosts of Babe Ruth and Lou
Gehrig were walking around in there."*

—MICKEY MANTLE

ON MARCH 21, 1951, AS THE NEW YORK YANKEES PREPARED TO PLAY
an exhibition game in Los Angeles against the Hollywood Stars,
an Associated Press photographer snapped a picture of 19-year-
old Mickey Mantle taking some practice swings during the team's
warmups. The fresh-faced Mickey appeared nervous. He still didn't
know where he would be playing that year, and he was concerned that
his good showing in spring training hadn't been enough to keep him
with the Yankees. Casey Stengel had benched him in the previous
day's game, a 5–0 shutout loss to the Chicago White Sox in Glendale,
his manager's adopted hometown. When Stengel finally sent him in
as a defensive replacement in the ninth inning, Mantle committed
an error on Nellie Fox's bloop fly ball. *The New York Times'* James
P. Dawson, the paper's boxing editor who was covering the Yankees'
spring training, had written in that Wednesday's *Times* that "Mantle

will get regular workouts when the Yankees leave California and demand for Joe DiMaggio diminishes."

The photograph of Mantle went out on the AP's national wire, where it appeared a couple of days later in *The Forum of Fargo-Moorhead,* Fargo's daily newspaper. That issue of the *Forum* made the rounds among athletes at Shanley High, including Roger, according to Gene P. Johnson, the teammate who later practiced law in Fargo. "I think it might have been Coach Cichy who first told us about Mickey Mantle," Johnson said in a 2008 interview. "How could you not have heard about Mantle? The fact that he was 19, barely much older than any of us at that time, that was what I think caught our attention. Nineteen and about to replace DiMaggio on the great New York Yankees. We all wanted to see what he looked like. And he looked like he might have been any of us." A few days later, *The Forum* carried an Associated Press story by Joe Reichler headlined, "Mantle Has Bright Future But Is Untested."

Around the country, as spring training advanced toward the beginning of a new season, young and old baseball fans alike were looking for news about the game's new phenom.

The Times' James P. Dawson, whose Baseball Writers Association of America membership dated to 1918 (a year before the Black Sox Scandal and a time when Babe Ruth was still with the Red Sox), had covered Ruth and Lou Gehrig and Joe DiMaggio, and was a pillar of modern day baseball to that point. In the first week of April, just a few days before Opening Day, Dawson seemed to make it official about Mickey Mantle and the future. Mickey had just raised his spring training exhibition games batting average to .462, walloping a home run and a double. "Mantle," Dawson wrote from El Paso, "gives every promise of developing into an outstanding baseball star."

"'What kind of a deal had this kid Mickey Mantle made with the devil?' At a place like Shanley, a Catholic school, that's what was on the minds of a few of us," recalled Gene Johnson. "How else could you explain a 19-year-old tearing up the big leagues like that? Or was he heaven-sent? Either way, he was out of this world."

Across America, the young baseball sensation Mickey Mantle had created a phenomenon among young teenage ballplayers who were reading anything they could in their hometown newspapers about the New York Yankees' unbelievable rookie who was barely older than many of them. In Milwaukee, Wisconsin, 15-year-old Anthony Christopher Kubek, a promising infielder at Bay View High School, was hooked. In Sumpter, South Carolina, it was another 15-year-old, Robert Clinton Richardson. In Alba, Missouri, it was 14-year-old Cletis Leroy Boyer, who would soon also be asking one of his older brothers, 19-year-old Ken—who the St. Louis Cardinals that same year would convert from a pitcher to a third baseman—if, in his minor league career so far, he had ever seen Mantle.

Add to those the names of promising high school prospects Ralph Terry, Tom Tresh, and Bill Stafford to name a few, and the picture becomes even clearer. Like Roger Maris, these players not only knew of Mantle before they became his Yankee teammates, but they also grew up as teenage hero worshippers long before they ever knew him. Baseball writers and biographers later explained why fellow Yankee players to a man supported Mickey in the 1961 chase of Ruth's record merely on the basis that he was the consummate "great teammate." But that was only part of the reason. By 1961, Mickey Mantle was more than that to these teammates. He was the essence of their boyhood, the teenager who had realized their high school dreams, the player who reminded them of the playground kid they had all been. And his impact on them would grow as they got to know him.

"Mickey often said he didn't understand it, this enduring connection and affection…" broadcaster Bob Costas would one day say of Mantle. He had grown up on Long Island, with a Mickey Mantle obsession that became as well-known as Bob Costas himself, with stories abounding of how he "might have the most famous Mickey Mantle card on the planet, even if it's not the most valuable." He carried a 1958 Topps Mantle card, No. 487 from that year's collection, in his wallet wherever he went on sports broadcasting assignments around the world. "People still ask me, 'Do you still have the Mickey Mantle card?'" said Costas. "It seemed like a sacrilege to throw it away, so I kept it in with my credit cards in my wallet." And he would often pull out his wallet to show it off: a special *Sport* Magazine All-Star Selection card that showed Mantle swinging a bat against a red background highlighted by dozens of small white stars.

In Queens, a young Yankee fan who grew up idolizing DiMaggio and hating Mantle when he came along suddenly changed his mind when "I realized something in a cold sweat: Mickey was actually closer to me in age [10 years older] than he was to DiMaggio [nearly 17 years younger]… Mickey was more like me, and I would have been scared shitless out there in center field. My heart went out to him." Stephen Jay Gould grew up loving Mickey Mantle and Tyrannosaurus Rex, eventually becoming a paleontologist at Harvard, a full-fledged baseball nerd convinced that the Mick was the best there ever was.

Mickey Mantle bonded a generation of boys and men in a way no religion, philosophy, or politician could. John F. Kennedy may have been a contemporary, but his charisma paled next to Mickey. What was it Costas also said about him? "We knew there was something poignant about Mickey Mantle before we knew what 'poignant' meant." Absolutely.

And it wasn't just Baby Boomer boys who were obsessed with Mantle. In Waco, Texas, Lidia Montemayor, who would go through high school and college without ever earning anything less than an 'A' in any course, could quote from memory Mantle's stat line for each of his seasons to date. Teenage boys couldn't compete with her in math, English, or science, and now they were also second best to her in reciting all the baseball statistical intimacies there were to know about Mickey.

Up in Roslyn, New York, there would be another young girl who was equally consumed with Mickey Mantle, her childhood hero. When she was grown up, Jane Leavy would interview Mickey as a sportswriter for the *Washington Post* and eventually authored *The Last Boy: Mickey Mantle and the End of America's Childhood*. Years later, while I was signing copies of my own Mantle biography in Manhattan, I was equally surprised to see as many middle-aged women as men lined up, all reminiscing about Mickey as I met them. Many of them were in tears, not a singular experience when it came to Mantle fans, who would sometimes burst out crying when coming face to face with their childhood hero.

In 1979, Mickey was paid an appearance fee by a New Jersey housewife to attend her husband's 40th birthday party. The husband couldn't control his emotions when Mantle showed up, bawling so much that Mickey himself was moved, even if he couldn't understand why he affected grown men this way. When he returned home to Dallas, Mantle impulsively shipped the man the pinstriped uniform the Yankees had given him when they retired his famous No. 7.

"One day I'm Mickey Mantle, a kid from Commerce, Oklahoma, that nobody outside my hometown knows," Mantle told me in one of numerous conversations in Dallas. "Soon I'm Mickey Mantle, a piece of merchandise like something you can buy at Neiman Marcus downtown. Doesn't make sense, does it?"

Mantle had that kind of impact on everyone.

It was the perfect time for a young American hero to come along. If Mickey Mantle hadn't lived, the Yankee broadcaster Mel Allen once said, he would have been invented. In a sense, then, Mickey Mantle, like most heroes, was a construction; he was not real. He was all that America wanted itself to be, and he was also all that America feared it could never be. The post-war America of the mid-20th century was like all societies with the need for heroes not because they coincidentally made them up on their own but because heroes like Mantle express a deep psychological aspect of human existence. They can be seen as a metaphor for the human search of self-knowledge.

In his time, Mickey Mantle showed us the path to our own consciousness through the power and spectacle of his baseball heroics, particularly his prodigious home runs often backlit by the cathedral solemnity of Yankee Stadium. In the atomic age of the 1950s, the tape-measure blasts in our national pastime took on the form of peacetime symbols of America's newly established military dominance. After all, Hank Greenberg, the first Jewish slugger in the game (who signed Roger Maris to his first pro contract), said that when he had hit his home runs from the mid-1930s into the 1940s, he was hitting them against Hitler, perhaps the greatest anti-Semitic symbol of all time.

For most of history, then, religion has been the main force of reproducing the dominant society's traits by sometimes using mythical figures to illustrate moral and societal principles that help form a common social conception of such things as death and gender roles. In the 1950s, as sport itself took on the role in our culture that religion had often played in the past, Mickey Mantle as the contemporary cultural hero contributed to American society's necessary business of reproducing itself and its values. As Mantle's close personal friend George Lois put it:

"Mickey Mantle was the last American hero. He was a walking shrine to an age of innocence and a symbol of a time when all was right with the world."

Even had he not reflected the times, Mantle would have been walking Americana. His career was storybook stuff, hewing more to our ideas of myth than any player since Babe Ruth. Mantle himself came to realize that Ruth and Joe DiMaggio, in a sense, represented a state of mind that never existed beyond the abstract. They were a mirage, just as he, too, would become an icon. A lesson to be reaffirmed, sportswriter Richard Hoffer once suggested about Mantle and perhaps heroes altogether, is that we don't mind our heroes flawed, or even doomed. In America, failure is forgiven of the big swingers, in whom even foolishness is flamboyant—and that the world will always belong to those who swing from the heels.

"When I was playing," Mantle would later say, looking back on his career, "I used to feel like everything was happening to some other guy named Mickey Mantle, like I was just me and this guy called Mickey Mantle was another person."

It may be that the unique relationship between America and baseball must be understood to fully appreciate Mantle's place in the equation—Maris' too. This was the age when baseball players were the princes of American sports, along with heavyweight boxers and Derby horses and the odd galloping ghost of a running back from down South or the occasional lanky basketball player in short shorts. Baseball players were the souls of their cities—Stan the Man in St. Louis; The Kid in Boston; Pee Wee, the Duke, Jackie, and Furillo in Brooklyn; and, of course, the incomparable Willie Mays for Giants fans. As 1950s historian Jacques Barzun was to aptly observe: "Whoever wants to know the heart and mind of America had better learn baseball...."

Long before Mantle and Maris, long before baseball became an industry of multi-national owners and millionaire players, Walt Whitman wrote, "Well, it's our game. That's the chief fact in connection with it: America's game. It has the snap, go, fling of the American atmosphere. It belongs as much to our institutions, fits into them as significantly as our Constitution's laws, is just as important in the sum total of our historic life."

Baseball is, to be sure, an American cultural declaration of independence. It has come to express the nation's character—perhaps never more so than during the intense, anti-Communist, post-World War II period, when a preoccupation with defining the national conscience might be expected, particularly defining the national self in a tradition that is so culturally middle of the road. As American Studies authority Gerald Early put it: "I think there are only three things America will be known for 2,000 years from now when they study this civilization—the Constitution, jazz music, and baseball...."

By the middle of the 20th century, baseball as an unquestioned symbol and performance-ritual of the best qualities of something called Americanism was an entrenched truism. The fictional literary character Terence Mann perhaps stated it more succinctly in the Hollywood film *Field of Dreams* when he says to protagonist Ray Kinsella: "The one constant through all the years, Ray, has been baseball. America has rolled by like an army of steamrollers. It's been erased like a blackboard, rebuilt, and erased again. But baseball has marked the time. This field, this game, is a part of our past, Ray. It reminds us of all that once was good and it could be again."

In a sense, then, baseball was the perfect metaphor for America's romance with nostalgia that would become engrained in the country as the game ceased being the national pastime. What could be more sentimental than a day at the ballpark, an experience that inevitably evokes the rich history of the sport, and can bring us back to a once-forgotten time? "It is the American game, that's just what it is," says Negro League legend Buck O'Neil in Ken Burns' *Baseball*, "and, actually, it makes you, me, I'm 81, but I can feel like I'm 15 when I'm talking baseball, I'm watching baseball, this is it, it does this, it can do this to any man, it brings you back."

Or, as Mickey Mantle once said in what seemed to sum up his connection with America: "I guess you can say I'm what this country's all about—I have to play ball. It's the only thing I know."

Perhaps fittingly, he reportedly made this remark to the Duke of Windsor when the English royal had visited New York in 1953. The former King Edward VIII, who abdicated his throne in 1936 to marry the American divorcée Wallis Simpson, attended his first baseball game when the Yankees hosted the Detroit Tigers on May 19. "Delighted" was his response when he was asked if he enjoyed it, and then he asked "to meet that 'switcher fellow'"—switch-hitter Mickey Mantle. The Duke of Windsor, while wearing a Yankee cap, was even photographed on the dugout steps with Mantle, Casey Stengel, and Phil Rizzuto.

"I've heard about you," the Duke of Windsor said to Mickey when they were introduced, according to the next day's New York newspapers.

"I've heard about you, too," Mantle replied.

The photograph with the Duke of Windsor became one of Mantle's favorites that Merlyn Mantle later proudly displayed in their home's den.

"The former king of England wanted to meet Mickey—can you believe that?" Merlyn said when she showed me the photograph. "Mickey's ancestors came here from England. What are the odds of an American boy of English blood growing up to become an American hero and then meeting the man who was once king of England? A charmed life if ever there was one."

8

Dante's Baseball Hell

*"You know, I was once named Minor League
Player of the Year... unfortunately, I had been
in the majors for two years at the time."*

—BOB UECKER

HOW GOOD A BALLPLAYER WAS ROGER MARIS RIGHT OUT OF HIGH
school? Was he as good as Mickey Mantle had been four years earlier?
Were either of them good enough to jump directly into the major
leagues? Still only 17, Mantle had hit .313 with seven home runs
playing 89 games in Class D in 1949, and the next year batted .383
with 26 dingers in Class C. Maris, then 18, hit .325 with nine homers
in Class C in 1953, following that with a Class B season batting .315
with 32 home runs and 111 RBI. In Mantle's third year, the Yankees
had him at spring training with the major league team. Even though
the suits thought Mickey needed more seasoning, Casey Stengel
insisted, "I gotta have Mantle in New York." The jump from Class C
ball to the majors was one few minor leaguers had ever made. Few have
ever had the backing and overblown hype from a manager who had
just won back-to-back World Series titles. Roger Maris certainly didn't
with the Cleveland Indians. He never had anyone in the organization

that championed him anywhere close to what Mantle had in Stengel. Or championed him at all.

But then, by his third season in professional baseball, Maris had fully established himself as the one thing an athlete without the support of a players' organization can least afford to be: a royal pain in the ass. In his two seasons, he had stubbornly refused to play where Cleveland's front office wanted him. Even as team executives had acceded to Roger's ultimatums, his unprecedented demands had, if not alienated, then certainly hardened the suspicions of some team officials about him. His rebelliousness had led to the firing of one of his managers, and that kind of reputation had to be unsettling to other managers in the Indians' organization, knowing that this Maris kid might be headed their way. Much might have been forgiven or forgotten over time, as recollections and reminiscences about the man who broke Babe Ruth's record recalled only the best. However, in the mid-1950s, what might have weighed matters most in Roger's favor were his own offensive production and the interest that the New York Yankees had begun to show in him.

The Yankees' interest in Maris dated back to 1955, his difficult season split between Class AA Tulsa and Class A Reading, when he was still Roger Maras. The Yankees weren't put off by Roger's run-in with Dutch Meyer, the Tulsa manager who would lose his job in the fallout, or by the drop in his batting average over the first two seasons. Yankee GM George Weiss had seen Maris' swing in spring training, and he heard about it from the team's minor league officials who were on the lookout for what Weiss felt was a most needed commodity: a power-hitting left-handed slugger who could take advantage of the short right-field porch at Yankee Stadium. During the 1961 chase of Ruth's record, Weiss would reminisce in an interview with the *New York Journal American* about shopping for Maris years earlier:

"We were looking for a left-handed pull hitter. In the past we had fellows like Tommy Henrich, Charley Keller, and Red Rolfe. But they were gone, and we couldn't get the right replacement. It was hurting us in that we weren't winning at home. On the road we were fine. But in the stadium there was trouble because of the lack of left-handed power. A ballclub, you know, should be tailor-made to its home park."

It would have seemed like the perfect time for the Yankees to secure Maris. The Indians were experiencing a fall to reality after their storybook 1954 American League championship year when they won a record 111 regular season games, breaking the 1927 Yankees' record of 110. You needed to look no further to understand their slide than second baseman Bobby Avila, who had a career season in 1954. He won the American League batting championship hitting .341, 60 points above his career average, and received *The Sporting News* Player of the Year Award. He also put up career bests in on-base percentage (.402), home runs (15), RBI (67), and runs (112). And the pitching staff, while solid, did not reach the heights of the 1954 squad.

From the Yankees' side, the lack of a left-handed slugger may have been overstated. The Yankees, who won 103 games in 1954, had a .701 winning percentage playing at Yankee Stadium. The second-place finish to the Indians, though, marked the first time since 1948 that the Bronx Bombers hadn't been in a World Series, ending a run of five consecutive world titles. But the Yankees needed pitching more than a left-handed bat as their once-formidable Yankee pitching staff was now suspect. The great Allie Reynolds had retired after 1954, and mainstays Eddie Lopat, Johnny Sain, Tommy Byrne, and Jim Konstanty were in their mid-thirties and no longer youngsters. Weiss was intent on rebuilding around 25-year-old Whitey Ford and 24-year-old Rookie of the Year Bob Grim.

Most other team general managers refused to trade with the perennial champions, but George Weiss was not one to take rejection easily. There had been more famous general managers in Major League Baseball, and some, like the Dodgers' Branch Rickey, would transcend baseball with the signing of Jackie Robinson to break the game's color barrier. However, no general manager could match Weiss for presiding over the greatest sustained run of excellence in baseball history. Under Weiss' guidance, from 1948 through 1960, the Yankees won 10 pennants and seven World Series championships. Weiss prided himself on the team's farm system that he had helped develop and run, so he considered the mid-century Yankees team to be his creation.

In 1955, though, he knew he needed to make a deal with someone and that turned out to be Baltimore's Paul Richards, who desperately wanted to improve the team that had finished 57 games out of first place. In the biggest trade in baseball history, Weiss and Richards made a 17-player deal that included no stars but substantially upgraded the Yankees for the next few years. Among the players obtained by the Yankees were starting right-handers Bob Turley and Don Larsen. The Orioles' side included their future starting catcher, Gus Triandos, his backup Hal Smith, and Yankee outfielder Gene Woodling.

Meanwhile, for Roger Maris, the 1955 season would be a character-maker. George Weiss later said that had been what he had learned from having Yankee scouts and minor league officials keep an eye on Roger. This was, after all, a nosy, squeaky-clean Yankee organization that had gleaned an FBI report on Mickey Mantle and had private eyes keeping tabs on Mantle, Billy Martin, and presumably Whitey Ford. "We watched him closely," the Yanks' GM said of the team's investigation of Maris. "We received reports on his personal habits and even assigned scouts to his hometown of Fargo, North Dakota, to find out about him. Everything we were told convinced us that he was the player we wanted."

Dealing for Roger, though, would have to wait. The Indians' own high-level brass thought Maris might fit well into its rebuilding of the team. The sky was the limit on Herb Score's future, and he figured to be Cleveland's ace for years to come. Maris had a strong 1956 season at AAA Indianapolis that vaulted him into the Tribe's plans for 1957, alongside 23-year-old Rocky Colavito, the 1956 Rookie of the Year runner-up with 21 home runs. General manager Hank Greenberg thought his Indians team had the foundation to compete with the Yankees for pennant runs in the near future. Of course, he couldn't have counted on Herb Score's tragic injury and the competitive and psychological impact that would have on the Indians. It was also now a decade since the end of World War II when major league teams began stockpiling and improving their war-ravaged rosters and farm systems, some more than others. As it would turn out, the Indians found themselves behind others in the post-war rebuilding. Some baseball historians and statistical experts like Bill James would eventually place the blame squarely on Greenberg.

Imagine if you could build a team in the 1950s around Hank Aaron, Ernie Banks, and Willie Mays? It's not fantasy baseball, but what might have been available to Greenberg. One of Greenberg's legacies would be that in his time as Cleveland's general manager, he sponsored more African American players than any other major league executive. Among them was future Hall of Famer Larry Doby, a player in the Negro leagues, who, in 1947, became the second African American to break baseball's color barrier and the first Black player in the American League. Doby developed into a seven-time All-Star center fielder, who, with teammate Satchel Paige, were the first African American players to win a World Series championship when Cleveland won the title in 1948. He also helped the Tribe win a then-record 111 games and the pennant in 1954, leading the league in home runs and RBI, while finishing second in the MVP Award voting. Doby would eventually become the second Black manager and be appointed to an executive position in the American League's office. But Doby's greatest contribution to Greenberg's career and the Indians should have been his recommendations that the general manager dismissed.

In 1949, on the heels of the Indians' World Series winning season, Doby personally told Greenberg that there were three outstanding young Negro League players he should scout and sign if he wanted to get a jump on other teams. These were players Doby himself had played with or knew about in the Negro Leagues, and he believed they could become major league stars, if given the chance. The players were none other than Aaron, Banks, and Mays—and Doby was insistent in his faith that they would change the course of the Indians' future. So Doby was understandably surprised and disappointed when they weren't at the Indians next spring training.

"Our guys checked 'em out and their reports were not good," Greenberg told his All-Star center fielder. "They said that Aaron has a hitch in his swing and will never hit good pitching. Banks is too slow and didn't have enough range [at shortstop], and Mays can't hit a curveball." This was an account presented by longtime *Cleveland Plain Dealer* Indians beat writer Russ Schneider in his 1996 team history *The Cleveland Indians Encyclopedia*. In 2002, *USA Today: Sports Weekly* attempted to debunk the story as myth, using as the basis that Aaron, Banks, and Mays were too young to have been scouted in the late 1940s, which isn't true, according to Negro League histories and biographies of the three players.

In 1949, Aaron, Banks, and Mays were young but already either playing in the Negro Leagues or soon about to be. Mays had been 17 when he began playing for the Birmingham Black Barons in 1948. Willie stayed with the Barons through 1949 before signing with the New York Giants in 1950. Banks was 16 in 1947 when he was first scouted by the Negro League's Kansas City Monarchs, before eventually signing with the Chicago Cubs in late 1953. Aaron was three years younger than Banks and Mays but signed with the Indianapolis Clowns in 1951, where he played for three months. Banks made his major league debut on September 17, 1953, at age 22. Mays began his career with the Giants in 1951, playing in that year's World Series against the Yankees. In 1954, Aaron began his historic 23-year career with the Milwaukee Braves. Imagine for a moment a Cleveland Indians team in the mid-to-late-1950s and beyond with Hank Aaron, Ernie Banks, and Willie Mays, along with Larry Doby and developing stars like Colavito and Maris.

But in the late 1940s and early 1950s America and the major leagues were still adjusting to a newly integrated national pastime. The landmark *Brown v. Board of Education* Supreme Court decision desegregating public schools would not be handed down until 1954 and its implementation would drag on for decades. The civil rights legislation outlawing housing, public accommodations, and voting was still more than a decade away. Through 1951, only six of Major League Baseball's 16 teams had at least one African American player on the roster. The Brooklyn Dodgers had taken the lead with Roy Campanella and Don Newcombe joining Jackie Robinson on a team that would soon push to the top of the National League, winning pennants in 1949, 1952, 1953, and finally a World Series championship in 1955. That was rare, however, and it would be years before any other major league team would field another team with at least a third of the lineup being African American.

In the mid-1950s, major league teams were small American oligarchies unchecked by law. In 1922, the U.S. Supreme Court had given baseball the rights that no business conglomerate would even dream possible. In *Federal Baseball Club v. National League,* the high court ruled that baseball was an "amusement" and that the leagues' baseball games, held then in more than a dozen states, did not constitute "interstate commerce" and so the country's antitrust laws did not apply to the game's wealthy owners. The irony could not have been clearer. The business that excluded the participation of Black players was now also legally authorized to act in much the same way that plantation owners had behaved in using the production of enslaved workers to further enrich themselves. The legal challenge that eventually brought down that rule effectively used that same argument. Once a player had been signed to a contract by a team, the rights to that player were retained by the team upon the contract's expiration. The player was the owner's property. All a player could do was to do as Maris had done in his early minor league dealings: deliver an ultimatum and be willing to quit if the team didn't budge.

"I've been a marked man ever since I got into baseball," Maris told *Cleveland News* Indians beat writer Hal Lebowitz early in 1957. "I've been called a brooder, a sore-head, a bad actor. I don't see it. Maybe it's because I show it on my face when I'm disgusted. I may look down, but inside me it's not that way. I never got down on myself. I have full confidence."

In the long run, though, the chip on his shoulder would pay off dividends for Maris, who would continue to brood and seethe over slights and perceived slights, not just over things that happened in the minors but even into his Indians rookie season in 1957. That was a year that began with such promise and potential Rookie of the Year talk. Through 16 games, Maris was one of baseball's top stories in the young season. He was batting .313 with three home runs and 13 runs batted in. The Indians had just climbed to .500. "This is the same Maris… who was classified as a 'brooder' by Tribe brass when he worked out in Tucson during spring training last year," a story in the *Sporting News* assessed the new Roger. "If this Maris seems a tough customer, it is only because he is such a competitor. He rebelled inwardly last spring because he wasn't playing… There has been no trace of moodiness or surliness in Maris this spring."

Then the fortunes of the Indians changed overnight—or two days later, in game No. 17 of the season. The Yankees came to town, and there followed the ill-fated first inning that destroyed the once-brilliant career of pitcher Herb Score. Three games later, on May 10, Maris sustained two broken ribs sliding hard into second base and catching Kansas City Athletics second baseman Milt Graff's knee in the chest. Roger was out of the lineup almost a month with incredible pain that made it impossible for him to swing a bat. But the Indians suddenly found themselves in the middle of an early season pennant race, and manager Kerby Farrell likely pressed Roger back into the lineup too soon.

Much was later made by some biographers who claimed Maris, though still hurting, had a brilliant early return, including two home runs in a four RBI day against the Detroit Tigers. Must have been in a different season or reality. The only four RBI game Maris enjoyed in the 1957 seasons came against the Tigers on April 18, the Indians' second game of the year. In fact, Maris struggled the rest of 1957: batting .188 for May; .253 with four homers and 11 RBI in June; .207 with just one homer and eight RBI in July; .186 with two homers and five RBI in August; and .246 with two homers and eight RBI in

September. Clearly, for Maris to have played in only 116 of the season's 153 games, this was a dramatically different ballplayer than the one whose first career home run had been a grand slam off Tigers pitcher Jack Crimian at Briggs Stadium in Detroit in only his second game in the majors.

In 1960, when Cleveland made the unpopular trade of Rocky Colavito to the Detroit Tigers for Harvey Kuenn, Indians fans began talking about the franchise being cursed. But if there was a curse on the team, it went back to at least the 1957 season. Maybe manager Al López jinxed the Indians with some Cuban *Santeria* curse when he stormed off after the 1956 season to become the new skipper of the White Sox. There came the horrific line drive off the bat of the Yankees' Gil McDougald that almost blinded Herb Score. Then two other 20-game winners from López's 1956 team, eventual Hall of Famers Bob Lemon and Early Wynn, slumped to below .500 records. This would also be Hank Greenberg's final season in Cleveland. So, if López's successor Kerby Farrell seemed desperate, he was. Desperate enough to risk the career of prized rookie Roger Maris, who had played amazingly well for him in AAA Indianapolis the previous year. He should have been shot, some Maris fans believed. Instead he was only fired.

"When I went back in the lineup, [Farrell] called me aside and explained that he knew I wasn't ready," Maris told *Kansas City Star* sportswriter Joe McGruff after his trade to the Athletics. "He told me not to worry and said that I had a job regardless of how I went. Well, I went lousy. And a few days later he called me in and said, 'Kid, if you don't start hitting, we're going to have to take you out of the lineup.'"

9

His Own Worst Enemy?

*"Roger had as much confidence in his
ability as any player I ever saw."*

—ROCKY COLAVITO

ROGER MARIS WAS PROOF THAT LIVING IN DENIAL CAN SOMETIMES DO
great things for your career. He had just finished his first season in the
majors, going from the prohibitive favorite for Rookie of the Year to
a sorry .235 batting average freshman on a bad sixth-place team who
was lucky not to have been sent down to the minors. But a Class AAA
demotion might have been his destination in 1958 if the new brass
of the Cleveland Indians hadn't wanted to keep a sheen on him for
trading purposes. Maris opened the new year on the trading block, just
not to the Yankees, who had again approached the Indians during the
winter meetings. By then, the Tribe's new general manager Frank Lane
had had his fill of Roger Maris. It may have been that the only baseball
people Lane disliked more than Roger were New York general manager
George Weiss, manager Casey Stengel, and the Yankees themselves.
He didn't like the Yankees' pinstripes, their winning ways, nor the way
they seemed to hold it over all of baseball. There was no way he was
going to give them a player perfectly made for their team.

For Lane, the last straw with Maris had been his refusal to play winter ball in Latin America. The Tribe's GM was a baseball traditionalist who had seen many ballplayers improve from one season to the next by playing through the winter. At the time, most major leaguers used the off-season to grow soft and fat, barely able to get ready for the new season through spring training. Playing winter ball amounted to the year-round conditioning that came into vogue in the free-agency era. Maris refused to be away from his young family for the winter, especially for only the $1,000 a month salary and demanded $500 more. Lane called winter-ball officials and secured the $1,500 amount that Roger wanted. Maris, though, could have tried the patience of Job. He told his general manager he still wouldn't go to Latin America and that he didn't think he needed the additional seasoning of winter ball.

"That did it," Lane would later tell *Baseball Quarterly*. "I made up my mind that this guy was going to be too difficult to handle to make it worth my while."

When he left for spring training in 1958, Maris had no idea that his time in Cleveland was near its end and that he had given the Indians his final ultimatum. True to his word, Frank Lane had just completed multi-player deals in which the Indians received two veteran All-Stars—Larry Doby, whom Hank Greenberg had traded away in 1955, and the ever-popular Cuban slugger Minnie Minoso. Doby was coming off back-to-back seasons when he batted .268 with the Chicago White Sox with 24 home runs and 102 RBI, and then hit for a .288 average, tied for a team-high 14 homers and drove in 79 runs. Minoso had batted .316 and .310 in the previous two seasons while driving home 88 and 103 runs respectively. They were aging players but Lane intended to join them with young star Rocky Colavito in a new outfield. Lane's plan was to use the left-handed-hitting Maris exclusively against right-handed pitching while waiting for the right deal, just not one with the Yankees.

Meanwhile, the Yankees had assigned legendary scout Tom Greenwade to birddog Roger Maris and the Indians. Lane was familiar with the story of Greenwade's discovery of Mantle (as well as how he signed him for peanuts) and he loved baseball people like Greenwade. Lane himself was equally a caricature of the consummate wheeler-dealer and had earned nicknames such as "Trader Frank," "Frantic Frank," and "Trader Lane." He and Greenwade were the lifeblood of the game.

"He was around here for a long time," Lane recalled of the great Yankee scout in an interview with author Maury Allen. "We knew he was there only to watch Maris. The Yankees were hot after him because they saw home run potential in that left-handed swing. The Yankees were pretty tricky about it, but they couldn't fool me. I would see Greenwade around, and I knew he was trailing Maris, and we'd get to talking. In that slow Oklahoma drawl of his he would start running Maris down. 'He can't do this and he can't do that.' When a scout from another ballclub starts doing that with your player, you know they're after him. They just want to get him for a cheap price."

Mickey Mantle was proof of that. Yet Mantle swore by Tom Greenwade, believing there was no one else in baseball whose word was better. Mickey had gotten to know Greenwade over the years and saw him as more than a scout. Born in 1904 in Willard, Missouri, Greenwade had been a pitcher who had played minor league baseball in the St. Louis Browns organization. After a bout of typhoid sidelined him, he went to work with the Internal Revenue Service. Then he connected with Branch Rickey, the Brooklyn Dodgers general manager who was looking for someone to scout players in Mexico, specifically a young Black Cuban shortstop named Silvio Garcia. This is the player

Branch Rickey first had in mind as the man who would break down baseball's color barrier. So in 1943, Rickey dispatched Greenwade to Mexico to scout Garcia, who at the time was considered the greatest shortstop Cuba had ever produced. But the Cuban youngster blew his chance, not on the field but off it. When Greenwade asked him what he would do if an opposing player insulted him with racial slurs, Garcia blurted out, "I would kill him."

Rickey returned to the drawing board, and in 1945 he sent Greenwade to check out Negro League shortstop Jackie Robinson. Was he the right player for Branch Rickey's sociological experiment? Greenwade returned to tell Rickey that he should sign Robinson but that he likely wasn't a major league shortstop but a second or first baseman. Based on Greenwade's recommendations, the Dodgers eventually signed Robinson and catcher Roy Campanella. But by then, Greenwade had been hired away by the Yankees, for whom he would sign not only Mantle but a litany or future major leaguers, among them: Elston Howard, Hank Bauer, Ralph Terry, Jerry Lumpe, Bill Virdon, and Bobby Murcer.

Roger Maris may have seen Tom Greenwade hanging around batting practice and the stadiums and even known he was a scout. It is unlikely, though, that he was aware of the deal talks whirling around him. But the writing, if not on the outfield walls, was on the daily lineups. Roger was the fourth outfielder and not playing regularly. No longer was Maris in any position to issue ultimatums, and the brash Bobby Bragan had told Roger he didn't give a damn what was on his mind or why he was brooding. He also didn't want to be a Yankee, or that's what he would say up until he was wearing pinstripes. The great irony is that his future, even at this low point of his career, possibly hinged on what the Yankees could do, above board or below it.

In the 1950s, at least for much of the decade, the New York Yankees had the added advantage of seeming to control not only their destiny but also that of the Kansas City Athletics. Originally this had been the Philadelphia Athletics, but it was now a shell of the great Connie Mack dynasty early in the century. In 1954, a Chicago real estate magnate named Arnold Johnson, who had financial ties to the Yankees, bought the Athletics and moved them to Kansas City, Missouri. His pinstripe connections were his long business association with Yankees owners Dan Topping, Larry MacPhail, and Del Webb. A year earlier, Johnson had even bought Yankee Stadium, although the league forced him to sell his share before he bought the Athletics. The Yankees' fingerprints were all over the deal. They had the major league rights to Kansas City. They owned the minor league Blues team that they quickly moved to Colorado, where the team became the Denver Bears. The entire deal did for collusion what Noah did for shipbuilding, but the Yankees got away with it. And it improved the team—the Yankees, that is.

The Kansas City Athletics effectively became little more than a major league farm team for the Yankees, who used the franchise for more quality playing time for players who otherwise might have been sent down to the minors. Over the next five years, New York and Kansas City made 16 trades that involved 59 players, sometimes with a revolving door effect that, of course, most often favored the Yankees. Players such as Bob Cerv went from the Yankees to the Athletics where, after developing into All-Star caliber, they were then dealt back to New York.

In one famous instance, the Yankees used the Athletics to circumvent the 1947 "bonus baby" signing rules put in place to prevent the richest of teams from signing all of the best young players and then stashing them in their farm systems. Prospects signed to large bonuses had to be placed on the major league team's 25-man rosters. Rescinded in 1950, the rule was revived and toughened in 1952, forcing teams to place bonus babies on their major league roster immediately upon their signing and keeping them there for two years from the signing date.

In 1955, the Yankees wanted to sign a teenage phenom from small Alba, Missouri, named Clete Boyer, who had been scouted by none other than fellow Missouri resident Tom Greenwade. Clete was one of seven brothers who all signed professional baseball contracts. Oldest brother Cloyd pitched for the Kansas City Athletics in 1955. That same year, future National League All-Star Ken Boyer broke into the majors with the St. Louis Cardinals, whom he would lead to a World Series title over the Yankees in his 1964 MVP season.

In future baseball histories, Greenwade would be credited with having signed Clete Boyer for the Yankees, for whom he played on two World Series championship teams and three other pennant winners. But he hadn't signed with the Yankees, who were just one of numerous major league ballclubs who pursued him. Signing Clete, though, would have cost Yankees dearly, beyond the $35,000 signing bonus that Boyer received. It would have forced the Yankees to use up one of team's prized roster spots on an 18-year-old not anywhere ready to help win a pennant. It also meant that Boyer wouldn't even be able to get any playing experience, even in the minors.

So the Yankees had their major league farm club, the Athletics, sign the young man. With the Athletics in 1955 and 1956, Boyer was able to play in 114 major league games, batting .226 with 47 hits in 208 at-bats. On June 4, 1957, two years after signing as a bonus baby, Boyer was traded by the Athletics to the Yankees as part of a 13-player swap. New York immediately shipped him to the minors, where he stayed until 1959 when he began the season with the Yankees before more seasoning in the minors and finishing for good with the major league team.

This then was the immediate baseball world that awaited Roger Maris in 1958. If Frank Lane, Cleveland's GM and baseball's consummate trader, couldn't find any seekers for Maris other than the Yankees, then there must not have been much of a market. For that, the Indians perhaps had only themselves to blame. Maris' brooding, stubbornness, and insubordination were hardly a secret among baseball executives, thanks to the Indians themselves. A baseball general manager would have to be crazy to want that kind of cancer in a team's clubhouse. Such a player would need to be another Babe Ruth to make the gamble worthwhile.

George Weiss and the Yankees didn't think Roger Maris was another Babe Ruth, but they needed a good left-handed slugger and were willing to take the risk. If Maris proved to be the trouble-making distraction that the Indians claimed that he was, Weiss had recently shown how swiftly he could deal with the problem and make it go away. Just months earlier, in perhaps the biggest Yankees story of 1957, Weiss had cut ties with the player who for many epitomized the heart and spirit of the Bronx Bomber dynasty of the decade: scrappy infielder Billy Martin, who had made considerable contributions to the championship teams of the 1950s. Martin had already been put on notice to avoid any trouble, especially since he was such a close pal of Mickey Mantle and Whitey Ford. Billy hadn't helped himself by causing a golf cart collision during spring training that had sidelined both Martin and Mantle. Then, early in the season, Martin was at the center of a nightclub brawl that made big headlines for days in all the New York newspapers and beyond.

Martin celebrated his 29th birthday on May 16 of the 1957 season with a party that began with dinner at the mid-Manhattan restaurant Danny's Hideaway, continued at the Waldorf Astoria, where singer Johnny Ray was performing, and ended at the famous Copacabana, where Sammy Davis Jr. was the attraction. Martin, the care-free divorced bachelor, was being treated by longtime teammates Mantle, Ford, Berra, and Bauer, along with their wives, as well as young pitcher Johnny Kucks and his wife.

Accounts of what happened at the Copacabana vary, except on the point that all hell broke loose. Led by Bauer, the Yankees apparently got into an argument with a group of bowlers seated next to their table. According to the players, the drunken bowlers began heckling Davis and called the entertainer "a jungle bunny," which touched a raw nerve among the Yankees after the racial harassment that Elston Howard often had to endure, especially during spring training in Florida. Their arguing continued near the men's room where, as bowlers and Yankees tried to hold back their own, some scuffling broke out and ended up with a fat, drunk bowler knocked out cold on the floor with his nose broken and other facial injuries.

Mantle recalled leaving Merlyn at their table to check on Martin, who had gone to the men's room. "I heard a loud crash," Mickey later said. "The next moment one of the drunks was lying in a heap by the cloakroom, knocked cold. I thought it was Billy. I turned around and saw a couple of other bowlers near the kitchen spitting curses at Hank. Whitey had a lock on his arms. I know this. Bauer never laid a hand on anybody. Neither did Billy. And the only thing I touched during the entire uproar was scotch and soda."

The Yankee players were quickly escorted out the back kitchen exit, but were spotted by a *New York Post* entertainment columnist who tipped off fellow reporters. It was generally believed that Bauer, who was being restrained in the men's room by his teammates, had been the Yankee who landed the punch—although Bauer vehemently denied throwing the punch. Several players and other witnesses claimed the bowler had been beaten up by a couple of bouncers from the club, but the issue was irrelevant. The newspapers sensationalized the story in typical large tabloid headlines that infuriated the Yankee front office, especially Weiss.

In a way that had become common after such incidents, Weiss summoned all the players involved for early morning meetings at the Stadium and refused to believe the Yankees had not been at fault, least of all Martin. Dan Topping also felt that his players had done something unseemly and fined them $1,000 apiece, except Kucks, whom he fined only $500 because his pay was significantly less. It made the Yankees appear all the more guilty, especially after the bowler filed a criminal complaint that led to the players testifying before a grand jury.

"At the grand jury, I remember Mantle standing in the middle of the room giving his testimony," Ford would later recall. "There was no chair, nothing. He was standing there and chewing gum and one of the jurors asked him, 'What are you chewing, Mr. Mantle?' 'Gum,' Mick said. 'Would you mind taking it out of your mouth?' Mick took the gum out of his mouth and there was no place to put it, so he had to hold it in his hand for the rest of the time he was being questioned."

Mantle elaborated in one of his autobiographies, recounting how he had not seen anyone throw any punches.

"Well," asked a grand juror, "did you see a gentleman lying unconscious on the floor near the Copa entrance?"

"Yes, I did," Mantle answered.

"All right. Do you have an opinion as to how this could have happened?

Mantle thought about the question and then, with a serious look on his face, said, "I think Roy Rogers rode through the Copa, and Trigger kicked the man in the head."

The grand jury broke out laughing, and an hour later the district attorney threw out the case for insufficient evidence. However, the damage to Billy Martin's career as a Yankee was done. On June 15, at the league trading deadline and almost a month to the day after the Copacabana incident, Martin was dealt to the Kansas City Athletics. George Weiss had finally succeeded in getting Martin away from his young star, but he would soon learn that Martin had merely been a symptom of Mantle's off-the-field behavior and not the problem.

"With Billy and me, drinking was a competitive thing," Mantle would recall. "We'd see who could drink the other under the table. I'd get a kick out of seeing him get loaded before me. Alcohol made him so aggressive. He's the only person I knew who could hear a guy give him the finger from the back of a barroom. We had some wild times."

Frank Lane was a man who could be equally as decisive as Weiss in getting rid of a troublemaker, which is how he handled moving Roger Maris. The trade began taking shape when Lane received a telephone call from Kansas City owner Arnold Johnson. Lane was no fool. He knew the Yankees were likely the instigators. Johnson's business connections with the Yankee owners were common knowledge. Still, Johnson claimed to be calling about Rocky Colavito.

"Rocky's too popular here now—they'd run me out of town," Lane told the Athletics' owner. "You take Maris instead. He's a better all-around player with more potential. He can run. He's a good outfielder. He's got a good arm, and one of these days he'll be a real good hitter."

Johnson told Lane he would have to think about it.

Maris was having a mediocre season, even though he was playing more often than had been in the Athletics' plans. By mid-June he had played in 51 games, getting 182 at-bats, but he was batting an unimpressive .225 with nine home runs and 27 runs batted in. Roger was having a horrible time, as were most players, in what became perhaps the most turbulent year in Indians team history. Much of the blame could be laid at Frank Lane's feet, though he put the fault on his new manager, Bobby Bragan, who later said he never knew what his general manager wanted. On June 26, only 67 games into the season, Lane fired Bragan, the shortest managerial stint at the time for a Cleveland manager.

Two weeks earlier, as the trading deadline neared, Kansas City owner Arnold Johnson called Lane at the Shoreham Hotel in Washington where the Indians were playing the Senators. Johnson was ready to make the deal for Maris. "I told Johnson I would make the deal for Maris on one condition," Lane recalled. "I didn't want Johnson passing him on to New York right away. I knew he would end up there later in any event, but I wanted to stall it as long as I could. Maybe my team would be strong enough to beat them by then."

Maris was on a flight back to Cleveland when the deal was announced on June 15. Along with pitcher Dick Tomanek and infielder Preston Ward, Roger went to the Athletics in exchange for infielder Vic Power, who was a four-time All-Star and winner of seven consecutive Gold Glove Awards, and utility man Woodie Held. Bobby Bragan broke the news to Maris and his two teammates while the Indians were in mid-flight. "I wasn't surprised Maris was traded," said Bragan, "considering who the general manager was."

In New York, some of the players who had become Yankees via the underground railway from Kansas City sensed what the deal would mean in the near future.

"Well, we just got Maris," said Ryne Duren, the fireball reliever who had been traded by the Athletics to the Yankees in the Billy Martin deal a year earlier to the day.

"Roger was shocked when he got traded," teammate Ray Narleski said. "He came over to my house in tears. I said, 'Roger, don't feel bad. You are going to Kansas City but will wind up with the Yankees.' I don't know if he liked that idea."

10

What'sis Name? Mantle?

"Everything Mantle is and everything he was going to be, that was me at one point. People who say I didn't like the kid didn't understand. He's everything I was, everything I am. He was *me."*

—JOE DIMAGGIO

IN 1950, MICKEY HAD GIVEN THE YANKEES A SNEAK PREVIEW OF WHAT to expect. That spring training, he had spent most of the time with other minor leaguers away from the attention of Casey Stengel. Without the benefit of the pre-spring training instructional camp for rookies that would begin the following year, Stengel could mostly only hear of the promising youngster from other coaches. In the sprints, Mantle had timed the fastest in the entire camp. It was Mickey's switch-hitting, however, that brought attention to the freckle-faced kid who was a virtual unknown. In an intrasquad game on the fourth day of camp, Mantle slugged home runs from both sides of the plate—shots farther than anyone could remember balls hit in spring training. The first time most of the rookies in camp even saw Stengel was after Mantle's second blast when the aging manager ran out on the field, waving a fungo bat as he chased after Mickey circling first base, asking other coaches, "What'sis name? What'sis name? Mantle?"

Then Mantle was utterly amazing in the 1951 spring training season.

Speed has always been an intangible quality in sports. Even in the sports where speed is not usually considered the most important of attributes, raw, natural swiftness afoot can be impressive. Stengel and his coaches at the team's instructional camp were immediately awe-struck by Mantle's foot speed. It was the kind of speed rarely seen in a power hitter, and it was one of the star qualities that he would later have in common with Roger Maris. In the early footraces of the 1951 spring training, Mickey outran other players by such margins that Stengel at first thought he was cheating with head starts. Stengel and the coaches had Mantle running sprints against everyone at the camp, including some of the roster players who were there under the guise of being "instructors" so as to not violate the restriction against major leaguers coming to camp before March 1. Mantle outran everyone. He was clocked running from home plate to first base, and his times were 3.1 seconds from the right-handed hitter's side of the plate and 3.0 seconds from the left-hander's side. No one in the major leagues was that fast.

That was also when Stengel began calling Mickey "Mantles." Some in camp thought the origin may have been in Stengel believing he had two Mantles because of his switch-hitting talent, which by itself was a rarity. At the time of Mantle's arrival, the American League featured just one regular switch-hitter, Dave Philley of the Athletics. Moreover, switch-hitting was seen as a device employed by hitters who were lacking other weapons. Of the switch-hitters that had preceded Mantle—among them Frankie Frisch, Red Schoendienst, and Max Carey were the best—nearly all were disdainful of the long ball. In

1951, the career leader in home runs by a switch-hitter was Rip Collins with 135. The idea of tape-measure power from both sides of the plate was enough to get anyone's attention.

As a switch-hitter, slugging home runs from both sides of the plate, Mantle quickly began to impress the other Yankees as well. Beyond running faster than any player Stengel had ever seen, his hitting talent and potential were prodigious. Only his defensive skills underwhelmed. Mickey had a tremendous arm, but he was no major league shortstop. In the minors the Yankees had left him at the position he had played in high school. But at Joplin in his first full minor league season, he had committed 55 errors, unusually high for a shortstop. But Stengel had other plans for Mickey. The thinking among some in the Yankees front office had been that Mantle might ultimately be converted into an outfielder. Once an outfielder himself, Stengel wanted to shift Mantle. So within days of Mantle's arrival at the instructional camp, Stengel made Mickey his own project, personally trying to teach him the new position. He then retained Tommy Henrich, the Yankee right fielder who had recently retired, to coach his young protégé. Stengel could barely contain himself and, in a burst of enthusiasm, invited the sportswriters at the camp to come watch.

"Mantles," Stengel told the writers, "is a shortstop and he ain't much of a shortstop, either. But he sure can switch-hit hard, and run as fast as anybody I ever saw. I've seen some pretty good runners and ol' Case was a pretty fair runner himself. You fellers be out here tomorrow and you might see this Mantle at a place that could surprise you."

Although they dismissed Stengel's comments as more Stengelese, the sportswriters who came by early the next morning caught Mantle taking outfield practice under Henrich's tutelage. The Yankees were determined to turn Mickey into a major leaguer, and Mickey was soon to learn that there was little room for sentiment. Yankee coach Frank

Crosetti worked with all the infielders, and the first thing he noticed about Mickey was his glove.

"Where'd ya get this piece of shit?" the former Yankee great asked.

Mickey didn't hear exactly what Crosetti said about the glove and perhaps didn't want to hear. Neither could he bring himself to tell him just how special the glove was. It was a Marty Marion autograph model, designed for infielders and endorsed by the shortstop on the great St. Louis Cardinals teams Mantle and his father had rooted for. The glove had been a Christmas present that his father had given him when he was 16 and which Mickey had used throughout high school and his two seasons in the minors.

"I knew exactly what it cost, for I had yearned after it for a long time," Mickey said of that special Christmas gift. "It was $22, about one-third of my father's weekly salary. And I knew, as all poor boys do, exactly what that amount of money meant in a family like ours. Of course, I doted on the glove with an unholy passion, loving even the smell of it, and I caressed and cared for it through the winter as if it had been a holy relic. But most of all, my heart was bursting with the realization of what a sacrifice like this said about my father's love for me and about his pride in my ability."

Crosetti never knew the story and might not have cared. The next morning he presented Mantle with an expensive, professional model glove that Mickey suspected Crosetti had even bought with his own money. Mickey put the glove his father had given him away, one of the first of many steps he would take over the next few years in attempting to break the unusually close bond with Mutt, both as father and coach.

Of course, plans to convert Mickey into an outfielder were already in the works. Although Mickey didn't realize it at first, the glove Crosetti bought him was a slightly bigger model designed especially for outfielders. Crosetti may also have been sending Mantle a subtle message: Perhaps it was time for Mickey to understand that his father had not known all there was to know about playing the game. That same day, Mickey used that glove in the intrasquad game that followed his outfield practice session with Tommy Henrich. He played center field, where he made one put out and acquitted himself without committing any mistakes. It was at the plate, however, that Mickey made the writers take notice. He lined a triple to center field in his first at-bat, then drove a home run over the right-field fence in his second time up.

"In Mickey Mantle," many of the sportswriters began reporting in their spring training updates, "the Yankees are grooming the successor to Joe DiMaggio."

That spring Mickey hit .402 in the Yankees' exhibition games, with nine home runs and 31 RBI, and reporters talked of him being the most exciting young player since Jackie Robinson, who four years earlier had broken baseball's color barrier with the Brooklyn Dodgers. In his first few exhibition games in Arizona, where the Yankees were training that spring, Mickey hit around .400 before the Yankees moved to California for a series of 11 games. Against the Pittsburgh Pirates, Mantle hit home runs from each side of the plate. Branch Rickey, the man who had signed Jackie Robinson for the Dodgers, was the general manager of the Pirates in 1951. Rickey could hardly contain himself after watching Mickey and at the game did something that was highly uncharacteristic of his conservative nature with money. He tore a blank check from his checkbook, signed his name and handed it to Yankee co-owner Dan Topping, who happened to be sitting next to him. "Fill in the figures you want for that boy," said Rickey, "and it's a deal." Topping smiled politely but left the check untouched.

The late author-journalist Dick Schaap remembered that "Mantle was so incredibly good on the field that even the men who praised him wondered, at times, whether they were maintaining their sanity." Jack Orr, who was then covering the Yankees for *The New York Compass*, reflected the general attitude among sportswriters in a column toward the end of spring training: "Some of us were kicking it around in a compartment on the Yankee train speeding through Texas. We worked over a couple of subjects, but, as always, we got back to the same old one. It was bed time when somebody said: 'Cripes, we've been going for three hours and we've talked about nothing but Mickey Mantle.'"

Pitching coach Jim Turner said he never saw anybody who could excite another ballplayer the way Mantle had already done. "When he gets up to hit," he said, "the guys get off the bench and elbow each other out of the way to get a better look. And take a look at the other bench sometimes. I saw [Pittsburgh Pirates slugger] Ralph Kiner's eyes pop when he first got a look at the kid. [Cleveland Indian] Luke Easter was studying him the other day, and so was [fellow Indian player] Larry Doby… Here's one sure tip-off on how great he is. Watch DiMag when Mantle's hitting. He never takes his eyes off the kid."

That spring, though, DiMaggio remained his typically stoic self in talking about the rookie who was being groomed to replace him. "He's a big-league hitter right now," DiMaggio told one reporter. "Who does he remind me of? Well, there just haven't been many kids like him. Maybe he has something to learn about catching a fly ball, but that's all. He can do everything else." In San Francisco, Joe's hometown, where the Yankees played an exhibition that spring, DiMaggio was asked if he resented Mantle moving in on his center field position. "Hell, no," said DiMaggio. "Why should I resent him? If he's good enough to take my job in center, I can always move over to right or left. I haven't helped him much—Henrich takes care of that—but if there is anything I can do to help him, I'm only too willing. Remember what I said back in Phoenix about those Yankee kids and how great they were? Well, the more I see of the ones we have now, the more convinced I am the Yankees won't even miss me."

"Mickey," said fellow rookie Gil McDougald, "had a spring training like a god."

Johnny Hopp, who would later be one of Mantle's roommates in New York, had the locker next to Mickey that spring and took to calling him "The Champ" because of his incredible streak of power hitting.

"You're going to make a million dollars out of this game, the Lord behold," Hopp said to Mickey after one spring game.

Mantle simply laughed. He was still unconvinced that he was doing anything special on the field. Despite all the hype about Mantle, there were also the skeptics. One of them was Stan Isaacs, Orr's fellow staff writer on *The New York Compass,* who was also critical of all the media hoopla being made over Mantle. He wrote: "Since the start of spring training, the typewriter keys out of the training camps have been pounding out one name to the people back home. No matter what paper you read, or what day, you'll get Mickey Mantle, more Mickey Mantle, and still more Mickey Mantle. Never in the history of baseball has the game known the wonder to equal this Yankee rookie. Every day there's some other glorious phrase as the baseball writers outdo themselves in attempts to describe the antics of this wonder: 'He's faster than Cobb... he hits with power from both sides of the plate the way Frankie Frisch used to... he takes all the publicity in stride, an unspoiled kid... sure to go down as one of the real greats of baseball... another Mel Ott.'"

Then came Opening Day of the season, which the Yankees were starting against the Senators on the road. When he arrived at Grand Central Station for the train trip down to Washington, D.C., Mickey still had no idea if he would be staying with the Yankees or be sent down to the minors along with a number of other rookies. The train the Yankees were taking to Washington that day was still typical of baseball travel in the early 1950s. Baseball and train rides were part of the fabric of the American culture. For teams, the train rides from city to city were the extension of the clubhouse. Players passed the time on long train rides through open fields with card games and baseball banter. The main diner with its Art Deco lights and etched glass dividers made an immediate impression on Mickey, who was still getting used to walking normally through a speeding train as he followed Casey Stengel from car to car toward the bullet-shaped smoking lounge. He practically forced himself to ask, "Casey, can you tell me something? Am I going to play at [minor league] Beaumont this year?"

Stengel winked. "I think you'll stay with us," he told Mickey. They were headed to the train car where the owners and general manager were riding. "When we get back there, just be quiet, and I'll do the talking." In the smoking lounge, Stengel told general manager George Weiss that Mantle was ready to play with the Yankees. Weiss shook his head. He thought Mickey was too young.

"I don't care if he's in diapers," Stengel insisted. "If he's good enough to play for us on a regular basis, I want to keep him."

Yankee co-owners Del Webb and Topping both agreed with their manager.

"George," began Webb, "they've been writing so much stuff about Mickey, I feel we have to keep him."

"The thing is, George," said Topping, "we're not opening in New York. We're opening in Washington. After two or three games under his belt, I think he'll be all right."

Mickey swallowed hard, trying to hide his excitement. He was going to be a Yankee. The contract talk that followed was like an afterthought for Mickey that, at the time, didn't seem to matter. Stengel himself negotiated Mickey's deal with Weiss, a contract, of course, structured to the Yankees' best interests. Under Mickey's rookie contract, he would get $7,500 for the season—which was $2,500 above the minimum but still a bargain for the player being touted as the successor to Ruth and DiMaggio. However, the Yankees' apparent generosity had a catch: If Mickey floundered and was sent to the minors, the Yankees would only be on the hook for the minimum.

Mickey returned to his train seat in a fog. He had just signed his first big-league contract. He had realized his dream of making it to the majors. He had achieved his father's dream. He thought about his father, Mutt, about his sacrifices not only on the long afternoons when he and his grandfather Charlie pitched batting practice to him but about how his father doted on him—down to saving a piece of his cupcake every day and bringing it home to Mickey in his lunch bucket after working a hard day in the coal mines. He looked out at the rain that was falling as the train sped toward Washington, D.C., and tears welled in his eyes as he thought about life back home.

As things turned out, though, the Yankees' entire opening series was rained out. Fittingly, Mantle's major league debut took place at Yankee Stadium on April 17, 1951. The Opening Day lineup Casey posted in the dugout had Mantle playing right field and batting third behind left fielder Jackie Jensen and shortstop Phil Rizzuto and ahead of DiMaggio, who was batting in the cleanup slot. Catcher Yogi Berra was batting fifth, first baseman Johnny Mize sixth, followed by third baseman Billy Johnson, second baseman Jerry Coleman, and starting pitcher Vic Raschi.

When he arrived in New York as a 19-year-old major leaguer, Mickey Mantle was the embodiment of what springtime in baseball can evoke, a symbol of innocence and hope. For the America then— and the America that nostalgia subsequently captured in the national conscience—Mickey was the eternal glory of youth. He was a country boy, innocent of the temptations of an urban jungle that was already becoming a predominant feature of American life. To be sure, that was the New Yorker's perspective, because seen through the eyes of his fellow Oklahomans, Mantle's arrival in New York was that of a hero venturing forth from the world of common into a region of glamorous splendor and fabulous forces.

Mickey himself would say that when he arrived in New York his view of the world wasn't much wider than the strike zone. "My childhood was part of what made me popular with the fans in New York and elsewhere," he said. "I was a classic country bumpkin, who came to the big city carrying a cardboard suitcase and with a wardrobe of two pairs of slacks and a pastel-colored sports coat."

"I remember my impression of him the first time I met him," Yankee pitcher Whitey Ford later said. "I thought, 'What a hayseed.'"

Yogi Berra had a similar recollection: "I remember he was a big, scared kid who we already knew could hit the ball out of sight. You know something else I remember? Even when he was a kid, we already knew he was a helluva guy."

On Opening Day at Yankee Stadium, Mickey was flabbergasted at the sight of the towering triple-deck stands already filling up. He had already been to Yankee Stadium before, when he joined the team for the final two weeks of the previous season. Mickey was ineligible for the World Series roster. However, at general manager George Weiss' invitation, he had attended the first two games of the Yankees' 1950 World Series against the Philadelphia Phillies. But on Opening Day of the 1951 season, Mickey now stared around the stadium for the first time from the playing field. As he studied the famous Yankee Stadium façade above the upper deck, Yogi Berra came up behind him.

"Hey, what kind of an Opening Day crowd is this? There's no people here." Mickey had quickly come to realize that the Yankee catcher didn't say things so much as growl them out. He stared at Yogi, then understood he was joking. Jim Turner, one of the coaches, came up to them.

"How many people watched you play at Joplin last year?" he asked Mickey.

"I'd say about 55,000 all season," he answered.

"Well, take a good look," said Turner. "We got about 45,000 here today for one game—almost as many people as saw you in Joplin all year."

Mantle gulped. "No," he muttered.

"Yes," said Turner, trying to put Mickey at ease. "And most of them came to see what you look like."

An hour and a half before the game, sportswriter Red Smith recalled watching Mantle looking nervously into the stands from the top step of the Yankees' dugout. From the bench, Stengel could only see Mickey from the chest down, but he noticed that the sole of one of his baseball cleats had torn loose. The Yankee skipper got up to talk to Mickey and then returned shaking his head. "He don't care much about the big leagues, does he?" Stengel said. "He's gonna play in them shoes."

"Who is he?" asked a visitor in the dugout who hadn't seen Mantle that spring.

"Why, he's that kid of mine," said Stengel.

"That's Mantle?"

"Yeah. I asked him didn't he have any better shoes, and he said he had a new pair but they're a little too big."

The visitor chuckled along with Stengel. "He's waiting for an important occasion to wear the new ones."

Stengel was also trying not to show his apprehension, not about how Mantle would do, but about this team he was patching up with Band-Aids, mirrors, and smoke. Pitcher Whitey Ford and infielder Billy Martin had been drafted and were lost to the team for this season at least. DiMaggio was ailing, and aging as well. The team's top three starting pitchers were all in their thirties. If this Yankees team were to compete for the pennant again, Stengel knew it would have to be with the help of at least two or three of their prized rookies. Gil McDougald looked ready to take over one spot in the infield. Mantle appeared set to play in the outfield. Then there was another highly touted youngster, Jackie Jensen, who had starred in the 1949 Rose Bowl for the University of California and to whom the Yankees had given a $40,000 signing bonus. A year earlier Jensen had been the spring training Golden Boy thought to be DiMaggio's successor. But Jensen had trouble hitting major league pitching. In the 1951 spring training, Stengel thought he could convert Jensen into a pitcher. That experiment quickly failed, and now the Yankees were hoping that Jensen might hit just well enough to stay with the team. For now, though, he was an afterthought.

On the dugout steps as he waited to take the field at Yankee Stadium for the first time in his career, Mickey Mantle couldn't keep his eyes off Ted Williams, who was taking practice swings outside the visitors' dugout. Joe DiMaggio had been Mantle's hero growing up, but it was Williams who was now still at his prime and would continue to be throughout the 1950s. Military service had taken away a couple of seasons in the 1940s, and would again during the Korean War. Williams was also coming off an ill-fated 1950 season when he broke his left elbow in the All-Star Game and played only 89 games. At age 32, Williams was already being acknowledged among his peers as the game's consummate hitter. Achieving that reputation was what Williams lived for.

As a rookie in 1939, when Mickey was not even eight years old, Williams had laid out what he wanted his epitaph to be. "All I want out of life," he had said, "is that when I walk down the street folks will say, 'There goes the greatest hitter who ever lived.'" This is the line that Bernard Malamud would appropriate and change ever so slightly—"Sometimes when I walk down the street I bet people will say, 'There goes Roy Hobbs, the best there ever was in the game.'"— for the mythical slugger in *The Natural,* which would be published in 1952. The 1951 season would also mark the 10th anniversary of Williams becoming the last major leaguer to hit .400. Williams had already won Triple Crowns in 1942 and 1947, and would go on to hit 521 home runs and finish with a .344 average.

The first time Mantle actually saw Williams play in person had been in September of 1950, when he had been brought up for two weeks after the end of his season at Joplin. "I saw Ted hit two home runs off Vic Raschi," said Mickey, "and I became convinced he was the greatest hitter I'd ever seen." Mantle had another reason on this Opening Day for not being able to take his eyes off Williams. Three players had been in the spotlight that spring: DiMaggio for what would be his last season, Mantle for his magnificent exhibition season, and Williams for his adamant refusal to play in exhibitions. During spring training just a few weeks earlier, Williams had set off one of the many controversies in his career by publicly criticizing the spirit of the Boston Red Sox fans, while praising that of the Yankees. Now, here at Yankee Stadium, Williams was the object of stares and admiration from fans and players alike.

Then, about half an hour before the game began, Williams walked over to the Yankee dugout to greet DiMaggio as photographers pressed around them. Mantle was surprised and embarrassed when photographers asked him to join DiMaggio and Williams in the picture. As Mickey moved in between them, Williams quickly acquainted himself: "You must be Mick." They shook hands, and then the three of them posed with Louisville Sluggers over their shoulders while camera shutters snapped.

Nearby a couple of other sportswriters were talking to Bill Dickey, the former Yankee catcher and manager who was now one of Stengel's coaches. They all turned to look at Mantle and one of the writers said, "Gosh, I envy him. Nineteen years old and starting out as a Yankee!"

"He's green," said Dickey, "but he's got to be great. All that power, a switch hitter, and he runs like a striped ape. If he drags a bunt past the pitcher, he's on base. I think he's the fastest man I ever saw with the Yankees. But he's green in the outfield. He was at shortstop last year."

"Gosh, Bill," said the writer, "do you realize you were in the big leagues before he was born?"

"He was born in 1932," said Dickey, misstating Mickey's birth year by a year, "and that was the year I played my first World Series."

Half an hour later, after the traditional Opening Day speeches at home plate, Whitey Ford walked out to the mound wearing his army uniform—he was still in the service—and threw out the first pitch.

Then Mantle's big-league debut began. At the plate, Mantle was fighting nerves and facing an enigmatic Red Sox starter that Boston had traded for during the winter. Southpaw Bill Wight, a tall, lanky Californian, had once been a rising young star himself.

As a 16-year-old he had been discovered by another of the great Yankee scouts, Joe Devine, a man whose signees included four who are enshrined in the Baseball Hall of Fame: Joe Cronin, Paul Waner, Lloyd Waner, and Joe DiMaggio. In 1946, Wight made the jump to the majors when he impressed perhaps the greatest of all Yankee managers,

Joe McCarthy. It was baseball's first year after the war-sapped roster years, and it would be the hard-drinking McCarthy's final season in a career in which he won nine league titles overall and seven World Series championships—a record tied only by Casey Stengel. McCarthy was looking for a left-handed starter to rebuild the team he had managed since 1931. That year, at a spring training held in Panama, Wight won a spot in the Yankee rotation, with the *Sporting News* reporting: "The southpaw operated with all the poise of a veteran, had plenty of stuff, and made even the customarily wary and cautious McCarthy grow exuberant."

Wight, though, didn't remain in the rotation in what quickly became an overall disappointing Yankee season topped by McCarthy's self-destructive drunken binge as manager. In late May, McCarthy resigned by telegram. Longtime catcher Bill Dickey took over for McCarthy, but he couldn't fix a team with clubhouse and front office disarray either. Dickey resigned September 11, and coach Johnny Neun oversaw the final weeks of a season in which the Yankees finished 17 games behind the Red Sox.

Wight later offered a poignant assessment of that Yankee season when he spoke about baseball's first season after World War II for the online oral history *This Great Game:*

"Most of [players returning from the war] expected their jobs back and they did, but they were all pretty rusty and some of them were never the same. That Yankees team was solid, with [Joe] DiMaggio, [Tommy] Henrich, and Charlie Keller in the outfield, but they didn't play that well their first year back, which was understandable. Joe D. hit around .290 and Henrich was around .250, so they didn't have their normal great years. Joe Gordon couldn't get going and we went through three managers that season [Bill McCarthy, Bill Dickey, and Johnny Neun], so the team finished third. I do remember Red Ruffing, the old master at age 41; he was still effective, with an ERA under 2.00.”

A year later, New York traded Wight, who became known as a journeyman pitcher. In 12 seasons pitching for eight different teams, he appeared in 347 games, compiling a 77–99 won-lost record and a 3.95 earned run average. Perhaps Wight’s problem in the majors was having played on mediocre teams. Notably, in his prime from 1948 to 1950, he pitched over 200 innings in each season, winning 15 and 10 games respectively in the final two years with the White Sox. The scouting report that teams developed on him was that Wight couldn’t get his breaking pitches over for strikes, something that he himself acknowledged.

“[Catcher Bill Dickey] was a general behind the plate and he was amazing at handling pitchers,” Wight said in an interview with baseball historian Ed Attanasio. “He always called for curveballs when I was on the mound, but I told him I don’t have enough control with breaking balls. So, I started shaking them off and he didn’t like that. He ran out to the mound and said, ‘Don’t ever shake me off ever again, rookie!’ I told him, ‘You don’t sign my paycheck, Dickey. You don’t even know me.’ Oh, he got mad when I said that. ‘You’re lucky to be on the ballclub at all kid, so don’t push it.’ To make his point, he called for four curveballs in a row after I got two strikes on the batter. I walked him and now I was mad. Dickey was used to working with pitchers like Lefty Gomez, Red Ruffing, and Johnny Murphy, who could throw all their pitches for strikes at any point in the count, so I guess he expected me to do the same.”

In 1951, the Red Sox thought enough of Wight to hand him the ball for Opening Day against the defending champs’ ace Vic Raschi, whose six-hit shutout would start the last of his three straight 21-game seasons. Mantle was batting third in the lineup, and the distinctive voice that announced his first at-bat from the public address booth at Yankee Stadium was also making his debut. Bob Sheppard would go on to announce more than 4,500 games between 1951 and 2007, where his words reverberated around the massive Yankee Stadium structure, and Reggie Jackson later famously nicknamed him the "Voice of God." Sheppard would be known by his signature announcing moments, though none more famous than:

"Now batting... the center fielder... Mickey Mantle."

Sheppard would earn a Monument Park plaque noting that he introduced both home and visiting players "with equal divine reverence." Each game he followed a trademark cadence in his announcements. He would introduce each player giving his position, uniform number, name, and repeated the number, during his first at-bat: "Now batting for the Yankees, the right fielder, number six, Mickey Mantle, number six." For each player's succeeding at-bat he communicated his position and name: "The right fielder, Mickey Mantle."

In many minds, including their own, Bob Sheppard and Mickey Mantle's names would be linked in Yankee eternity. Sheppard once told a WABC radio interviewer that he had a special affection for the natural resonance of many Latino players' names: Salomé Barojas, José Valdivielso, Álvaro Espinoza. "Anglo-Saxon names are not very euphonious," he said. "What can I do with Steve Sax? What can I do with Mickey Klutts?"

For Sheppard, though, there was no name that could match the sound of "Mickey Mantle." It was his favorite name to call, and he fondly remembered Mantle, in retirement, once telling him: "'Every time you introduced me at Yankee Stadium, I got shivers up my spine.' And I said to him, 'So did I.'"

It was a memorable connection that would begin inauspiciously enough. After Sheppard introduced him in his Yankee Stadium debut,

Mantle broke his bat on the first major league pitch he saw, almost beating out the infield grounder. He popped up in his second at-bat and came to the plate for the third time in the sixth inning with the Yankees leading 2–0, nobody out, and runners Phil Rizzuto at first and Jackie Jensen at third. Bill Wight was still on the mound for the Red Sox, pitching well but getting no offensive support. Waiting on deck, DiMaggio called Mantle aside and spoke to him. It was as much to relax Mickey as to offer a tip against Wight on his third at-bat against him. DiMaggio was familiar with Wight and knew he had trouble throwing a curveball for a strike. Sit on his fastball, DiMaggio advised.

Mantle nodded, stepped to the plate, and connected off Wight for his first major league hit. Batting right-handed, Mickey hit a fastball past the outstretched glove of shortstop Lou Boudreau into left field, driving in the runner from third base. Mantle's hit continued the rally for a three-run inning that would seal the game.

As he scooted back to first base from the wide turn toward second, Mantle momentarily caught a glimpse of DiMaggio looking at him, a small smile across his face, nodding in Mickey's direction, and giving his heir apparent a sign of acceptance.

"I would have given anything for his approval," said Mantle. "And I'd gotten it."

11

Phenoms and Tailspins

"Casey Stengel saw the potential in his swing, his power, and the quickness of his bat and recognized that Roger Maris was the perfect player for Yankee Stadium."
—MAURY ALLEN, BASEBALL HISTORIAN

ANXIETY AND PANIC ATTACKS ARE NOT USUALLY ASSOCIATED WITH heroes, especially baseball stars. Courage, coolness, cockiness, even arrogance, yes. But nerves are also part of the game. Most great players perhaps have a better rein on their fears or hide the insecurities and nervousness with the stoicism of an experienced professional athlete. Underneath, however, their tears and tantrums offer a glimpse of a virtue that most men of their time held in bitter disdain: authentic human emotion. In Maris and Mantle, especially in their rookie and early seasons, one witnessed fear and hope colliding—the hero's anxiety, his frustration, his confusion, and his elation all colliding with each other as he pursued his dream of success and conquest. And it was a challenge both Roger and Mickey had to face alone because few could see through their masks of self-confidence what was really going on within them.

Although their rookie seasons were six years apart, there were striking similarities in the hardships they each confronted, the emotional impact it took on their lives, and how they had to find the character within themselves to keep the setbacks from either ending or impacting their careers. Years later, in separate interviews, they each would credit their loved ones—Maris: his wife, Pat; Mantle: his father, Mutt, and his New York girlfriend, Holly Brooke—for believing in them and reminding them to especially believe in themselves.

In his rookie season, Mantle's sensational spring training and early season success gave hope that he would be an immediate star. After Opening Day, he drove in two runs in another Yankee victory the next day. He had three hits in five at-bats a few games later, and was suddenly off to a .320 start.

Then in Chicago on May 1, Mantle hit the first of his 536 career home runs. In the sixth inning, with one out and Yankee ace Vic Raschi, who had doubled, on second base, Mantle stepped into the left-handed hitter's box against right-hander Randy Gumpert. Some reports maintained that Gumpert, who had pitched for the Yankees after World War II, including the 1947 World Series championship team, tried to fool Mantle with a changeup. Gumpert had a different memory of the pitch. "I threw him a screwball that didn't screw much," he said years later. "Mickey smacked the ball in dead-center field right into the bullpen… it must have traveled 450 feet in the air!"

Beyond the right-field fence in Comiskey Park, Yankees backup catcher Charlie Silvera, who was in his usual spot in the bullpen, saw the ball land and picked it up. Silvera knew, as did almost all of the Yankees, that Mickey would want that ball. In the clubhouse, Mantle inscribed the ball "My first H.R. in the Majors, May 1, 1951, 4:50 p.m. Chicago, 6th inning off Randy Gumpert."

Once back in the Yankee dugout, Mantle was still breathing hard and trying to contain himself when he saw Joe DiMaggio slowly getting off the bench. DiMaggio, who in his last season would play in only 116 games and had not been in the lineup that day, was nursing a new injury that would sideline him the next two weeks. Mickey figured the weary Yankee Clipper was just getting ready to retire to the clubhouse for the day. Instead DiMaggio surprised him.

"Joe came over to me on the dugout bench and said, 'Mickey, Gumpert oughta thank you. You just put him in the history books,'" Mantle would recall. "I wasn't sure what the hell he meant until later. He meant people would remember he was the first pitcher I homered against. So I guess Joe knew I was going to amount to something."

Three days later, the Yankees were in St. Louis to play the Browns in Sportsman's Park. In the stands that day were Mickey's mother, his Oklahoma girlfriend Merlyn, and her mother. Mantle hit another home run. A reporter approached Merlyn after the game and asked her what she thought of Mickey's homer. "I expected it," she said. "He promised me he'd do it."

Soon Mickey was leading the league in average, RBI, and home runs. And strikeouts. That happened as Mantle's slump crept in almost as quickly as the name he had quickly made for himself, and unraveled his confidence at the plate. The pitcher's "book" on Mickey already spread around the league: he was a sucker for high fastballs just above the letters. Mantle also didn't have the discipline not to chase those pitches, or the patience to drive outside pitches to the opposite field. By mid-July his batting average had fallen to .260, with Stengel unable to communicate with his young star about making changes to his swing and his at-bats. Mantle just continued to strike out. In Cleveland in mid-July, Bob Lemon struck him out three times. In the dugout, Mickey smashed two of his bats against a wall. At other times, he smashed his fists against walls after striking out. Stengel threatened to fine him, but Mantle's outbursts continued unchecked. At his wits' end, Mantle tried to lay down a two-strike bunt with a runner in scoring position in the bottom of the ninth inning, but fouled the bunt attempt for an out to end the game. Stengel was furious. "Nice going, son," he said to Mickey in front of his locker. "You sure fooled us. Next time I want you to bunt, I'll give you the sign."

A few days later, Mantle was demoted to the Yankees' then-AAA minor league team, the Kansas City Blues.

Roger Maris' early rookie season heroics in 1957 were similar to Mantle's outstanding start. After his 3-for-5 debut, in his next game Roger belted an 11th-inning grand slam that capped a five-run victory. Throughout his rookie season, Maris wore No. 32, not switching to No. 5 until his second season. After his trade to Kansas City, he wore both No. 35 and No. 3. He never wore No. 9 until he joined the Yankees in 1960. Throughout 1957, Roger used only one bat, a 35-inch, 33-ounce Louisville Slugger—the H&B signature model O16 that company records show was part of a shipment delivered to him during his final minor league season in 1956. The bat, showing visible heavy game use and a 13-inch crack in the handle—identified by his No. 32 written on the knob in vintage black marker—sold at auction in 2007 for $3,525.

Like Mantle, in his rookie season Maris impressed sportswriters and opponents, possibly more than he did people in the Indians organization. No one had been more taken with Mickey as a rookie than his manager Casey Stengel, and it may be just coincidental that in 1957, it was the same Stengel who was singing Maris' praises. On May 8, the day after the tragic line drive injury to Herb Score, Maris plastered a pitch off right-hander Al Cicotte deep into the right-field stands for a two-run homer that finished a rout of the Yankees. So deep was the grief over the devastating Score incident that Stengel wasn't as upset by the 10–4 routing. He had put the guilt-torn Gil McDougald back into the lineup, and his shortstop delivered three hits. Then, he had blurted out to some Indians beat writers: "What about the kid in center field, you don't think he has power? He hits a ball pretty good for a young man and why wouldn't you like to have him if you could?"

The writers, puzzled about whether the Ol' Perfessor might have been talking about Mantle, who had homered in the third inning off the Tribe's Early Wynn, soon deciphered the "Stengelese" to realize he was talking about Maris. Stengel had seen the future: not only a left-handed pull-hitter to capitalize on the short porch at the Stadium but also a power hitter to put in the lineup behind Mantle, much as the Yankees had once used Lou Gehrig to back up Ruth and keep opposing teams from pitching around the Babe. In the team's hotel that night, Casey laid that out at dinner with George Weiss, as if his general manager hadn't already had those thoughts. The story goes that Stengel even bragged about it, telling a reporter the next day, "That kid in center, Maris, I like him. I told George to buy him."

The late baseball author and historian Maury Allen believed that Maris reminded Stengel of Babe Ruth more than anyone else, more than even Mantle, whom he had compared to the great Bambino in Mickey's rookie season.

"Stengel had been around professional baseball since 1910. He had seen them all. He often remarked at the incredible skills of Babe Ruth, the player he considered by far the best in the game's history. He had first seen Ruth in the World Series in 1916. Perhaps there was something in Roger Maris that made him think of his old Boston and New York opponent, Babe Ruth. He would keep an eye glued on the doings of young Maris for the next three seasons."

But just hours after having been the subject of Stengel's bragging, Roger Maris' rookie fortunes had changed. By then the Yankees were in Baltimore, trying to keep from extending a two-game losing streak. The next day, Stengel awoke to read in the morning newspapers about his 4–1 loss to the Orioles as well as of the sliding injury that would stop Maris' hot rookie run and eventually ruin his tenure in Cleveland. Roger was sidelined, out of the lineup, and in such pain that he could not even take batting practice.

Not unlike most ballplayers on the disabled list, he had to watch games in street clothes sitting in the stands and readily recognizable. It made him an easy target of sportswriters like the *Cleveland News'* Howard Preston, who couldn't understand why, if a ballplayer was healthy enough to be walking around, why he couldn't be out on the field. "Here was a chance for him to sit in a seat behind the catcher," Preston wrote of the injured Maris, "to watch what the pitchers threw, to see—up close—the mannerisms of some of the players he will be playing against for many years. But he was a spectator, that's all, way up in the stands." To which perhaps the only reply is the one Mantle made after his brief time in sports media.

"You don't realize how easy this game is," Mickey said, "until you get up in that broadcasting booth."

Amen, but then, this is the second guessing that all injured professional athletes have to put up with from coaches, managers, front office people, and the news media. How injured is too injured not to play or practice? How much pain can an injured athlete endure to play and be productive? Or even half productive? Mickey Mantle, of course, is the poster boy for having played virtually an entire career in pain. Sad and tragic because of the physique: bulging shoulders and arms and Popeye-like forearms. "The body of a god," teammate Jerry Coleman once marveled. "Only Mickey's legs were mortal."

In Game 2 of the 1951 World Series, the rookie Mantle—playing right field with DiMaggio in center—took off after a fly ball off the bat of fellow rookie Willie Mays of the New York Giants, caught one of his spikes in a drainpipe covering, and ripped up his right knee. He would never play another pain-free game. The injuries were like a biblical plague: pulled muscles and sprains; fractures and abscesses; to knees, hips, shoulders, ribs. But it was the rookie injury that robbed him of his once great speed and necessitated wrapping both legs in tape, mummy-like, before each game. "He is," his manager Casey Stengel once lamented while observing the leg-wrapping in the clubhouse, "the best one-legged player I ever saw play the game. You can only imagine what he would've accomplished on two legs."

All this was after his career low point, the minor league banishment, a time when he was so depressed that he called his father in Oklahoma, telling him he wanted to quit.

Maris had threatened to quit when his demands weren't met in the minors, but the injury in his rookie season was different. All he wanted was the time to heal properly and then, once healthy, to groove his swing again. However, this was Cleveland, a small-market franchise and a team much closer to mediocrity than the pennant champion of three years earlier. The Indians were headed to a sixth-place finish in an eight-team league and a next-to-last-place finish in home attendance. Both the manager and general manager would be fired at the end of the season. Maris had a hang-up about playing for the Yankees, but the Indians weren't in the same financial stratosphere at the Yankees. What was the joke he had overheard that spring? What's the difference between the New York Yankees and the Cleveland Indians? The last Yankees World Series championship team picture wasn't in black-and-white. Teams weren't equal, and there was no draft system yet in baseball. Roger could have signed with any major league team interested in him, and several had been. Instead Maris picked a team that seemed to be the butt of baseball's joke of the year.

From where Roger stood, the Indians organization also didn't know what they wanted of him. They had two Hall of Famers, Hank Greenberg and Tris Speaker, giving Roger contradictory advice of what the Indians expected of him. Greenberg, the general manager, wanted him to be a pull-hitting left-handed slugger. Speaker, in an advisory and coaching role for his beloved Indians, continually pressed Roger to drive the ball to the opposite field. The conflicting demands on Maris were as far apart as the two ancient hitters' styles and eras. Speaker, a great early century hitter, had belted only 117 homers in his 22-year playing career that ended in 1928. Greenberg, whose career ended in 1947, had been a pure slugger with less than half of Speaker's hits.

"By the time they finished with me," Maris said, "I didn't know what I was doing."

As his rookie season unfolded, Roger also had a more personal concern weighing on him. Pat was pregnant and expecting their first child. The baby was due July 25, a date when the Indians were scheduled to be on the road. So there was a strong possibility that Roger wouldn't be with Pat when she went into labor at home in Parma, Ohio, about 15 miles from Municipal Stadium. In the 1950s, paternity leaves were unheard of in professional sports, and it would be decades before there would a shifting of the tides on the national perception on the role of fathers. Additionally, Roger had reason to worry. Pat would later miscarry during another pregnancy and also experienced difficulties in other pregnancies, even requiring hospitalization while expecting Randy in 1961. "I went to the ballpark and went through the drills," said Maris. "But I'm quite sure that I wasn't concentrating on the business at hand. My mind was often back at the house. How I was wishing we would soon learn something definite about my wife's condition: whether or not the baby was safe." Roger was talking about his wife's 1961 pregnancy, but it could easily have been about expecting a baby in 1957.

As the Marises feared, Roger was with the team in Baltimore when daughter Susan Ann was born on July 31. Her birth, though, happened to coincide with an open date on the Indians' schedule, and the team arranged for Maris to fly home to see his new baby before joining the team for its next game in New York.

Where had Mantle been when his first child, Mickey Jr., was born on April 12, 1953? He was at Ebbets Field, playing an exhibition game against the Dodgers. How he learned of the birth may have been fitting. As he stepped up to the plate, he and the entire ballpark heard from the address announcer: "Ladies and gentlemen… now hitting… number seven… Mickey Mantle… Mickey doesn't know it yet, but he just became the father of an eight-pound-12-ounce baby boy."

Although he would be known as Mickey Jr. the rest of his life, Mickey's first-born son was technically not a "Jr." He was named Mickey Elvin, after his father and grandfather. Little Mickey was more than a month old before Mickey was given time off to go home to meet his son. Even then, Mickey might not have been given the time off had he not developed a rash over much of his body that became inflamed whenever he perspired. When the team doctor instructed Mantle not to play for a few days, Stengel gave him the time to go home and see his baby and his wife. The rash quickly cleared up, and Mickey just as quickly became bored of staying at home with his young family. When a photograph of Mantle out at a fishing hole appeared in the newspapers a few days later, he got a call from Stengel ordering him to be on the next plane.

In typical fashion, Merlyn accepted having to bear childbirth, and later child rearing, by herself. "When you sign up to be a baseball wife," she said, "you forfeit your right to bitch about not having your husband at the hospital when you go into labor. That's part of the game—a phrase every baseball wife needs to keep handy."

However, that wasn't how Roger and Pat Maris felt about what they were willing to give up to baseball. Or perhaps that was just one of the ways that Roger Maris, the man, was different than the teammate to whom he would always be linked in people's minds, like Ruth and Gehrig. Where family was involved, Maris bled blood, and his immediate family was probably more connected with his professional life than anyone else who ever played the game. He had shown that in the minors when he had been willing to give up baseball if it meant taking him away from his loved ones during the winter, the only time he could be close to them for any length of time. Could that, then, have explained in part the slumps into which he would get mired almost every season? Through the prime of his career, Pat was pregnant through the baseball season almost every year. After Susan's birth in 1957, Roger Jr. was born in November 1958; Kevin in August 1960; Randy in August 1961; Richard in November 1963; and Sandra in 1965. In another year, there had also been a miscarriage.

As the great Pittsburgh Pirate Ralph Kiner, who the Indians assigned as a special instructor to Roger in the 1957 spring training, later observed: "When Maris had his slumps, a lot of it was psychological."

So could Maris' slumps simply have borne out findings in the *Journal of Obstetric, Gynecologic, & Neonatal Nursing*, which concluded there are high levels of distress in expectant fathers who are positively involved during the expectant mother's pregnancy?

12

Fathers and Wives

*"No boy, I think, ever loved his father
more than I did. I would do nearly
anything to keep my father happy."*
—MICKEY MANTLE

IN HER BEST YEARS, MERLYN MANTLE MAY HAVE BEEN THE ENVY OF possibly every woman in America, and held in near Madonna-like status by their husbands at a time when only the beautiful, loving wife of the young Massachusetts senator who would soon be elected president of the United States commanded such high regard. In that decade of American prominence after World War II, in what some likened to a cathedral in the Bronx borough of New York City, she had watched her husband perform spectacular athletic feats that had much of the nation proclaiming him the symbol of his time. But he was also a fragile hero to whom we had an emotional attachment so strong and lasting that it defied logic. And yet he was perhaps the most compelling sports figure of our lifetime. He was also complicated. No one knew this better than his wife, who would endure betrayal, abuse, and alcohol addiction from the only man she ever loved. Mickey Mantle would have been the first to say he was no Roger Maris when it came to marriage and family life. In that, the Mick was far closer to the Babe than Maris ever would be.

Merlyn herself readily admitted that her Mickey had a fucked-up relationship not only with her, but with all women. She blamed her emotionally cold, distant mother-in-law for part of that. Mickey had such a screwed-up relationship with his mom that he wouldn't allow her to babysit any of his four sons. Merlyn also put part of the fault on Mantle's half-sister Anna Bea, who, as a teenager along with some of her friends, had sexually abused Mickey when he was a child. Finally, Merlyn felt that Mickey's dad, Mutt, had to shoulder some responsibility because of the obsession he had with his oldest child.

And yet Merlyn possibly owed her marriage to her late father-in-law, Mutt Mantle, and the emotional influence he wielded over Mickey. In 1951, at Mantle's lowest point after his demotion to the minors, it hadn't been Merlyn to whom Mickey had turned for loving support and encouragement, even though they had dated for two years and were engaged to be married. Instead the slumping and distraught Mickey Mantle, his confidence shaken and his career at stake, had cried on the shoulder of the secretive, unknown Holly Brooke. She was an actress seven years older than Mickey, whom he had met during his first weeks in New York. Mantle had fallen in love with her, later that summer even asking her to marry him, and possibly would have, except for his father's deathbed opposition the marriage. After the 1951 World Series, diagnosed with a terminal illness and with only months to live, Mutt had begged his son to marry Merlyn, "one of your own." When had Mickey ever disobeyed his father or not done everything he could to please him?

So, on December 23, 1951, with his father barely able to stand and Mutt's best friend serving as best man, Mickey married Merlyn in Commerce, Oklahoma.

The Mantle wedding was a stark contrast with that of Patricia and Roger Maris. Even his mother's disapproval could not dissuade Roger from marrying the woman he truly loved. For Pat's part, as a newlywed, she wanted to be with Roger wherever he was playing. In late 1956, she joined her husband in going to the Dominican Republic, where he was playing winter ball with the *Estrellas Orientales,* the Eastern Stars. There, an incident that might have normally upset Roger was quickly defused by the humor of his new bride, who was taking in the Latin American trip as a honeymoon. It all had to do with the last name, Maris, which Latin fans mistook as plural for *Mary.* "In the Caribbean they called him Mary," recalled Roger's brother-in-law Walt Seeba. "Somehow the people there got confused and thought he was the Blessed Virgin." Blessed be Roger Maris, yes!

In 1957, the first pregnancy had kept Pat at home during the season. In the coming years, pregnancies and caring for her young family also prevented her from attending most of his games except for a few each season. She would often write Roger letters, but Maris wasn't much of a letter writer. So he would phone home often, pouring out his heart and frustrations via long distance. "The truth is we're an average small-town American family and proud to be just that," Pat would later write in *Look* magazine. "The fact that Roger is not just an average baseball player hasn't changed the way we think or the way we like to live."

Pat's counterpart, Merlyn Louise Johnson Mantle—who always looked like a tiny, platinum-blonde high school cheerleader at various stages of life—was a quiet woman who had never yielded to self-pity, though she might have had reason. The wives of American heroes—be they soldiers, astronauts, public servants, or athletes—too often are seen as only extensions of their spouses. Few recognize their sacrifices. And that, sadly, they often live with and love a stranger—a husband they not only don't know but for whom they will do almost anything, even if it demeans them. Merlyn was married to Mickey for 43 years, until his death in 1995, and had four sons with him, but the man was an utter stranger to her much of their lives. So much so that she sometimes joked that she raised five boys—her four sons and her husband. She was married to someone who was part created image and the other part a mystery to himself. What Merlyn may have known best was Mickey's glory, which she also basked in.

Merlyn also knew about Holly Brooke, almost from the beginning of their long love affair in 1951. It hadn't mattered to Mickey that he was engaged to his high school sweetheart, who was still in Oklahoma. Holly Brooke was stunning, as beautiful as any of the starry-eyed young actresses who hung around the Stage Deli or Danny's Hideaway in those days. "I thought she looked a little like Rita Hayworth," Mickey said years later. "I had never seen anyone that beautiful in the movies. You know how people wondered later why Joe [DiMaggio] would fall so hard for Marilyn Monroe? Well, when you've grown up the way Joe did in San Francisco and I did in Oklahoma, poor and the smell of fish and coal in your nostrils that you want to choke, and then someone like that—someone you would only see in your dreams or on the movie screen—taking any kind of interest in you, well, there's no goddamn way you're going to walk away from that."

Mickey began seeing Holly every day that the Yankees were in New York. Holly showed him the New York nightlife, which he wouldn't see with any of his Yankee teammates that year. "I guess I developed my first taste for the high life then," Mantle later said, "meeting Holly's friends, getting stuck with the check at too many fancy restaurants, discovering scotch at too many dull cocktail parties."

However, that wasn't exactly true. Mickey didn't get stuck with many checks. That's something that he quickly learned from Holly— that his celebrity and fame opened doors and were a commodity that he could trade on. The Stage Deli especially was often Mickey's security retreat from the intimidation of the big city. Max and Hymie Asnas, who owned the delicatessen, befriended Mickey and often made him special meals that were not on their menu. "Like all shy people," said Mantle, "I had a hard time going into new restaurants, not knowing whether to grab a table or wait to be shown, afraid to order something different for fear of making a jerk of myself, unable sometimes to tell the waiter from the busboy. But in the Stage Delicatessen I might have been in my hometown." Much the same was true at Danny's Hideaway and many of the places where he went, where there was always someone picking up the tab. If another guest wasn't paying for Mickey and whomever he was with, the places he went to were always too happy to comp him his meals and drinks. It was a big deal to have a New York Yankee who was a regular hanging out in your place, and early in the season, Mickey was the toast of the town.

"Mickey was the prince of the city," Holly said. "And he was having the time of his life. He loved every minute of it."

In Mantle's own words, Holly Brooke—a young, divorced mother from New Jersey—would become "the love of my life," and would hold on to his affection for years. The New Yorkers who knew her, or, more accurately, knew of Holly, dismissed her as the Broadway showgirl who, in the spring of 1951, had been involved in some reportedly sketchy scam to take advantage of the dazzling Yankee rookie. But she and Mantle would carry on a love affair even after Mickey's marriage later that year and through much of his Yankee career. It ended only after she married a Broadway producer in the late 1960s who later left her well taken care of.

"I became the showgirl who tried to scam Mickey Mantle," Holly reminisced in a series of interviews with me from 2006 until her death in 2018. "Oh, if they had only known. I loved Mickey. Mickey loved me. Mickey had great years in his career. I was with him in New York those years, too. Many of his fans would tell you that 1956, when he won the Triple Crown, was his favorite year. And it was his best season. But if you had asked him, he would have said that 1951 was his favorite year. It was his favorite year because it was our year."

So who was this Holly Brooke who captured the heart of Mickey Mantle as no girl or woman ever had?

Holly Brooke had been born Marie Huylebroeck in Bayonne, Hudson, New Jersey, a girl so striking and lovely that in 1948 she won the Miss New Jersey pageant, qualifying to compete for Miss America. There was only one problem. She was a divorcée, a violation of the pageant rules. She also was a 23-year-old single mother with a young child. Any scandal was quickly avoided when Huylebroeck agreed to quietly relinquish her newly won crown. A cover story was quickly produced, and she was quietly succeeded with a new Miss New Jersey.

"I knew I was beautiful and had talent and I guess I just wanted to see how I kind of stacked up against other beautiful, talented women," she told me in explaining why she had even entered the pageant, knowing she was in violation of its rules. "And if anyone in the pageant had said to me, 'Young lady, you're going to win,' I would have dropped out or not even entered. I wouldn't have wanted to put myself in that kind of predicament. Who would?"

The experience, though, was a validation for a Jersey girl with grand dreams and great expectations but an unusual name of Belgian and French origin. The Americanized pronunciation of Huylebroeck was Holly Brook, and as a teen that was the artistic name she chose, spelling it Holly Brooke. She moved to Manhattan, where she appeared in several small parts in off-Broadway productions and bit rolcs in films.

By early summer of 1951, she was effectively living with Mickey Mantle and spending every off-the-field moment with him when the Yankees were home. His Yankees teammates, those who knew of the relationship, feared she was a femme fatale who would ruin Mickey. Mantle would call her his first and great love. All was well as long as Mantle played well and continued to hit the way he had in the early weeks of the season. Mickey, however, had begun drinking heavily and had no control over his growing problem, especially since he could always find someone to pay for his drinks or buy the booze he would take home with him.

"He moved from the Concourse Hotel to 53rd near the Stage Delicatessen—I think they were on the fourth floor—and he wanted me there all the time," Holly told me in one of our interviews, "and I couldn't because I had to work as an actress and model. I would come there after my work, and sometimes I'd work on a movie until 10 or 11 at night. One night I came home late, and he had started drinking and was so sick that I had to stay there with him all night, rubbing his back and helping him to the bathroom because he was so sick he kept throwing up. I felt bad that I hadn't been home earlier, and I kept telling him, 'Mick, you can't keep doing this. This isn't good for you.'"

Was Mickey Mantle just a 19-year-old kid who couldn't hold his liquor or was he already hooked, already an alcoholic, something he would finally admit years later but which in his rookie season was quickly becoming a problem?

"I remember the first weekend the Yankees were home and me telling him I had to go home for the weekend, and Mickey begged me not to go," Holly recalled. "And I said, 'Mick, I've got to. I see my son on weekends.' I had already told him I was a working mom, and that my family kept my son during the week, and I'd go home on the weekends. He said, 'Well, okay, Holly, bring him up here, and we'll spend the weekend together.' I couldn't believe he'd said that, but I thought, 'Well, let's see.' And I brought my son Harlan up, and I swear Mickey took to him like he was his own."

Mickey Mantle was on a skyrocketing rookie start that seemed impossible to maintain. He was hitting like a veteran All-Star. He was keeping nightlife hours that maybe only Babe Ruth could have maintained. He was dating a gorgeous actress and he was even talking about marrying her and adopting her son. And he was still four months from turning 20. Hell, the kid couldn't even legally buy a drink. Then, almost overnight, he couldn't buy a hit, and that wasn't the kind of thing someone can buy for you. The Yankees sent him down to Class AAA ball, and the slump continued. Mantle was so bad he was making pitchers doomed to the minors look like Cy Young winners. But Mickey's real slump wasn't on the diamond—it was in his head.

So what was happening with Mickey back in 1951? His condition was never diagnosed at that time, but it appears that at age 19 his symptoms fit the profile for someone suffering with panic disorder. Mickey was suffering from stress, his self-worth and confidence having taken a serious jolt from his demotion to the minors. "When Mick retired," Merlyn said later, "a big chunk of his self-esteem went out the window. I question whether he ever had much to begin with...."

Baseball slumps, according to Kevin Elko, adjunct professor to the Sports Medicine Fellows at the University of Pittsburgh School of Medicine, are largely fueled by panic. "The panic," said Elko, a consultant to several professional sports teams, "has become a condition. More than any other variable, panic is the malady." Former Yankee outfielder George Selkirk, Mickey's manager at Kansas City, and some of the other Blues coaches had begun to suspect that Mantle's problem was a case of nerves—that maybe Mantle just didn't have it. However, it may have been something far more serious: a hint of possible panic disorder. Years later, a therapist working with Mantle and Merlyn concluded that "Mickey is totally controlled by fear. He is filled with fear about everything." At the height of his slump, each time Mantle came to bat, he was overcome by sudden surges of overwhelming fear that came without warning and without any obvious reason. It was more intense than the feeling of being "stressed out" that most people experience.

"Depression was a regular part of my life," Mickey admitted in a 1993 interview with sports broadcaster Roy Firestone. "At times, I thought about killing myself."

At times, I thought about killing myself.

When he was sent down to the minors, Mantle's world came crashing down around him. "It is a depressing thing being sent down to the minors, and I felt low," he said later. "I thought I had missed my big chance. I figured they had looked at me and didn't want me. I felt like running off and hiding someplace where there was no baseball. Perhaps it wouldn't have been as hard to take if there had been no ballyhoo. But now the big bubble had burst, and I felt I was the laughingstock of the league. The same newspapers that billed me as a superstar in April were now saying I was through."

The only thing Mickey felt he had going for him that summer was Holly Brooke, with whom he was talking by long-distance telephone calls almost daily.

"I was calling him 'Mickey Mouse,' a pet name only his mother had used before," Holly said, almost word for word to what had appeared in a 1957 *Confidential* magazine exposé. "More than once, Mickey would ask me how I felt about marrying him, owning him 100 percent… permanently. But he always answered his own question. 'No, I guess not,' he'd say. 'You'd never be happy in a little town like Commerce.'

And he was right on that. Other towns were different though. For instance, I remember flying to Columbus [Ohio] to see him and buck up his spirits. I'd planned to stay one night but wound up staying three days. That was in 1951 when the big blow fell and the Yankees shipped him off to their Kansas City farm club. When he heard the news, Mickey broke down and bawled like a baby. He often called me from there and other minor league towns, asking me to fly out and spend a few days with him because he was so lonesome." Brooke also wound up with one of the few existing photos of Mantle in a Kansas City uniform, which he inscribed, "To Holly, with all my love and thoughts."

Soon, however, Holly was concerned enough to put her life in New York on hold and immediately join Mickey in Kansas City. "He called me and said he needed me," she told me. "But this was different than whenever he had said that before. He sounded desperate and helpless. When I got to Kansas City, he looked terrible. He had been drinking too much and sleeping too little. All I could really do was console him and to try assuring him things would get better. But he was at the lowest period of his life to that point and feeling sorry for himself."

No amount of loving, however, could restore his confidence on the ballfield. He gave up and called his father to tell him their dream was over. He was no minor league ballplayer, much less a big-league one. Mutt had been reading about his son's troubles in the newspapers and shared Mickey's agony. But it was the desperation in Mickey's voice that concerned Mutt most. He thought that maybe a visit from his family might help, or at least ease Mickey's anxiety. Almost immediately he packed Lovell, son Larry, daughter Barbara, and Merlyn into the car for the five-hour drive from Commerce to Kansas City. Mickey was staying the Aladdin Hotel. But Mutt, the family, and Merlyn hadn't expected to find a woman staying in the same hotel room with Mickey, who didn't even begin trying to explain Holly Brooke to his mom, dad, and fiancée. When I asked him about this years later Mickey just shook his head, his mouth half open as if still disbelieving the scene and the looks that Merlyn and Holly exchanged.

"I was living there, and boy, was I glad to see him," Mantle said, stressing just that he focused on his father, who was left alone with his son. "I wanted him to pat me on the back and cheer me up and tell me how badly the Yankees had treated me and all that sort of stuff. I guess I was like a little boy, and I wanted him to comfort me."

"How are things going?" Mutt asked Mickey.

"Awful. The Yankees sent me down to learn not to strike out, but now I can't even hit."

"That so?"

"I'm not good enough to play in the major leagues," Mickey said. "And I'm not good enough to play here. I'll never make it. I think I'll quit and go home with you."

"I guess I wanted him to say, 'Oh, don't be silly, you're just in a little slump, you'll be all right, you're great,'" Mantle later said. "But he just looked at me for a second and then in a quiet voice that cut me in two he said, 'Well, Mick, if that's all the guts you have, I think you better quit. You might as well come home right now.'"

Mickey wanted to tell him that he had tried, but he knew better than to argue with his father when he was in the mood he now found him in.

"Mickey, you can't have it easy all your life. Baseball is no different than any other job. Things get tough once in a while, and you must learn how to take it—the sooner the better. It takes guts, not moaning, to make it. And if that's all the guts you have, I agree with you. You don't belong in baseball. Come on back to Commerce and grub out a living in the mines for the rest of your life."

139

Then Mutt said the words that tore into Mantle's heart:

"I thought I raised a man, not a coward!"

After saying hello to Mutt, whom she had met earlier in New York, Holly had retreated to the bathroom while Mickey's mother, his brother, sister, and Merlyn had gone back out into the hallway. Merlyn later said she heard much of what Mutt had said to Mickey through the door, as did Holly in the bathroom. As for Holly and Merlyn, Holly said they exchanged tentative glances but didn't speak to one another.

Mickey would later say that Mutt's lecture that night "had been the greatest thing my father ever did for me. All the encouragement he had given me when I was small, all the sacrifices he made so I could play ball when other boys were working in the mines, all the painstaking instruction he had provided—all of these would have been thrown away if he had not been there that night to put the iron into my spine when it was needed most.

"I never felt as ashamed as I did then, to hear my father sound disappointed in me, ashamed of me," Mantle said. "I have wondered sometimes exactly what it was. I know that I wanted my father to comfort me. He didn't. He didn't give me any advice. He didn't show me how to swing the bat any different. He didn't give me any inspiring speeches. I think that what happened was that he had so much plain ordinary courage that it spilled over, and I could feel it. All he did was show me that I was acting scared, and that you can't live scared."

Indeed, throughout both his childhood and adult life, fear was the one emotion that ruled him and motivated him as both a boy and a man, as both a player and a husband. It began as a mixture of fear and respect for his father, much as it is for many youngsters who are pushed to succeed in any endeavor that is as meaningful to a parent as to the youngster, if not more so. But Mutt's influence over Mickey—Mutt's ability to motivate his son with the fear of disappointment—would extend far beyond Mickey's childhood as well as beyond baseball. Mickey's marriage to Merlyn during the Christmas holidays that year would be an act possibly more out of love and fear of disappointing Mutt than out of love for Merlyn. In later years, Mickey would measure himself as a husband and father to his own father and, of course, pale in the comparison because anything short of perfection would have failed his father.

Mutt, the family, and Merlyn stayed around to watch that night's game, which perhaps was all that Mickey needed. He slugged two monstrous home runs, as if this was his great spring training season all over again. Mantle's horrible slump was over, and his bat let everyone know it, especially the doubters on the Blues. He hit 11 home runs, three triples, nine doubles, drove in 50 runs, and batted .361 over the next 41 games, putting the Blues in the middle of their own American Association title race. But that ended when the Yankees recalled Mantle back to the majors. Kansas City–native Calvin Trillin would later lament his own frustration with baseball, blaming it on the Yankees stripping his beloved Blues of their power-hitting young star. "I hate the Yankees," he wrote. "They called Mickey Mantle up from Kansas City right in the middle of a hot pennant race with the Indianapolis Indians."

If Mickey Mantle could do this for the intelligentsia of Kansas City, imagine what impact he must have had on the fans in the cheap seats.

Soon-to-be rookie phenom Mickey Mantle, 19, chats with his family at their home in Miami, Oklahoma, on April 12, 1951. In front (left to right) are Mickey's father, Mutt Mantle; mother, Lovell; brother Larry, 10; and Mickey; and in back (left to right) are twins, Ray and Roy, 15; and Barbara, 13. (AP Images)

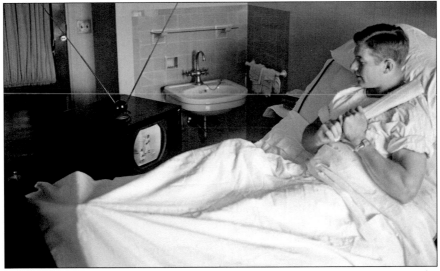

Mickey Mantle watches Game 3 of the 1951 World Series on television at New York's Lenox Hill Hospital on October 6, 1951, recovering from the career-altering Game 2 knee injury that would rob him of his once blinding foot speed. (AP Images)

Mickey Mantle relaxes at home with his wife, Merlyn, and sons, Mickey Jr. (holding a bat) and David, in 1956, after his Triple Crown–winning season when he led the American League in home runs, runs batted in, and batting average. (AP Images)

Roger Maris of the Kansas City Athletics in 1959.

(Icon Sportswire via AP Images)

New Yankees outfielder Roger Maris in 1960. (AP Images)

On October 2, 1960, Mickey Mantle (No. 7) and Roger Maris (No. 9) couple their Yankees jerseys to make 79, representing the combined total home runs the pair hit in 1960 for the Yankees (Mantle with 40, and Maris with 39). Little did they know that was nothing compared to what was to follow. (AP Images)

Mickey and Roger Maris visit Yankees spring training camp in St. Petersburg, Florida, on February 25, 1961. (AP Photo)

Roger and Mickey celebrate a 7–6 victory over the Washington Senators in New York in July 1961. Mantle belted his 26ᵗʰ and 27ᵗʰ homers to drive in the first four Yankee runs. Maris hit his 28ᵗʰ, a two-run walk-off to win the game.

(John Lindsay/AP Images)

In a September 1961 visit to Yankee Stadium, Harry Truman chats with Roger and Mickey about their historic home run chase. (AP Images)

Roger and Mickey chatting with actress-singer Doris Day on the set of Touch of Mink. (AP Images)

Mickey and Roger look over a telegram from fans encouraging them in their battle for the home run record late in the 1961 season. (AP Photo)

Claire Merritt Ruth, widow of Babe Ruth, poses with Roger and Mickey in August 1961, as the two Yankee stars are in the midst of their assault on the Babe's record. (AP Images)

October 1, 1961: Roger watches his record-breaking 61st home run leave Yankee Stadium.

(AP Images)

Roger poses with Sal Durante, the fan who caught his historic 61st home run, in the locker room at Yankee Stadium.

(AP Images)

President John F. Kennedy and Roger Maris pose at the White House on April 27, 1962. (William J. Smith/ AP Images)

Roger Maris with his wife, Patricia, late in the 1961 season. (AP Images)

Roger Maris, Mickey Mantle, and Joe Pepitone pose for a photo after their 8–3 win over the St. Louis Cardinals on October 14, 1964, in Game 6 of the World Series in St. Louis. (AP Images)

Roger Maris in St. Louis on Monday, August 5, 1968, announcing that he will retire from professional baseball at the end of the season. Maris hit 61 home runs in 1961, breaking Babe Ruth's record. At left is St. Louis Cardinals manager Red Schoendienst, and at rear is general manager Bing Devine. (AP Images)

Mickey Mantle hangs up his uniform in the Yankee Stadium locker room on Mickey Mantle Day, June 8, 1969. (Marty Lederhandler/AP Images)

Pallbearers (in pairs from front) Whitey Ford (left) and Yogi Berra; Bill "Moose" Skowron (left) and Hank Bauer; and Johnny Blanchard (left) and Bobby Murcer, lead the casket of Mickey Mantle out of church after his funeral on August 15, 1995, in Dallas, Texas. (John Roca/New York Daily News/AP Images)

Here Mickey is pictured at Baylor University Medical Center in Dallas, Texas, on July, 11, 1995, one month after receiving a liver transplant. He would die just over one month later, on August 13, 1995. (NewsBase/AP Images)

In Maris' first appearance at Yankee Stadium since 1966, he stands with his old teammate, roommate, rival, and friend Mickey Mantle on April 13, 1978, to help celebrate and hoist the championship flag for the 1977 World Series team. (Bettmann/ Contributor/Getty Images)

Roger (left) and Mickey (right) talk for the NBC TV cameras before a 1984 game at Yankee Stadium.
(Photo by Focus on Sport/ Getty Images)

Mickey and Roger pose for an August 1961 LIFE magazine photo shoot in the midst of their historic chase. (Bob Gomel/ The LIFE Images Collection via Getty Images)

13
The Fabled No. 7

"When I was 20 years old, I was a better ballplayer than [in my prime]. I could hit better, run faster, and throw better. Yet they farmed me out to the minor leagues."

—MICKEY MANTLE

IN MID-AUGUST, MICKEY'S TORRID TEAR THROUGH CLASS AAA PITCHING soon convinced the Yankees, who were knee-deep in an American League pennant race, that they needed Mantle's hot bat back in the lineup. But they would have to stand in line for his services. On the other side of the world, the Korean War, now in its second year, was quickly depleting U.S. military troops. More than 33,000 Americans would eventually die in combat, and twice that number were wounded or captured as prisoners of war.

The Selective Service was drafting 42,000 men each month just to keep the troop level up, and now Uncle Sam wanted Mickey Mantle. It didn't matter that he had already been rejected twice—declared 4-F as physically unfit for service because of the bone disease that had almost cost him a leg as a teenager. Mickey's medical records bore out that he had been hospitalized for extensive treatment of osteomyelitis in 1946 and again for a flare-up in 1947. Osteomyelitis happened to be one of the medical conditions that the government had decided was automatic grounds for denying entry into any of the branches of the military because it was a disease that could recur at any time. If that were to happen while in the service, the government would be liable for paying a disability pension for life—conceivably hundreds of thousands of dollars in pension payments and medical bills.

But after all the national attention surrounding his fabulous spring training that year, Mickey Mantle was no longer simply the unassuming youngster from Oklahoma. "My dad wrote… that a lot of people were asking why I wasn't soldiering in Korea," Mantle recalled of a letter he received as the season began. "To be candid, the war was the furthest thing from my mind. Certainly I knew about the mounting casualties, the talk going around that General MacArthur was planning an all-out fight against Communism, even thinking of dropping an atomic bomb on China. Well, I could understand how some people felt, especially those who resented seeing young, apparently healthy guys hitting baseballs while their own sons and husbands were being killed in battle."

In his biography of Casey Stengel, author Robert W. Creamer claimed that the Yankee organization, seeking to quell growing criticism about Mickey's 4-F status, went so far as to ask the Oklahoma Draft Board to re-examine Mantle's case. Indeed, no one was more aware of the potential public backlash and harm over Mickey's draft status than the Yankee brass, especially general manager George Weiss, who soon enough would begin developing a protective attitude toward Mantle. Weiss had an aristocratic gentility about him, and he saw Mickey as a naïve, vulnerable country boy, completely out of place in the big city. Unfortunately for Mantle in 1951, as the hailed successor to Ruth and DiMaggio and with the spring training exploits to prove it, he had become virtually a walking expression of the American culture's irrationality, as he would be throughout his career and even beyond. He was loved for what America thought he should be—a personification of the country's own aspirations; he was vilified for the human vulnerability that kept him from realizing those expectations.

Despite being rejected a second time for military service, Mantle continued receiving criticism questioning his courage for not fulfilling his "military obligation." In fact, it seemed that the hate mail and public taunts increased the more that the legitimacy of his draft exemption was mentioned, even throughout the rest of the decade. "Mantle began to receive vituperative hate mail and as the debate raged around him, the shy, uncommunicative boy shrunk deeper and deeper into his shell of silence," Yankee historian Peter Golenbock wrote in *Dynasty, The New York Yankees, 1949–1964*. So in late August 1951, Mickey underwent a third physical by Army doctors at Fort Sill, Oklahoma, and was once again classified 4-F because of the osteomyelitis.

The next day, the Yankees recalled Mantle back to the majors.

When Mickey arrived in the Yankee spring training camp in 1951, an uncanny sense of destiny and history was already at work. The man with the acumen to first pick up what was happening was not the manager, Casey Stengel, nor anyone else in the Yankee's upper echelons. Rather it was a man who for more than half a century worked in virtual anonymity with the Yankees, obscure except among the Yankee players and the Yankee family. He was Pete Sheehy, the clubhouse attendant, a short, wispy man who had been with the Yankees since 1926.

"I was waiting for the [Yankee Stadium] gates to open one day when I was 15," Sheehy once recalled, "and the clubhouse man then, Fred Logan, brought me in to help him do some things. I was sitting on the trunk later when he asked me to come around the next day. I've been here ever since. I never said much. He called me 'Silent Pete.' The 'Silent' wore off but the 'Pete' stuck. My real name is Michael."

For the next five decades, Sheehy endeared himself to Yankee players for whom he did more than pick up their towels and their dirty clothes from the floor where they dropped them. Michael "Pete" Sheehy kept their secrets, treated them kindly, and made them feel like they belonged. In 1951, he greeted Mickey Mantle, as he did each new Yankee, with a note instructing him to call a "Mr. Wolf." The note which he'd given Billy Martin had asked him to call a "Mr. Lyons." Roger Maris was to call a "Mr. Bear." The number was always the same: the Bronx Zoo. Until his death of a heart attack at the age of 75 in 1985, Sheehy was rarely ever noticed or in the newspapers. One rare exception occurred on July 4, 1939, the day the dying Lou Gehrig was honored at Yankee Stadium. After the ceremonies, a fight broke out near home plate. Nearby a photographer snapped a picture of Sheehy zealously protecting the ailing Yankee legend from being trampled in the brawl. Until his death, Sheehy kept a copy of that photograph in a back room of what later was memorialized as the "Pete Sheehy Clubhouse."

By 1951 then, Sheehy obviously recognized that there was a historic symmetry to the Yankees' line of succession: Lou Gehrig had assumed the superstar role after Babe Ruth; Joe DiMaggio's debut had come at the end of Gehrig's career; and now Mantle appeared headed to join the Yankees in DiMaggio's last season. Sheehy was known as one of the few people that could joke around with the somber, stoic DiMaggio, who was like an ice god emotionally. Sheehy loved to tell the story of the time DiMaggio asked him to check out a red mark on his backside.

"Hey, Pete, take a look at this," Joe said. "Is there a bruise there?"

"Sure there is, Joe," Sheehy replied in a matter-of-fact tone. "It's from all those people kissing your ass."

Sheehy's duties included assigning new players uniforms, and Billy Martin distinctly remembered his introduction from Sheehy to the Yankee uniform when he reported in February 1950 to a pre-spring training instructional camp in Phoenix. "All the young players always got high uniform numbers," Martin recalled. "But when Pete gave you a low number, you knew you were gonna stay with the club. He gave me No. 12 at first, but when I went in the service he told me, 'I'm gonna give you something smaller when you come back because your back's not big enough for two numbers.' That's how I got No. 1. I remember my first thought when I met him was that I was awed. Here's the guy who took care of Babe Ruth and Lou Gehrig. But he treated all of us the same—like we were all Ruth and Gehrig."

Sheehy, in particular, had to keep track of uniform numbers that were not already worn by a player or retired to honor Yankee legends like Ruth and Gehrig. One of the great though not well-known stories of the Yankee clubhouse was that Sheehy had originally issued the young Joe DiMaggio No. 18 when he joined the team in 1936. It was a number that had previously been worn by a tempestuous pitcher named Johnny Allen, who was traded to the Cleveland Indians. As he got to know DiMaggio and sensed that he would be the historical successor to the legacies of Ruth and Gehrig, Sheehy decided Joe should wear No. 5. When numbers were first put on uniforms, most of them had been issued according to the player's place in the batting lineup. So Ruth, as the third batter in the Yankee lineup, was given No. 3, and Gehrig, who followed Babe in the batting order, was issued No. 4. When Mantle arrived at the Yankee instructional camp amid such feverish anticipation in 1951, Sheehy didn't hesitate in issuing him the only number that made historical sense—No. 6. "Around this club,"

Sheehy told Dick Schaap, "you always had the feeling that great things would happen. It started with Ruth and kept going on."

Six months later, when Mantle returned to New York from Kansas City, one of the first people he went to see at Yankee Stadium was Pete Sheehy to get his uniform. For years, the traditional story has been that Sheehy decided to give Mantle a new uniform number—No. 7—on the chance that perhaps his former No. 6 might bring back bad memories of how Mickey's hot start had gone so stunningly bad.

"To be honest," Mickey later said, "I didn't put any stock in whether I was wearing No. 6 or No. 7. But after I had No. 7 on for a while, no one was gonna take it off my back."

Years later, however, Holly Brooke would disclose the story of how Mantle truly switched to what would become his famous number.

In 2014, in one of our numerous conversations in recent years, I visited with Holly and found her unusually emotional as she discussed Mickey's return to New York after his minor league exile to Kansas City.

"Above Grand Central Station, there used to be this incredibly, fabulously opulent apartment that looked like a palace that the original architect built as part of the original design, and in 1951 I knew someone—I knew a lot of people even then—who arranged for me, for us, to stay there one night that summer," Holly recalled. "And so Mickey and I spent one of the greatest nights of our lives there. It was a romantic, magical evening. We made love all night. We were both young and in love, and he wanted to marry me and spend the rest of our lives together."

Her eyes welled up, and Holly cleared her throat. She was recovering from a bad cold that came on over the holidays and hadn't retreated much, and her face slackened, making her voice parched and masking the gentle lilt of earlier conversations about days now more than six decades ago. Although small and fine-boned, any hint of frailty was deceptive. She was a hard-edged New Yorker at heart, and, from her 10th-floor apartment just off Central Park near Trump Tower, had the view of Manhattan to match. As she sipped her afternoon tea, it was evident that her mind remained sharp, unbothered by her age. Holly would be 91 that coming June—June 7, she emphasized because the number had always been special. So special, she said, that in that late summer of 1951, when she was in Kansas City living with the love of her life, she had begged that when he returned to New York from his minor league demotion he ask the Yankees to change his uniform, giving him the jersey with the numeral seven.

"'It will bring you luck,'" she told me she said to Mickey. "'I promise.'"

Mickey Mantle would do just that when the Yankees called him back to the majors that August, tearing up Triple-A pitching with a vengeance with the Blues. Some skeptics feared that Mantle, who would not turn 20 until the end of October, was washed up for good when he went into a slump after a magnificent start to his rookie season. However, Casey Stengel had dismissed that kind of talk, telling reporters who asked if Mickey was finished playing, "You wish you were through like that kid's through."

On August 22, 1951, the Yankees' new prodigal son returned to New York, arriving with Holly on a Super Chief train at Grand Central Station and passing through what was then known as the "Kissing Room," where travelers once embraced their sweethearts, friends, and family, and offering cozy access to the Biltmore Hotel above. That was where Zelda and F. Scott Fitzgerald had honeymooned, she whispered to Mickey as they snuggled arm in arm with the crowd.

"I don't know if Mickey knew who F. Scott Fitzgerald was," said Holly, smiling as she dreamily remembered that day. "I shouldn't say that. He was a very smart man. He just didn't like to show it, but his mind was like a steel trap. Once he heard or saw something, he knew it by heart. I suspect that's what helped make him such a great hitter and ballplayer. But I think he enjoyed being seen as that good ol' country boy.

"We had a drink at the Kissing Room. We had come in a day early, and Mickey didn't have to report back to the team until the next day. He didn't want to go to the Concourse Plaza where they had a room for him. That was all the way out in the Bronx, and we were in Manhattan and at Grand Central Station, and we had the day to ourselves, and I had come to think that we would have the rest of our lives together as well.

"'Holly, I want you to marry me,' Mickey said to me that night. He had said it earlier, but I think, returning to New York, he knew he now had it together. The Yankees wanted him back in the majors, and this time he knew he was going to stick with the team for good, and that he would live up to all they were expecting of him. We had talked about marriage. He had talked about marriage. He had talked about wanting to marry me and about adopting my son. But this time was different. He was so insistent. And when he asked me to marry him this time, it wasn't like the other times.

"He knew the only person who could stand in our way was his father. But Mutt had seen us together in Kansas City, just as he had seen us together here in New York before Mickey was sent down. And in Kansas City, I think he saw in Mickey's face his determination to be with me. There in front of me, Mickey said to his father, 'Dad, so what if she's older than me? She's seven years older than me. Mom was 10 years older than you when you married her, and she had been married before as well. If it can work out for you and Mom, why couldn't it work out for Holly and me?' I thought Mutt was going to cry. He left our room, and I wouldn't be surprised if he did shed a tear later.

"You could tell that Mickey had hit a soft spot. So that night back in New York, Mickey says to me, 'Dad won't like it. You saw what he's like. He wants me to marry Merlyn, but I can't. I'm not in love with her. I'm in love with you. So I'll bring him around.' And, of course, I said, 'Yes, Mickey, I'll marry you. I love you.' And he told me he loved me, too. 'You're the love of my life, Holly.' And that's how we left it. Mickey was going to talk to his father—'Come hell or high water,' I think is how he said it—and we were going to get married as soon as the season ended. Mickey said the only thing that would be more perfect was if the Yankees won the World Series as well."

14

Baseball, the Soap Opera

*"Mickey was great to Roger and
me. He never acted like a star—he
was more like a class clown."*
—JOE DeMAESTRI

IN JOE DIMAGGIO'S ERA, AND certainly in Ruth's, a youngster would have
had to live in New York to personally take in the visual image of how
his Yankee hero looked, how he walked, how he swung the bat, and ran
the bases. No verbal description on radio, no matter the broadcaster,
could compare to the real images of ballplayers transmitted across the
country through television broadcasts of games in the coming years.
The phenomenon of fans outside Major League Baseball cities seeing
their heroes as a game unfolded started near the end of DiMaggio's
career, when television sets began being mass produced. The Giants-
Dodgers 1951 playoff series, ending dramatically with Bobby
Thomson's pennant-winning home run, was the first to be televised
across America. The impact on the fans' perception of players they
might previously have only read about or seen in newsreels at theaters
was as visceral as what a young fan experienced his first time at Yankee
Stadium, multiplied over and over.

In 1946, there were 17,000 television sets in the country. By 1950, Americans had 4.4 million television sets. Then TV exploded in the country with 15 million sets sold in 1951 alone. By 1953, two-thirds of American homes had at least one TV. By 1960, there were more than 50 million television sets throughout the land, influencing what Americans wore, did in their leisure time, bought, and talked about. Like radio before it, the development of broadcast television during the 1950s helped baseball immensely. Television not only brought the games into the fans' homes, it allowed the kids to see their favorite players in action. The fact that two of baseball's "golden eras" ran concurrently with the advent of radio in the 1920s and television in the 1950s is probably not a coincidence. Unlike the 1920s, this era also featured a healthy baseball-card market. The influence of TV was so evident by 1955 that Bowman's final set was designed to show its players inside a television screen.

For Mantle, the television boom coincided with the best six-year period of his career, from 1953 to 1958, when he established himself as the most feared hitter in the game and arguably its best player. In that stretch, Mickey averaged 36 home runs, 102 RBI, 122 runs, 114 walks, a .320 batting average, and played in five of his 12 World Series. Mantle and the Yankees became what seemed like regulars on the nationally televised *Game of the Week*, which began as a Saturday event and eventually featured Sunday games and occasional doubleheaders. While the telecasts included most of the top major league teams, the Yankees appeared most often. Hall of Fame Cardinals pitcher Dizzy Dean was one of the announcers, along with Buddy Blattner, who was later replaced by Pee Wee Reese. With Mantle in his glory years, they had a ready-made star attraction ideal for a medium designed for Saturday afternoon heroes. The intricacies involved with Mantle's switch-hitting talents were often dissected

154

and explained to an enthralled national audience that had never seen ballplayers close up and personal in their own dens and living rooms. Every Mantle at-bat invariably included a close-up shot of the unique way he held his bat, with the little finger of the bottom hand curled up underneath the knob.

"I wonder why he don't just use a longer bat," Dean once observed.

"Dizzy," shot back his sidekick Blattner, "that's why you were a pitcher and not a hitter."

"Yo're right, pahd'ner. Yo're right!"

Coming into tens of thousands of American homes on Saturday and Sunday afternoons via their television sets, Mickey Mantle established himself every bit the cultural hero as Lucy, the Lone Ranger, and the Beaver. Mantle's swing, whether he was hitting a home run or striking out, was simply another of the fast-moving images on the small screen. There is a certain mystique of genuine Americana surrounding classic '50s television hits that still lives on to this very day. It is easy to forget that the comparatively crude technology of black-and-white television was, in the 1950s, every bit as cutting-edge and exciting as the internet half a century later. The beautiful, rhythmic performers who inhabited this domain became the new cultural heroes. The electronic media made it possible to preserve each facial expression and each inflection of a singer's voice as well as each nuance of a baseball hitter's stance. Celebrity, too, was born of exposure to audiences upon a vast stage. The public became consumers of popular culture, connoisseurs of its various kinds of rhythms. Millions watched Mantle hit home runs or just strike out, but always with that famous swing that seemingly began at the core, uncoiled from his legs and trunk in a movement of sheer power, and finished as if he had swung from his soul. No other player did that.

For Mantle, however, no amount of hero worship could soften the bumps of real life. By 1958, two years after the most glorious season in Mickey's career, Merlyn had come to see that the "fantasy time," as she called it, had extracted a high price. The previous year, she and Mickey had moved their family to Dallas—to a four-bedroom home on an acre of land, costing $59,500, in the Preston Hollow section of the city—in part to be closer to a major airport but primarily because life in tiny Commerce, Oklahoma, had become a three-ring circus, with little chance for privacy. "People were knocking at their door all hours of the night, wanting to borrow money," recalled Mantle's golf friend Marshall Smith. "They'd come over and use their bathroom. Can you believe that? People just wouldn't leave them alone."

Was Roger Maris ready for that American baseball hero's lifestyle, the loss of privacy, and his family taking a backseat to his fame? Roger was introverted and unprepared for the tumult that he would eventually unleash. Maris preferred to go about his work and be left alone. Not especially articulate, he hated questions that had nothing to do with baseball. As teammate Tony Kubek would observe: "No one in any sport endured more pressure over a more prolonged period than Roger." It was not that Maris was standoffish with teammates, as much as that he was not like Mantle, the consummate teammate who had been a teenage hero to many of the younger Yankees. They had now spent years in the clubhouse with Mickey, watching him tape up his damaged legs daily just to play and quietly wincing at the pain he endured. Would it be any wonder that most of them would prefer Mantle over Maris to break Ruth's record if it had to be broken?

"Mickey was thought of as the 'true' Yankee," said second baseman Bobby Richardson. "Roger had been traded in from Kansas City. I think Roger understood. He was an unusual ballplayer. He didn't care about individual honors."

On December 11, 1959, the Yankees sent the quartet of Norm Siebern, Hank Bauer, Marv Throneberry, and Don Larsen to the Kansas City A's in exchange for Roger Maris, Kent Hadley, and Joe DeMaestri. There was excitement among the Yankees about having obtained Maris, but their memories were not so short as to be cautioned by the dashed hopes behind Siebern. About the same age as Maris, Siebern was a left-handed hitter with extra-base power who had been seen as a potential star when he arrived in the big leagues with the Yankees in 1956, a promising candidate to fill the team's hole in left field and play alongside Mickey Mantle. But injuries sidelined Siebern, who then also fell out of favor with manager Casey Stengel over a couple of misplayed fly balls that lost a 1958 World Series game, although the Yankees still won the Series.

Siebern lost fly balls in the sun or in the lights, which had been turned on to accommodate television. This happened in left field in the old Yankee Stadium where, because of the notorious afternoon October shadows, Yogi Berra once famously said, "It gets late early there." It hadn't mattered that Siebern hit .300 and won a Gold Glove that season. The mercurial manager lost faith. Casey benched him for the last three games of the World Series and played him less in 1959. Thankfully for Siebern, the trade to Kansas City removed him from Stengel's dog house. With the A's, Siebern recovered his confidence, moving permanently to first base and becoming a three-time All-Star, hitting 25 home runs with 117 RBI in his best season, 1962.

Roger Maris, though, would quickly make teammates and fans forget Siebern and Hank Bauer, whom he would replace in right field. "The press hadn't written how good he was," said Yankee reliever Ryne Duren. "Roger Maris was the best all-round player I ever played with, even better than Mantle. I'm not saying he was a greater talent, but he was more consistent and probably as good as any player I ever saw because he did everything right."

Writers covering the Yankees were especially surprised by how they hadn't realized Roger's size. "There is nothing small about Maris," wrote *The New York Times*' Arthur Daley. "He's a 197-pound six-footer who doesn't look it. His build is compact and symmetrical. In street clothes or baseball uniform he seems ordinary in size—or less. But when he's sitting in front of his locker in the Yankee Stadium clubhouse, a truer appreciation of his physique instantly hits the eye. His upper arms and shoulders are heavily muscled. In the vernacular of the trade, 'he strips big.'"

For Mantle, getting himself mentally into the 1960 season had been one of the most difficult challenges of his career to that time. The 1959 season had been one of his toughest, and fans had placed much of the blame for the team's disappointment on Mickey's shoulders. The booing of Mickey by Yankee fans became so strong that at one point Mantle momentarily simply gave up. After striking out twice in one game, he went to bat the third time and intentionally took three straight strikes. The displeasure of fans in the Stadium was matched only by Stengel's own outrage. Mantle on several occasions had shown his own disgust at the booing by saluting his tormentors with a defiant middle finger of an upraised fist. In this instance, however, a subdued Mickey knew he had been wrong and apologized to his teammates. But once again, the Yankees' fortunes in the middle of the season were crippled by Mantle's injuries. During one stretch, Mickey came up to bat with 57 men on base—and he drove in only four of them. Mantle drove in only two runs in the entire month of August.

Throughout the slump, Mickey never slowed down his drinking and his nightlife, or his emotional outbursts against the fans and the press. Exasperated, Stengel publicly referred to Mantle as his "greatest disappointment." It was not surprising, except to Mickey, when Weiss opened the Yankees' 1960 contract negotiations by demanding that Mantle take a $17,000 pay cut from his $72,000 salary. Mantle responded by holding out during the first two weeks of spring training, before finally agreeing to a $7,000 pay cut. In trying to make up for the lost training time, Mickey aggravated the old injury to his right knee. He also was bothered by the right-shoulder injury from the 1957 World Series, suffered when second baseman Red Schoendienst had fallen on him during a botched pick-off play. It was an injury that affected his hitting and would reduce the strength in his once-powerful throwing arm over the remainder of his career. Hurt and embittered as he might have been, Mantle still found time to unwind. That spring training, he and Whitey Ford were among a group who were rescued naked and treading water in St. Petersburg Bay after the boat on which they were partying caught fire and sank.

Mantle and Maris, then, were the ideal imperfect pair of buddies for the soon-to-be counter-culture decade of the 1960s—Mickey, the hard-drinking, devil-may-care slugger; and Roger, the moody, petulant star seemingly angry at much of the world. Butch Cassidy and the Sundance Kid would have only one thing they didn't: they robbed banks. But Mantle and Maris would steal the hearts of American sports in their few brief years together.

Ruth, Gehrig, DiMaggio, Mantle. The history of the Yankees bled with the triumphs and lows of legends of the past, which is exactly what Mickey seemed now, 10 years after his tumultuous rookie season, of which he sometimes spoke as if it had happened a generation ago. "I got into trouble with the press early, because I was scared," Mantle told one reporter in 1960 about a time when Maris was still a sophomore in high school. "I was young when I came to New York, and I got misquoted, well, maybe not so much misquoted as it came out not sounding like me talking. I was scared and I didn't really know how to handle it, so if you misquoted me, I just wouldn't talk to you anymore, and if you came up in a group around my locker, I wouldn't talk to anybody, which made the whole joint mad."

Mickey Mantle, the guy who was supposed to break all the records, had been booed, heckled, and hanged in effigy for not doing so. Mick was used to it. So much so that in the coming years whenever Maris was booed, Mantle would sometimes joke, "Hey, Rog, thanks for taking my fans away."

Mantle, of course, had been through his own chase of Ruth's record in 1956. He had a decade of familiarity with the New York press, and he had been through the tedious, trying cycle of being asked the same question dozens of times after a ball game—questions that often were silly, naïve, sometimes stupid, and seemingly intended to goad players into making brash comments suitable for the next day's newspapers. More importantly, Mantle had come to understand that in the world of journalism there rarely appeared to be embarrassing questions, only embarrassing answers. Mickey had been through his own combative periods with the beat writers, and he had learned through experience what to say and what not to say. Mickey also knew, as do most ballplayers, that the pressures related to breaking records are usually not pressures athletes themselves feel first but instead the pressures that come to be placed on them by the constant attention by the news media.

On top of it all, Mantle had learned to court the writers, much as Stengel had. Sportswriter Bert Sugar was among those who noticed the growth and change in Mantle. "Particularly at a bar," said Sugar, "where he liked his scotch. Mickey had no pretense. He wasn't hung up on being Mickey Mantle. I'd run into him in places like Mr. Laff's, Runyan's, Tucker's—bars where sports guys hung out. And he'll always say, 'Hey, why don't you come over and say hello?' In a bar, Mickey was quiet—he wasn't a noisemaker. He was very comfortable being in a crowd. He was happy being accepted as a person rather than Mickey Mantle. We'd tell one another jokes. He loved jokes, the longer the better. He didn't like one-liners. He went for good ol' boy humor—I'm framing this, pre-1990s—you know, politically incorrect women jokes were the brunt of it. Mickey Mantle was a frat boy at heart."

15

A Historic Debut

*"Sure I played, did you think I was born
at the age of 70 sitting in a dugout
trying to manage guys like you?"*

—CASEY STENGEL

WHEN ROGER MARIS SHOWED UP AT HIS FIRST SPRING TRAINING WITH the Yankees in 1960, he was a three-year big-league veteran with little inclination for small talk, especially about himself. Fortunately, the Yankees coaching staff at the time included baseball veterans with much more experience than Maris and without his protective chip on his shoulder. Among them was major league journeyman Wally Moses, who couldn't take his eyes off Maris when he first saw him. Like Maris, Moses had been a left-handed hitter, though without the power. In his best season, in 1937 with Connie Mack's Philadelphia Athletics, he had slugged 25 home runs while batting .320 with 208 hits. In his 17 seasons, Moses banged out 2,138 hits, more career hits than 49 non-pitching position players who have been inducted into the National Baseball Hall of Fame. But then, Wally Moses had been discovered by fellow Georgia native Ty Cobb, and was no run-of-the-mill slap hitter. No less than Ted Williams befriended Moses when he joined the

Red Sox in midseason of 1946. The outfield of the American League pennant-winning Boston team that fall had Williams in left, Dom DiMaggio in center, and Wally Moses in right.

"I remember Dom DiMaggio and Ted Williams coming to our house," recalled daughter Judith Moses Latham, who was eight in 1946. "Ted Williams was considered a very antisocial person, but he and my father had a very good relationship. There was a picture taken one afternoon where he and I were sitting at our piano bench playing 'Chopsticks' together."

Earlier that season, while with the Chicago White Sox, Moses had endeared himself to Williams because of an incident in a game between the two teams. "Now, Wally Moses was a nice, quiet little guy, never raised his voice at anybody," Williams said, recalling that in this game, umpire Nicholas "Red" Jones cleared the White Sox bench, with Moses pleading: "'Red, I've been in the big leagues 11 years. This is my 11th year in the big leagues. [It was actually his 12th.] I've never been thrown out of a game in my life. Honest to Pete, I never said a word to you on the bench. I was way over in the corner. I never said a word.' And old Red Jones, I'll never forget... He said, 'Wally, I want to tell you. It's like this. It's just like a raid on a whorehouse. The good go with the bad.'"

Years later, watching Maris for the first time at the Yankees spring training camp, Moses immediately thought of Williams. As a fellow left-hander, he couldn't help but admire Williams. Moses was among the Red Sox teammates who would often surround the hitting cage, as if gathering for a religious ritual, just to watch Williams take pregame batting practice. He studied Boston's Splendid Splinter as if doing research, which, in fact, he was. It helped him understand the science of hitting, eventually leading him to become one of the game's first coaches specializing in hitting.

In Ted Williams, he had the consummate hitting expert. Teddy Baseball was always the willing instructor, talking hitting with Moses at length. Six decades before the talk among hitting coaches had turned to changing a batter's "launch angle" and preaching against the ages-old credo of "swinging down" at the ball, Williams was already doing so. Williams believed that all good hitters had "upswings" but that the secret of hitting for power was in not swinging late on pitches and instead in the bat hitting the ball out in front of the plate.

This was the advice Wally Moses had begun passing down to other hitters, among them two-time batting champions Ferris Fain of the Philadelphia A's in 1951 and 1952 and Richie Ashburn of the Philadelphia Phillies in 1955 and 1958. Yankees' catcher Elston Howard, who batted a career-high .348 in 1961 and would go on to an MVP season in 1963, credited his improved hitting and increased power to Wally Moses' coaching. "We decided in the spring that I ought to close my stance and ease up on my swing, I was swinging my head off the ball," said Howard. "Moses told me to swing with my arms—use my wrists—not my body. I also began using a heavier bat, a 36-inch, 35-ounce one. I used to use a 33-ounce one."

But it was in Maris that Moses saw the hitter who most reminded him of Ted Williams. The swing was compact, disciplined, and upward—similar to Williams' distinctive uppercut. It also began from a surprisingly upright stance, like Williams used, with just the slight forward bend from the waist. Williams' feet were further apart in his stance, his hands held his bat lower, and he used a more noticeable hitch of his hands. But from the top of the hitch, his swing was almost identical to Maris' complete swing.

"I told Roger that when we began working," Moses said in an interview with *Sports Illustrated's* Frank Deford in 1968. "He just looked at me. 'I'm not Ted Williams,' he said. 'There was only one Ted

Williams.' But guess what? It turned out that in 1957, when Roger joined the [Cleveland] Indians, he'd been watching and studying Ted every chance he could. Ted hit .388 in '57, and he hadn't been that bad in his last three seasons. Heck, what was he, 41 when he retired? So the Indians played the Red Sox, what, 22 times each season in each of Roger's seasons in Cleveland and another 22 times the season he was with the Kansas City A's? Which means that Roger got a chance to see Ted take batting practice over 60 times, not to mention a couple of hundred at-bats. You think he didn't go to school on that? Roger was locked in on Ted Williams. Was it coincidence that when Roger joined the Yankees in 1959, he ended up wearing uniform No. 9, the same number as Ted?"

By coincidence, uniform No. 9 became available in 1960 because for the previous eight seasons it had been worn by right fielder Hank Bauer, who was part of the Yankees' multi-player trade with Kansas City that brought Maris to the Bronx.

"What number were you with the A's?" Yankee clubhouse attendant Pete Sheehy asked Maris when he showed up at spring training in 1960.

"No. 3," said Maris.

Sheehy smiled as he gave him a you-gotta-be-pulling-my-leg sheepish grin. His first year on the job had been the greatest season any Yankee player ever had, and Babe Ruth, of course, had worn that number.

Maris returned the smile. "I guess only Babe Ruth ever wore No. 3 with the Yankees," he said.

"Well, you'd be surprised," said Sheehy. "Actually, seven other players wore No. 3 after the Babe."

"Really?"

"They didn't retire the number until the Babe died in '48," said Sheehy.

"Anybody else famous wear No. 3?"

"Cliff Mapes," said Sheehy.

"Cliff Mapes?" Maris had never heard of him. "And he's famous?"

"Cliff Mapes," said Sheehy, "is the only Yankee to ever wear Babe Ruth's No. 3 and then Mickey Mantle's No. 7. When the Yankees retired Babe's number in '48, they gave Mapes No. 7. He still had that number when Mantle came on in '51, and Mickey took No. 7 after he came back from the minors. In the time he was away, Mapes was sold to the Browns."

Hollywood could not have scripted a smoother landing for Roger Maris. He was, after all, the all-business ballplayer ideally made for the corporate image of the Yankees, which was the consummate, bottom-line sports organization perfectly made for Wall Street. The incomparable sportswriter Robert Lipsyte may have captured the essence of Roger Maris best when he described him in his first days at Yankee Stadium in *The New York Times*: "Maris, at 25, looked cold, forbidding. His bristly crew cut stood guard over a strong face of few expressions. His nose and chin were prominent, his eyes small, his lips thin. His matter-of-fact Midwestern intonations masked a passion for baseball. He came to the ballpark early to run, shag flies, and bask in the fellowship of the clubhouse, where he was considered a decent, hard-working, talented regular guy."

Pete Sheehy epitomized the common man with whom Maris most closely identified, and they quickly formed a close bond that would cement itself in 1961. At the height of that year's chase of Babe Ruth's home run record, Sheehy made sure that the training room, which was off-limits to reporters, was well-stocked with beer, water, food, and anything Maris and Mantle might need after a game. Mantle often didn't need this escape, but Roger did. At season's end, he gave Sheehy a $500 tip in addition to what he had already contributed to a players' honorarium. Was it any wonder that Sheehy was later quoted saying: "Roger Maris was my all-time favorite Yankee. If you knew Rog right, he was a grand guy."

That was no easy accomplishment for strangers around Maris, as he had written in his memoir of the 1961 season, *Roger Maris At Bat:*

"There is no halfway with me. When I take a liking to someone, then I really like him and stick by him unless one day he proves I was wrong in the first place. Usually when I met someone for the first time, I'll stay in the back seat on the outside until I make up my mind about him. I am always careful with new acquaintances until I am sure whom I'm with….

"Sometimes it is said that people think I'm tough to get along with just because I say what I think and don't follow the crowd. That's all right with me. If people are going to like me, they are going to have to take me as I am. If they don't like me, then there's no way I can change them. In fact, I wouldn't even make an attempt. My friends know me and understand me. The others don't count anyway."

Much to his surprise, Roger quickly felt at home with his new team. The Yankees made no secret of their enthusiasm to have him on the team, and Mantle and Whitey Ford were generous and kind in their hearty welcome. Maris responded with a remarkable debut in pinstripes on a chilly April 19, 1960, in what would become one of the two best Opening Day performances in team history. It was against Boston on Patriots Day, before the second-biggest Opening Day crowd ever at Fenway Park. It was a Yankee premier that teammate Ralph Terry may have helped by loosening up any pregame jitters on Maris' part by pitching batting practice. One pitch in particular came in on

Roger's hands. If he had swung and hit the pitch, Maris might have broken his bat.

"Oooh," cooed Maris. "That was my game bat."

He was about to change bats when Mickey Mantle grabbed it and checked out the weight and the balance,

"Rog, this is a hell of a bat," said Mantle. "I think I'll use it."

Maris laughed and quickly grabbed it away. "It doesn't matter," he said.

Hitting leadoff, Roger smashed two home runs while also collecting a single, a double, a walk, and four RBI in a 4-for-5 day at the plate and an 8–4 Yankees win. Maris' homers were a two-run round-tripper in the fifth inning off starter Tom Brewer and a solo dinger in the eighth off left-hander Ted Bowsfield. Mantle went 2-for-3 in the game and walked twice. Only Babe Ruth may have had a better Opening Day as a Yankee. In 1932, when he was 37 years old, Ruth hit two home runs with five RBI in a 3-for-5 day and 12–6 victory over the Philadelphia Athletics. Understandably, Maris' performance immediately brought comparisons to Ruth.

The opener also happened to be the first game at Fenway in Ted Williams' final season. He slugged a milestone eighth-inning homer off Jim Coates. It was his 494th career home run that moved him ahead of Lou Gehrig into fourth place on the all-time list. Only Babe Ruth, Jimmie Fox, and Mel Ott had hit more home runs at the time. The game was especially touching for Roger, as he watched Boston mayor John Collins, wheelchair-bound from polio, roll himself out near the pitching mound to throw the first pitch. Maris' older brother Buddy had been stricken with polio at the age of 18, ending his own athletic career as a freshman in college. In 1955, Collins and his four children contracted polio while he campaigned for a seat on the Boston City Council. Collins' children recovered but the disease forced him to use a wheelchair or crutches for the rest of his life. Maris took note of Collins in the wheelchair and some weeks later sent the Boston mayor a note, acknowledging his courage and telling him about his own brother's polio.

"What a genuinely nice gesture," Collins told me in an interview years later. "I sent him a thank you. I think it was late in the season, and they were in a tight pennant race. But somehow he found the time to send me a signed baseball. Gotta love the guy, even though he was a Yankee!"

It was a time when Roger Maris took in all he could of his new surroundings, his teammates, and especially the small Yankee Stadium right field, where he had to play as well as attempt to capitalize on its short porch. It had been constructed with Babe Ruth in mind, even though he was fully capable of Ruthian 400-foot blasts that would have cleared most parks. But the House That Ruth Built had also specifically been catered to turning the Babe's moderate fly balls and hooked line drives into home runs. The Yankees were banking that Maris, too, could capitalize on such an inviting target. Roger was having a spectacular year. After batting leadoff in his first two games as a Yankee, Roger was moved to the clean-up slot behind Mantle. But he did not hit his first home run as a Yankee at the Stadium until May 3, when he connected against Detroit's Bob Bruce. Maris was leading the league in home runs and runs batted in while also making fans forget about the popular Hank Bauer in right field with his outstanding defensive play. The feeling was mutual. Although he did not like the big city atmosphere of New York, Maris was happy to be with the Yankees. "Don't ever let anybody tell you they don't like coming to a team like the Yankees," said outfielder Bob Cerv, Maris' roommate, who had also come to the Yankees from Kansas City. "The Yankees are over the track and up the hill."

Maris was the new kid in town. In midseason, he filmed a commercial for Camel cigarettes, and there were other endorsements in the works for shaving cream and razor blades. Clearly, he seemed at peace with himself, as an August 13, 1960, story in *The New Yorker* suggested: "This is perhaps the most tangible evidence that he's had so far that he is a success in his chosen occupation." Roger even consented to a pregame interview. "The newcomer has been hitting so many home runs that at times he has been ahead of Babe Ruth's home run–hitting pace of 1927... As Maris picked up his glove and rose to leave, we asked him how he felt about his chances of breaking Babe Ruth's home run record. 'Nobody's ever going to break that record,' he said. 'Not me or anybody else.'"

No one is ever going to accuse *The New Yorker* of placing a curse on the subjects of its interviews like the bad luck sometimes associated with athletes featured on the cover of *Sports Illustrated*, but that story marked a dramatic change in what had become a storybook 1960 season for the Yankees. With Mickey rebounding to old form, the Mantle-Maris combination in the No. 3 and No. 4 spots of the batting order quickly became fodder for Ruth-Gehrig comparisons and a slew of nicknames. One Detroit writer called them "the buzz-saw team." Another dubbed them "Double M for Murder." Yankee announcer Mel Allen referred to them as "the gold dust twins" and "those magic marvels." Then there was Stengel's own description of the pair: "The fella in right does the job if the other fella doesn't."

Years later, whenever Mickey Mantle thought back to when Roger Maris joined the Yankees in 1960, his mind would inevitably drift to their manager, Casey Stengel. Mantle's own relationship with Stengel was complicated and often misunderstood. It was not a surrogate father and son relationship, as much as Casey and his defenders wanted it to be. Sadly, even later, there would never be the resolution to their differences. "I'm not sure I'd gotten smarter as I'd grown older or whether Ol' Casey was now just really old because more and more of what he said was no longer colorful and eccentric—he was more and more just a senile old bastard," Mantle told me in 1970 over some Chateaubriand at the Fairmount Hotel in Dallas. "He wasn't making sense, not that I ever really thought he did, but he was now leaving people he talked with shaking their heads. Like they no longer thought him clever and funny and wondering if he'd finally lost his marbles. I think he had. Like wanting to turn Yogi into a third baseman that spring. That idea lasted all of a couple of days of Yogi taking ground balls at third. Or trying to move Roger from right field to left before realizing that Roger was the perfect right fielder. And damn if we didn't pay a price for Casey's lamebrain ideas in the World Series that fall."

Stengel also had been drinking more in recent years, often staying up until the early hours of the morning entertaining writers with his stories. He had been known to occasionally doze off in the dugout in the middle of games, but players were noticing that it was happening more frequently. Now even the old Stengel charm had worn thin, particularly with his players, although writers continued their fascination with his double-talk and the lively copy it made. Often it amounted to little more than stream-of-consciousness rambling. The best example of it in a public setting may have been his 1958 testimony before senator Estes Kefauver's subcommittee looking into proposed legislation exempting baseball from antitrust laws. Stengel was among a number of baseball people called to testify, including Mantle, Ted Williams, Stan Musial, and the Yankees Del Webb. But it was Stengel who would be remembered for his answer about whether the Yankees would continue to monopolize the World Series.

"I got a little concerned yesterday," Stengel began, "in the first three innings when I saw the three players I had gotten rid of, and I said,

'When I lose nine what am I going to do?' And when I had a couple of my players I thought so great of that did not do so good up to the sixth inning, I was more confused. But I finally had to go and call on a young man from Baltimore that we don't own, and the Yankees don't own him, and he is doing pretty good. And I would actually have to tell you that I think we are more the Greta Garbo type now from success. We are being hated. I mean from the ownership and all, we are being hated. Every sport that gets too great, or one individual…"

The senators seemed unsure what to make of what Stengel had just said, so they called on Mantle. Mickey was nervous about what to say, so when he was asked his views on applying antitrust laws to baseball, he said the first thing that came to mind.

"Well," Mickey began in that country drawl of his, "after hearing Casey's testimony, my views are about the same."

The strait-laced Capitol Hill hearing room erupted in laughter.

What ultimately cost Stengel his job was losing the confidence of the team's co-owners Del Webb and Dan Topping, who had made him a rich man besides giving him a place to leave a legacy in the game. Casey was the highest paid manager in baseball, with an unheard-of annual salary in excess of $80,000, plus bonuses and the team's profit-sharing plan given to all full-time employees except the players. In 1960, Stengel's profit shares were already $158,747.25. Webb and Topping, though, were shrewd businessmen. They demanded results and after the disappointment of 1959, Stengel's retirement was hastened by the Yankees loss in the 1960 World Series to the Pittsburgh Pirates on Bill Mazeroski's famous home run in Game 7.

The loss was universally blamed on Stengel's decision to not start Whitey Ford in Game 1, which would have allowed the southpaw ace of the staff to start three games in the best-of-seven series. Stengel's mismanagement of his pitching staff was critical. Within days of blowing the World Series, Stengel was fired, with Yankees co-owner Dan Topping saying he had grown too old, which prompted Ol' Casey's best response to old age:

"I'll never make the mistake of turning 70 again."

Ol' Casey. They already called the quirky Yankees manager that in Mickey's 1951 rookie season, though Mantle wasn't sure how old his manager had been at any time. He wasn't really sure until 1960, when the Yankees in midseason honored Stengel at Yankee Stadium. In May, the team had commemorated the 50th anniversary of Casey's debut in organized professional baseball. He turned 70 on July 30, but the celebration at the stadium was postponed, as was that day's game with the Kansas City Athletics, because of a rainout. The birthday festivities took place the next day between games of a doubleheader, which the A's spoiled by winning the first game 5–2 in 11 innings.

Roger Maris took in that Stengel birthday celebration with amusement. He was learning that his aging manager was as unpredictable as he was hilarious. Five days earlier, Stengel had raised eyebrows with a stunning lineup change. He penciled in Maris, who had been batting either third or cleanup in the lineup, to the leadoff spot against Cleveland's All-Star left-hander Dick Stigman. The lineup change made no sense to anyone but Stengel. Maris drew a walk in the sixth inning, scoring on Mantle's 25th home run that seemed to spark the Yankees who were in second place, trailing the White Sox.

When they swept a double-header a couple of days later, the Yankees were back leading the American League. But then the Athletics came to town and spoiled Casey's birthday by knocking them out of first place again. Stengel was in a foul mood despite receiving countless gifts from the team and fans. When a knife was handed to him to cut his birthday cake, Stengel pretended to slit his throat while muttering that he "might use it on himself" if his team continued playing like they had so far that season. Maris looked at Mantle, whose scowl suggested he didn't think Casey's remark had been funny. Maris agreed.

The White Sox, the defending league champions, were no pushovers, even as team owner Bill Veeck was talking about selling his shares in the ballclub to possibly start a new franchise in Southern California. Veeck, after all, was an innovator. That season, his White Sox became the first major sports team to put player names on the backs of uniforms. Sadly, though, they also were the first to misspell a player's name on a uniform. During a road trip to New York, Ted Kluszewski took the field at Yankee Stadium with his name misspelled. His uniform shirt had a backwards "z" and an "x" instead of the second "k" in his name.

The incident caused some laughs among players in the pregame ritual of batting practice and warm-ups, where players inevitably exchanged small talk with opposing team players. Mantle and Kluszewski knew each other from the four All-Star games on which they'd played on opposing sides. Maris later said he had watched Mantle being loose and friendly with Kluszewski, much the same way he was with Yankee teammates. Mickey had been friendly and welcoming with Maris, and over the season's first months he had come to accept Mantle as genuinely friendly.

Now in 1960, the Yankees were making a second-half comeback despite Mantle's performances, in which he switched between being fabulous one day and in a funk the next. But all that changed with a Mickey Mantle turnaround that can be dated to have begun August 14, the day after the publication of *The New Yorker* story about Maris. On that day, in a doubleheader with the Senators, Mantle failed to run out a routine double-play ground ball. Mantle's gaffe was in stark contrast with the all-out hustle by Maris, who, running from first base to second, barreled into the knees of the second baseman as he tried to break up the double play. It proved to be a costly mental error on Mantle's part, as he hadn't bothered to move more than a few feet from the batter's box. Roger was injured on the play, bruising his ribs so badly that he would be out of the lineup for weeks.

Disgusted with himself as the double play ended the inning, Mantle waited near the first-base foul line for someone to bring him his glove. Instead, he saw Bob Cerv emerge from the dugout. Fed up with Mantle's erratic play, Stengel was pulling Mickey out of the game. A chorus of boos rained down from the stands and grew even louder as Mantle, humiliated in front of his home stadium, walked back to the dugout. "It don't look very good, us trying to win when the man hits the ball to second or third and [Mantle] doesn't run it out," an exasperated Stengel told reporters after the game. "That's not the first time he's done that. If he can't run, he should tell me. If he wants to come out, all he has to do is tell me. Who the hell does he think he is, Superman?"

With Maris injured and sidelined, the anti-Mantle fans at the Stadium had all the more reason to boo and jeer him as they did when Mickey's name was announced for the game the next day. Veteran Yankee followers believe it was the loudest, fiercest booing ever heard at the ballpark, and Stengel would later say, "In all my years in baseball, I never saw a city that booed a man so much before he went to work." For years, beginning with his rookie season, Mantle had endured an unprecedented amount of booing, heckling, and abuse, reflecting a glimpse into the dark side of sports fanaticism. Dick Schaap, in his early biography of Mantle, wrote of an incident in which a young teenaged woman waited for Mantle outside the players' entrance to the stadium before a game. When Mickey arrived in a cab, the young woman ran up to him and began punching him and pulling his hair, explaining later, "We don't like him because he's stuck up." Other angry fans would greet him with derisive remarks like, "Look, here comes the All-American out."

Broadcaster Red Barber believed that Mantle was paying the price for all the premature praise that Stengel had heaped on him, including the comparison to Yankee immortal Babe Ruth, and that Mantle was subsequently unable to match on the field. "He's booed," Barber theorized, "because he's not a colorful player like Babe Ruth. Ruth was a freewheeling guy on and off the field. He had magic, but Mantle isn't a showman." But Mel Allen, known as the "voice of the Yankees," felt that the booing had less to do with ancient Yankee history but with the more recent Yankee legend, Joe DiMaggio. Mantle was playing in a stadium at a position still haunted by the memory of DiMaggio and by fans whose adoration of the Yankee Clipper at times approached idolatry.

DiMaggio, though a son of San Francisco, had come to personify New York's ethnic diversity, with his popularity the bond for the melting pot's confluence of cultures. DiMaggio also had the luxury of not having to play in the era of television, as Mantle did. The magic and mystique of the game and its heroes could often be stripped away by televised pictures that left little to the imagination. As David Halberstam would write in the *Summer of '49* about the pennant race in which DiMaggio figured prominently: "…radio was an instrument that could heighten the mystique of a player, television [through overexposure] eventually demythologized the famous." Allen, too, would come to feel the same way. "The unfortunate thing about Mickey," he said, "is that he followed DiMag in center field. No matter who played center field after DiMaggio, that person would be booed. Fans resented that Mantle was supposed to be another DiMaggio. DiMaggio fans believed nobody could ever be another

DiMaggio. When Mickey came up at 19, they started booing. They're still booing."

The booing and heckling of Mantle was not just from Yankee fans. Once Mantle glanced into the stands where the verbal abuse was especially bad and noticed that it was coming from several vendors at Yankee Stadium. Former stadium vendor Curt Schleier later recalled a gracious incident between Mantle and some autograph-seekers that surprised him. "Even Mickey Mantle stopped for me," he said. "He first gently inquired if I was 'one of the bastards that was booing me yesterday?' After I assured him I wasn't part of a group of vendors that had razzed him the day before, he signed too."

The day after the worst of the booing in 1960, Mantle rose to the occasion in a game that many Yankee writers believe ultimately changed the minds of some of his harshest critics in the stands. Playing the Orioles, Mantle hit a game-tying home run in the fourth inning, eliciting some cheers among the boos and leading Mickey to do something that was extremely un-Mantle-like. As he trotted from home plate back to the dugout, Mickey tipped his cap to the fans—something he rarely did because he said he never liked to show up a pitcher off whom he had homered. When Mantle came up to bat in the eighth inning, the Yankees again trailed. The Orioles had a chance to retire him on a pop up behind the plate; however, the ball was dropped, giving Mickey one more chance. Mantle then drove a Hoyt Wilhelm knuckleball into the right-field seats for a two-run home run that put the Yankees back on top, and proved to be the game-winner. Yankee historian Peter Golenbock singled out that game and those Mantle heroics—rising up after the disastrous performance the day before—as the day that the booing of Mickey at Yankee Stadium stopped.

"I wanted to be good tonight more than I ever wanted to be good in my life," Mantle said after that game. "I don't know what I would have done if I had had another bad day like yesterday."

This also marked the beginning of a time that would be among the Yankees' most fabled for years to come. The Yankees closed out the 1960 season by winning their final 15 games. They did it with a revived pitching corps led by Ford, Ralph Terry, Art Ditmar, and Bob Turley; the re-emergence of the defensive play in the infield with Bobby Richardson, Tony Kubek, and Clete Boyer; and the power-hitting game spearheaded by Mantle and Maris. Mickey hit 40 home runs to lead the league, and Maris, missing considerable time with the rib injury, finished one homer behind him. But Roger edged out Mantle for the league's MVP Award in the closest balloting at that time. In his first season in pinstripes, Maris made his second All-Star team and led the league in RBI and slugging. At season's end, Stengel lavished more praise on Mantle than at any time since spring training of his rookie season: "I believe the most powerful factor has been Mickey Mantle, who hit 40 home runs and drove in 90 runs and played 50 hours through three doubleheaders on a bad knee without asking for relief or flinching. He has worked hard and hustled and in my mind he is the most valuable player."

After a long decade, however, the Stengel-Mantle relationship was nearing its end. Shortly before the end of the season, in the middle of the Yankees' 15-game winning streak, Webb had informed Stengel that this season would be his last as manager. Although Stengel did not want to retire, Webb insisted. The plan was for Ralph Houk to become the new Yankee manager and to make the transition as smooth as possible. Houk was one of Stengel's coaches and had been a minor league manager in Denver when Webb had been president of that team.

Stengel agreed to go quietly, though Webb might have been better off to wait, as the World Series loss was universally blamed on Stengel.

"He didn't start Whitey in [the opening game of] the series," Mantle would later recall. "Whitey shut them out twice. We outscored them something like 58 runs to 23, something like that. We surely had the best team. That was the only time that we got beat in the World Series where I felt that the best team lost, and I believe it was because Casey didn't start Whitey in the first game."

One could argue that Stengel had historically mismanaged Whitey Ford. Over the course of his 16-year career, Ford compiled a 236–106 record, for the third-best winning percentage in the history of the game at .690. But Mantle and others generally agree that Whitey's record might have been even better if Stengel had used him in the normal pitching rotation that most teams with strong pitching staffs used. Instead, Stengel used Ford every fifth day and sometimes held Ford back from a rotation start against a weak team to pitch him instead against the best teams in the league. Not only was Ford not reaping the benefit of some easy starts, he also wasn't getting enough starts to have a chance at winning 20 games, the benchmark of pitching greatness at the time. The result was that Ford never had a 20-game win season under Stengel, and enjoyed his best success the year after Casey was ousted, posting a Cy Young Award–winning 25–4 record in 1961. Ford's best record under Casey had been in 1956 when he won 19 games.

Mantle often blamed himself for costing Whitey a 20-win season, having committed a costly fielding mistake that decided a 1–0 game against the Orioles in Ford's last start. "I didn't have the heart to face Whitey after the game," Mantle said, thinking back on that game. "I was almost in tears. I dreaded the thought of facing Whitey, but he made it easy for me. He came up to me in the clubhouse, put his hand on my shoulder, and said, 'Forget it, Mick. Let's have a beer!'"

Customarily, the ace of the staff gets the starting nod in the World Series opener, as the Pirates' Vernon Law did in the first game at Forbes Field in Pittsburgh. Ford was ready to start for the Yankees. "I was sure I was going to pitch the first game of the World Series," Whitey would recall. "But Casey started Art Ditmar instead. He said he wanted to save me for the first game at Yankee Stadium [Game 3 of the Series], which really ticked me off. It was the only time I ever got mad at Casey. I felt I should have pitched the first game, so that I could pitch three times if it became necessary."

Ditmar never made it out of the first inning, and the Yankees lost a 6–4 game that Ford was confident he could have won. The Yankees won the next two games by scores of 16–3 and 10–0. Ford's start in Game 3 was the first of his two shutouts in the Series. Mantle hit two home runs in Game 2 and another in Game 3. Mickey's home runs at Forbes Field included a tape-measure blast to a desolate part of center field where only Babe Ruth had ever hit a ball. Pittsburgh bounced back from being virtually pummeled out of contention with 3–2 and 5–2 victories in Yankee Stadium before Ford pitched again in shutting out the Pirates, 12–0, at Forbes Field to force Game 7.

But for all the power shown by the Yankees, the Series was decided by Pirates second baseman Bill Mazeroski's dramatic home run in the bottom of the ninth inning, giving Pittsburgh a 10–9 victory in the slugfest, and making the Bucs one of the most unlikely World Series champions. The Yankees were stunned. They had outscored the Pirates 55–27, out-homered them 10–4, and out-pitched them with Ford's two shutouts. Just look at who was named the MVP of the series: not a Pirates player but the Yankees' Bobby Richardson, the only time in history that the award has been given to a member of the losing team. The loss was a bitter disappointment for the Yankees.

In the clubhouse, Mantle retreated to the trainer's room, where he cried uncontrollably, unable to reconcile himself with the defeat. In addition to his three home runs, Mantle batted .400, drove in 11 runs, scored eight runs, and walked eight times. "I was so disappointed," he said. "I cried on the plane ride home."

Ford wouldn't talk to Stengel on the flight back to New York. "The way I was pitching," said Ford, "I know I would have beaten them three times, and we would have been world champs again. But Stengel was stubborn."

16
Yankees in Camelot

"My going off after the record
started off as such a dream."
—ROGER MARIS

THE 1961 SEASON DID NOT BEGIN WITH ANY HINTS OF AN ASSAULT ON Ruth's 1927 record. But then, in 1927, Babe Ruth himself had an unspectacular start, mustering only four home runs in April. But if Ruth wasn't the reborn Saint George capable of slaying any dragon he met, he was at least, as biographer Leigh Montville called him in *The Big Bam,* "the patron saint of American possibility."

"Sixty, count 'em, 60!" the Babe had boasted in 1927. "I'd like to see some other sonofabitch do that!"

In going after Ruth's record, it didn't matter how you started. It hinged on how you did in the home stretch of weary September games. The Babe hit 17 home runs in September of 1927. If Mickey Mantle had hit that many dingers in September of his 1956 Triple Crown–winning season, he would have established a new record with 64 home runs. He had 47 homers coming into the final month. Mantle wasn't alone in collapsing under the pressure of September. In 1932, Philadelphia Athletics slugger Jimmie Fox took 48 home runs into September in his assault on Ruth's record but could hit only 10 round-trippers in the final month. In 1938, Hank Greenberg of the Detroit Tigers—who would later be Maris' general manager in Cleveland—was on track to possibly match Ruth. Greenberg entered September with 46 home runs. But he could only belt 12 more the rest of the way.

September especially took its toll on Mantle, who was said to treat each failure at the plate like a personal Armageddon. "My father taught me to hit home runs," he would say. "There were no lessons for striking out."

In 1961, Mickey Mantle got off ahead of Ruth's 1927 pace, hitting seven home runs in the season's first month. Roger Maris, on the other hand, hit his first and last home run of the month on April 26 and was batting a lowly .204 at the end of the month. What turned Maris' fortunes around was the decision made by the Yankees new manager, Ralph Houk, to switch Mantle and Maris in the batting order. For much of his career, Mickey had batted third in the lineup, the spot traditionally reserved for the team's best hitter. For much of 1960, Maris had hit in the clean-up slot, where the manager usually pencils in his most powerful hitter. Mantle was comfortable in either slot, and Houk concluded the lineup would be strengthened by the switch. He was right. In the clean-up spot, Mantle made Maris the beneficiary of good pitches to hit. Teams would pitch to Maris rather than pitching around him for fear of putting him on base and having to pitch to Mantle with a runner on base. His MVP season in 1960 had established Maris as a legitimate star in the league, but no one was ready to place him on the same level as Mantle. In 1961, Maris never received an intentional base on balls. More importantly, Maris immediately broke out of his slump, hitting 11 home runs in May. Mantle also continued his strong start, and had 14 home runs at the end of May. At the same point of the season in 1927, Ruth had 16 home runs.

Having Mantle and Maris switch spots in the lineup was just one of the major changes Houk made when he became manager. In one of their first meetings during spring training, the new Yankee skipper took Mantle aside and said: "Mickey, I want you to become the leader of this team. It's your team." Mantle had never been the rah-rah type to give clubhouse speeches, but Houk explained that what he wanted and expected of him was to lead through his example. To some extent, Mantle had already been doing this. His unselfishness in playing through pain, in helping younger players with their transition to the big leagues, in being "one of the guys" instead of the isolated icon he could have been, had made him the most beloved teammate on the Yankees. In his own self-deprecating way, Mickey would later say that he suspected that Houk had also privately asked Ford and Berra to become the leaders of the team. But Houk had not.

Mantle didn't realize just how much he needed a change in managers until the season began. Mickey Mantle had been 28 years old in his last season playing for Stengel, but the "Old Perfessor"—the nickname Stengel had enjoyed being called—still treated him the way he had when he was 19. Berra, Ford, and Mantle were grown men playing a boys' game who were treated like youngsters in the patriarchal environment that existed under Stengel. There was also no players' union in baseball at the time, and no players' representative on the team—and no officially designated player in a leadership or captain's role. The impact on Mantle especially was critical. Years later, Mantle would acknowledge that his father had died before he had ever come to terms with him and their relationship. Mutt had always dealt with him on an adult-child basis, and so, too, had Stengel, both on the field and off. In spring training of 1961, new manager Ralph Houk would help Mickey to finally break free of his childhood.

Houk had been a rarely used reserve catcher with the Yankees from 1947 to 1954. He went on to manage a farm team before becoming a Yankee coach and had seen first-hand the love and admiration Yankee players had for Mantle. Houk had been in the same clubhouse with DiMaggio and knew the selfish, self-absorbed side of the Yankee Clipper that remained hidden from the public. He knew that DiMaggio had been the fans' favorite, but knew that Mantle was a players' player.

Houk would also begin changing the way Stengel had run the team. Casey's platoon system, which had minimized or ruined some careers, was discarded. A regular four-man rotation was implemented that would make Ford a 20-game winner for the first time in his career. Gone, too, was Stengel's doghouse, as well as his manner of criticizing players or destroying their confidence as he had done with Clete Boyer in the 1960 World Series. Stengel would be especially remembered among many of his players for the cruelty and insensitivity in his treatment of those who were not the stars of the team.

There was a moment in that 1960 World Series against the Pirates that drove this home. In the second inning of the opening game, after Yogi Berra and Bill Skowron had singled, Clete Boyer was called back to the dugout as he walked to the plate to bat. Boyer, about to have his first at-bat in his first World Series, was shocked to learn that Stengel was pulling him for a pinch-hitter—in the second inning of the Series' first game, for crying out loud. Stengel later explained that he was playing for a big inning, though pinch-hitter Dale Long flied out and the Yankees did not score in that inning. Boyer left the dugout for the clubhouse, where he cried at his locker for half an hour with teammates vainly trying to console him. To his credit, Boyer bounced back to compile an .833 OPS in that World Series, even though Stengel used him in only four games. "Everybody hated him," Boyer said of Casey. "When he came out of his mother, the doctor slapped *her.* "

It can be argued that without Houk at the helm, the legendary 1961 Yankees, and Maris and Mantle's chase of Ruth, never take place. For the Yankees, the arrival of Ralph Houk marked a transition into the emerging new era of 1961 when the world seemed to be turning upside down. While the unofficial theme of the Kennedy presidency may have been Camelot, there were soon showdowns with Fidel Castro and Nikita Khrushchev. Americans watched their new young president in live, dazzling press conferences. Then there was Maris and the Mick. Roger Maris failed to homer in his first 10 games, but by the end of July he had 40 home runs, six games ahead of Ruth's 1927 home run pace. "My going off after the record started off such a dream," Maris said. "I was living a fairy tale for a while. I never thought I'd get a chance to break such a record."

It was this "fairy tale," as Maris called it, that some fans and reporters were determined to bring down to earth by pitting the two sluggers against each other in a petty, personal rivalry. Unlike Mantle, Maris remained rooted to his small-town mindset. When outfielder Bob Cerv rejoined the Yankees early that season, he and Maris began sharing an apartment in Queens, away from the spotlight of Manhattan. It was a perfect setting for Maris, as Cerv had been one of his best friends from his time with the Athletics.

In 1961 Cerv was in his third stint with the Yankees. He had been a rookie with Mantle in 1951, been dealt away to the Athletics in 1957, traded back to the Yankees in 1960, and then taken in the expansion draft by the Los Angeles Angels, where he played 18 games in 1961, before returning to the Yankees again. He was one of those players who had not had an opportunity to blossom under Stengel's platoon system. In Kansas City, however, he got a chance to play regularly over three full seasons, during which time he hit 69 home runs and enjoyed his best year in 1958, when he hit .305, slugged 38 homers, and drove in 104 runs.

By 1961, now in his mid-thirties and a year away from retirement, Cerv was best suited as a pinch hitter and occasional outfielder on the talent-rich Yankees. When he rejoined the Yankees early that season, "Maris was starting to get recognized," Cerv later recalled, "and it was starting to be too much downtown." Maris and Cerv were joined in the apartment later in the season by Mantle, though the exact way that came about is not altogether clear. The popular story surrounding Mantle moving in—and repeated again in Billy Crystal's HBO film *61** recounting the Mantle-Maris home run derby—was that it had been Maris' idea in trying to save Mickey from his drinking and carousing. But Cerv and fellow-Yankee Tony Kubek remember it differently. According to Cerv, Mantle one day said, "'Hey, can I move out with ya?' Just like that. Nothing more. 'Sure,' I said, 'we don't care.'" It was Kubek's recollection that Mantle moved in of his own initiative. Mickey, Kubek felt, was spending too much money living at the St. Moritz Hotel in Manhattan. Kubek also believed that it was Mantle who was concerned about the pressure that was being placed on Maris and wanted to help out. "Mickey had been through it so many times," Kubek recalled, "that I really believe he thought he could help Roger by moving in and giving support."

Just when the pressure began seriously affecting Maris is uncertain. It became noticeable to some teammates in midseason, before the All-Star Game. When Roger hit his 27th home run, his record pace became impossible to dismiss. A reporter asked him if he had a chance to break the Babe's record. Although he had been asked about Ruth's record before, this may have been the first time the question was asked in the context of where he was in the historic chase.

"How the fuck do I know?" Maris answered brusquely.

The response was honest, but it also was full of the hostility building up within him.

At the time, Roger was ahead of Mickey. Maris led through game 73 but Mantle hit two homers in game 74 to tie Roger at 27. But Maris had another surge, homering in game 78 to lead 32–28. Three games to go before midseason, and Roger was more than halfway to Babe Ruth's record. But then Mantle bounced back again and led through game 117 on August 12, when Maris tied up the race at 45 home runs apiece. In 1927, Ruth hadn't hit 45 home runs until September 6, when he and Lou Gehrig were both tied with the same number. Coincidentally, Mantle, like Gehrig, would never take the home run lead again. Maris went on to become the first player to reach 50 before September, homering against the new expansion Angels in Los Angeles on August 22, then slugged No. 51 on August 26 against the Athletics in Kansas City. Mantle was left in the dust.

"The Yankees did not want Roger to break the record," said Maris' Cardinals teammate Mike Shannon, to whom Roger later shared his frustrations of 1961. "They never set anything up. They never protected him. Hell, yeah. He knew that. If it was going to be broken, they wanted Mantle to break it."

In 1961, only perhaps Mantle could truly empathize. In the course of being roommates, a deep friendship developed between Mantle and Maris despite their differences in personalities and habits. Part of their bonding was through being teammates, but obviously the key ingredient in their friendship was their chase of Ruth's home run record. At various times, reports circulated that their on-field rivalry had developed into a feud. It was little more than New York tabloid sensationalism. Those "feud" stories rarely, if ever, mentioned that they were roommates for the obvious reason that such a detail would have seriously lessened the validity of those accounts.

"It seemed the more pressure was on Maris, the closer he and Mickey became," Whitey Ford would recount. "Not that there wasn't a good-natured rivalry between them, a sense of competition. That was only natural. They both wanted to lead the league in home runs, and they both wanted to break Ruth's record. This was normal, and the competition brought the best out of both of them. Then, when Mantle got hurt and he knew his chances of breaking the record were over, he rooted for Roger as much as anybody."

What Mantle couldn't help Maris with, however, was his actual day-to-day handling of the reporters' questions. Where Mantle's answers were often short, humorously self-deprecating, or mundane, Maris would make the mistake of being too honest or brutally frank in answering questions. He would appear noticeably impatient about answering the same question over and over. At other times, he would become verbally combative but lacked the intimidation that Mantle could have when he didn't want to answer a reporter's question.

Journalists like *Newsday's* Steve Jacobson believe that the growth of television changed the attitudes of newspapers at the time. Newspapers, seeking to combat the popularity of television, decided that they must not only report about the game but "an effort had to be made to delve into what the athlete was thinking and what his response was." In the days of Ruth, baseball writers wrote about what happened at the park and nothing else. Perhaps this has something to do with how Ruth, a man with infinitely more bad habits than Maris, was viewed as a man who could do no wrong, while Maris, a family man, was treated like a pariah. The harshest articles written about Maris were a series by Jimmy Cannon, who was irked that Maris missed an appointment with him, and a piece by UPI's Oscar Fraley, who thought Maris had snubbed a child asking for an autograph. Cannon ripped Maris in 1962 for purportedly snubbing him, calling him "the whiner" and accusing him of "treacherous smallness," "lingering rudeness," and "self-worship." Also that spring, Fraley called Roger a "one-year wonder" and a "zero."

Unfortunately for Maris, he wasn't protected by the Yankees from the media the way that Mark McGwire would be by the Cardinals in 1998 when he broke Maris' home run record. Maris' experience, in fact, would serve as a lesson for how the news media's demands on McGwire would be handled by his team. But in 1961, the Yankee beat reporters were virtually unchecked in their freedom in the team clubhouse after each game, with only the trainer's room and the showers being off-limits.

Maris would ultimately become the public's whipping boy, taking the onus of great expectations off of Mantle. Author Robert Creamer was among those who would personally witness the transformation in Mickey. "Mantle changed quite a bit in 1961," Creamer recalled years later. "Mantle hit 54 home runs himself, but now it was Maris who was hounded by reporters. As Roger bore the brunt of the media pressure, Mickey became almost genial and was much more responsive to questions from reporters he knew." In the past, Mantle had been almost impossible to interview at length, a point that was underscored in a story Creamer recounted of fellow *Sports Illustrated* writer Gerald Holland's experience with Mickey: "Holland had run into the same wall of indifference that Mantle habitually erected against writers. But Holland had understood that Mantle was a country boy and country people tend to dislike pushy strangers. So he visited Mantle at home in Oklahoma, but he stopped asking questions, stopped talking to him almost entirely, except for perfunctory remarks like 'Yup' and 'Nope' and 'Pass the sugar.' He was getting Mantle used to him. Finally one day, Mickey said, 'Well, are you going to ask me questions or what?' Holland's story was a gem."

As the home run derby intensified, so too did Maris' unpopularity among some of the writers and among some longtime Yankee fans, undoubtedly including many who had previously booed Mantle. When Maris took the lead in the home run race, it may have been the best thing that ever happened to Mantle. The fans had found a new scapegoat and began booing Maris, who happened to play the same position as Ruth. Clete Boyer was among the Yankees who saw this incredible turnaround in the way fans had suddenly became Mantle supporters in the chase of Ruth's record. "Mickey got booed because Casey Stengel built him up to be something he wasn't," said Boyer. "Mickey was supposed to hit 1,000 home runs. When he didn't, the fans got on him. Roger took the pressure off Mickey. They never booed Mickey again. It became good guy-bad guy. The press, everybody, wanted Mickey Mantle to break Babe Ruth's record."

Historically, Ruth's record had been the most sacred in the game. He was credited with revolutionizing baseball with his power, and his name was part of the nation's language as a sports icon larger than the game itself. Perhaps no one inside of baseball held Ruth in higher esteem than the commissioner, Ford Frick. A personal friend of Ruth's who had even been his ghostwriter, Frick became concerned midway through the season that Babe's record might finally be broken. His concern was not without some merit.

In 1961, baseball experienced its first expansion, with the American League adding the Los Angeles Angels and a new Senators franchise in Washington to replace the team that had moved to Minnesota. Frick and others worried that expansion, with the introduction of at least 20 more pitchers, had weakened the overall level of pitching in the league.

Additionally, expansion had meant increasing the number of games each team played that season to 162, eight more games than the season in which Ruth had hit 60 home runs. Frick could do little about the allegedly weaker pitching that Mantle and Maris were facing, except to lament the situation. The expanded schedule was another matter. On July 17, Frick ruled that anyone who broke Ruth's home run record—or any other record as well—would have to do it in 154 games for it to be considered as having bettered Ruth's mark, otherwise it would be regarded as an altogether separate record in the books. Practically speaking, it would be a record with an asterisk.

The additional pressure of the commissioner's decree was yet another distraction in the media circus that had formed around the two sluggers. The frenzy surrounding them was not limited to Yankee Stadium, but extended throughout the league. Security guards had to escort Mantle and Maris in and out of the ballparks. The lobbies of the Yankees' hotels were regularly filled with journalists not only from newspapers but also from radio and television stations, each wanting their own interviews with the duo. Through mid-August they were even with 45 home runs apiece, before Maris surged ahead. On September 2, Maris hit his 52nd and 53rd home runs. The next day, Mantle hit two home runs to pull within three homers of Maris.

The betting money among fans and almost everyone around them was still on Mantle.

They didn't really know Roger Maris and his power of mind in proving critics wrong.

17
Power of the Outsider

*"Maris later told his friend Mike Shannon
that the ambition to beat Mantle in 1961 had
been a calculated affair. He had been goaded
into it, he told Shannon, by the fans."*
—DAVID HALBERSTAM

THEY SAY THE SOUL OF A NEW YORK CITY SUMMER IS HEDONISTIC IN
the most selfless way imaginable. Some make a game of watching how
others endure the heat, or wilt in the unrelenting sun. In the dog days
of summer in 1961, few people could take their eyes off Roger Maris,
Mickey Mantle included.

Mickey kneels down in the cathedral of Yankee Stadium. Of course
he does—he isn't religious, he just happens to be in the on-deck circle,
rubbing the rag of pine tar across the handle of his bat as he watches
Roger dig in at home plate. Watching the two of them, it's impossible
not to see that they are as different as night and day. Maris' muscles
seem to flow; Mantle's bulge. Maris is visibly high-strung and intense;
Mantle playfully laid back. Maris appears comfortable deferring to
Mantle, the longstanding star of the team, on everything except what

they are both chasing. Then, as Mantle continues to watch, Maris swings from his heels. The crack of the bat is deafening.

"This could be 56!" booms the excited voice of Mel Allen, the familiar Yankees radio broadcaster. "She's going… going… GONE! Maris has hit number 56… four behind the Babe, and it's only September 9…."

Almost an hour later, a pack of sportswriters surround Maris in the Yankee clubhouse, according to the next day's newspapers.

"Rog, what's it feel like to be this close to Ruth's record?" one writer asks.

"It doesn't feel any different than it did yesterday," says Maris.

Another writer jumps in. "Didya know that with your homer today, you and Mantle have already overtaken Ruth and Gehrig for most home runs by two teammates in a single season?"

"No, I didn't know that," says Maris, who hollers to Mantle. "Did you, Mick?"

Nearby, Mantle looks up. "Nah. How many did Gehrig hit?"

"Forty-seven," the second writer tells Mantle.

"Fuck, 47? I already got 52. I've beaten Gehrig," says Mickey, quickly looking at Maris. "It's up to you to beat Ruth."

There's a roundhouse of laughter as the writers scribble furiously.

Later in the training room, Mickey's immersed in a whirlpool, sipping on a beer. Maris is getting rubbed down on the training table, Yankee clubhouse attendant Pete Sheehy recalled in a 1976 interview with me as he recounted the scene between Mantle and Maris.

"Mick, I'm losing hair," says Maris. "I'm losing sleep. Something I don't get. How come going for the record doesn't seem to get to you?"

Mickey considers it with a sip of beer.

"It does," Mantle says finally. "It did in '56."

"I read where you had 47 going into September?"

"Then I only hit five more the rest of the way," says Mickey.

"What happened?"

"The Babe," says Mantle. "He rose out of his grave and kicked me in the balls."

"What?"

The trainer finishes the rubdown on Maris. He's been listening in.

"Mickey pulled a groin muscle," the trainer tells Roger.

Mantle takes a long swig of his beer. "I was seein' the Babe on the street, in cabs, in bars. Of course, it wasn't, and I mighta been drinkin' too much." Mickey points to the beer Maris has just opened. "Someone else's ghost becomes your monster."

"Tell me 'bout it," says Maris, putting his beer down.

"It's like naming a kid 'Junior,'" says Mickey

"What's wrong with that?"

"Nothing personal," says Mantle. "Well, actually it is." He pauses and remembers something from the past.

"You know, a couple of years ago, Merlyn and the boys were flyin' back to Dallas, and I guess Mickey Jr. was playin' in the aisle. Well, some guy thought he was cute and asked him what his name was. Merlyn says he said, 'Mickey Mantle Jr.' Real proud and all. Well, the guy must've thought here was this little kid who wants to grow up to be Mickey Mantle and made a joke about it. Mickey Jr. started cryin' cause the guy didn't think that was his name. Imagine having to go through life like that."

Mickey is weepy eyed and reflective, as is Maris.

As different as they were, they were bonded that summer, as they would be the rest of their lives, in a pursuit not for fame but for immortality in sports, which are often confused as the same, though they aren't. Mickey would have countless friends and many teammates over his lifetime, but Roger Maris would remain special.

197

"Roger is the man I wish I could have been," Mantle told me during one of our conversations in the early 1970s. There was no arguing with him. You couldn't tell him that all men are different. They may be equal in the eyes of the law, the founders of America, or perhaps even some religions, but they are different, and one man's character may be as ill-fitting on another as their clothes. As someone to admire, though, you could do a lot worse than Roger Maris.

Back at Yankee Stadium, Mantle the next day slugged his 53rd home run of the season. The M&M Boys had 18 games in which to catch Ruth, but the pressure was mounting to the point of being almost unbearable. Maris was chain-smoking Camels, and his hair began falling out in patches. Pressure and criticism of Maris was also coming from unexpected sources. Hall of Famer Rogers Hornsby, considered by some at the time to be the greatest pure hitter to ever play the game, entered the fray, telling reporters, "Maris has no right to break Ruth's record." For the most part, Maris internalized the pressure. "He became a nervous wreck," said longtime friend Whitey Herzog.

Houk recalled that "Roger'd say things honestly, without thinking about them, and they'd be exaggerated. Somebody asked him if he really wanted to break Babe Ruth's record and Roger said, 'Hell, yes' and that was big news. Why wouldn't he want to break the record? Rogers Hornsby, I think it was, said, 'Wouldn't it be a shame for a hitter like Maris to break Babe's record?' And Roger said, 'Screw Hornsby.' He said it half kidding, but the writers were jumping on things like that, and now that's in the headlines: Maris Rips Hornsby."

In Detroit, Maris set off another negative reaction from fans and media after hitting home run No. 57. When the ball bounced back onto the field, Tigers All-Star right fielder Al Kaline threw it to Maris for a souvenir. "When the writers asked me about it afterward, they said, 'Gee, wasn't that nice of Kaline?'" Maris recalled. "I said, 'Well, any of the players would have done that.' I didn't mean to knock Al. It was very nice of him to do that. But any right fielder in the league would have done that. I would have done that for Al, that's all I meant. That's not how it came out in the tabloids. They made it sound like I was knocking Al. By the time they finished with me, the fans thought I was a bomb ready to go off."

Mantle was also feeling the pressure. Or perhaps his drinking and carousing betrayed him because, even while living with Maris and Cerv, his playing around had continued. Now in September, in the home stretch of the most important challenge of his career, he felt utterly sick and rundown. He feared that his fast life might have caught up to him. In addition to feeling physically exhausted, he had developed a cold and upper respiratory infection that lingered on a road trip to Chicago, Detroit, and Baltimore. Mel Allen, the Yankee broadcaster who was privately pulling for Mantle in the home run derby, saw Mickey and urged him to immediately see his doctor, Max Jacobson. The "Voice of the Yankees" couldn't praise Jacobson enough. His patients included Elizabeth Taylor, Lauren Bacall, Ingrid Bergman, Leonard Bernstein, Judy Garland, Humphrey Bogart, Marilyn Monroe, and President Kennedy no less. The wonderful doctor specialized in giving vitamin shots that Allen said would "fix you right up."

Upon returning to New York, Mickey hurried to an appointment with Dr. Jacobson that Allen had made for him, not suspecting that it would be the doctor's visit he would come to regret for the rest of his life. Jacobson gave Mantle a shot in his hip that Mickey later said made him scream in pain. No one is certain what went wrong, but something did. Walking back to his hotel on Jacobson's advice, Mantle became delirious and eventually made it into bed with a fever, and feeling worse than before he had visited the doctor. He couldn't play in the next day's game, and eventually checked in to Lenox Hill Hospital.

Doctors found an infection where the shot had been given, requiring them to lance the injection spot and make a three-inch cut in the shape of a star over the hip to permit the area to drain. It looked like a war wound. There was a hole in Mickey's hip big enough to fit a golf ball, leaving him bedridden. Mantle's part in the chase of the Babe was over. After the shot, Mickey started only two games and finished the historic season as an also-ran with 54 home runs.

For Maris, however, this wonderful if troubling season would become a personal triumph into baseball immortality that would not be fully appreciated until years later. On the 154th game of the season, he hit home run No. 59 in Baltimore against pitcher Milt Pappas, and barely missed another that would have tied the Babe's record. He had failed in his record-setting quest within the time frame set up by the commissioner, but the season was far from being over. Proof of that was the media and national attention on Maris that continued unabated through the final eight games. Roger Maris' pursuit of the Babe, much to Frick's chagrin, was still on. In New York in the 158th game, with Ruth's widow in attendance, Maris tied Babe Ruth's record. In one baseball purist sense, Roger had actually beaten the Babe to No. 60. Maris hit his 60th home run in his 684th plate appearance that season. Ruth didn't hit his 60th until he had stepped into the batter's box for the 687th time in 1927.

"The minute I threw the ball," Baltimore Orioles pitcher Jack Fisher later admitted, "I said to myself, *That does it. That's number 60.*" Today just a footnote in one of the most memorable subplots in Major League Baseball history, Fisher had the eyes of the baseball world upon him as he delivered a high curveball to the plate on September 26, 1961. Maris' thunderous left-handed swing smashed the ball violently an instant later, bouncing it off the concrete steps of Yankee Stadium's upper deck and down onto the field, where Orioles right fielder

Earl Robinson retrieved the ball and tossed it to umpire Ed Hurley. Through first-base coach Wally Moses, the ball was delivered back to the Yankees dugout just as Maris completed his customary speedy trot around the bases.

Then, to everyone's surprise, Maris took a day off. In 1973, in a previously unpublished interview, author Peter Golenbock asked Roger if the tension had just become too much.

"Pressure, as far as playing the ballgame, there was no pressure," Maris said. "Playing was the easiest part of it. Mentally, it'd just gone pretty strong—the press before and after ballgames and everything—continuous questions, continually trying to be on your guard, because there were a certain few who were looking for you to make a slip—I'm not trying to knock anybody, but you know sometimes when you're answering one guy's question, someone else butts in with another thing, and another guy comes in on half of what you said, and they misinterpret. Through all the pressures, the continuous questions being fired at you, the pressure was quite strong. Mentally I needed time off… I had already hit the 60th. Steve Barber was pitching, a left-hander. I don't ever believe I hit Steve that strongly. I managed to get a few hits off him, but not that strongly. I was having enough pressure mentally that I just felt I needed the day off, and of the remaining ballgames that I had left, to me this was the best day to take. This is when I asked Ralph for the day off, and I got the day off."

Maris returned to the lineup on Friday when he went hitless and then homerless on Saturday. Finally, on Sunday, October 1, facing Boston in the final game of the season, Maris stepped into the batter's box in the fourth inning at 2:42 PM Eastern time.

"Fast ball is wide," said broadcaster Red Barber on WPIX-TV after the first pitch. "He lays off of it. Ball one."

Maris checked the cleats on his right shoe. Then banged his bat against the side of the sole, knocking off some dirt.

"Low. Ball two."

The crowd booed.

"The crowd is reacting negatively," said Barber. "They want to see Maris get something he can swing on."

Maris fidgeted by running his right foot over the batter's box. He dug in again and took two short swings while Stallard wound up and delivered, just as Maris unloaded his swing.

The sound of a solid crack was deafening.

"There it is," says Barber.

Right fielder Lou Clinton went back to the short wall, looking up at a ball clearly headed out of the field. The ball rose toward the right-field stands, just to the right of the Yankee bullpen some 360 feet from home plate, falling about six rows deep into a wild confusion of grappling fans. And there a 19-year-old Brooklyn youngster named Sal Durante caught the ball on the fly and moments later was escorted by security guards with his precious souvenir to the Yankee dressing room.

"Sixty-one," cried Red Barber. "Five thousand dollars for somebody. He got his pitch. It's five thousand dollars."

It was a reference to the reward that San Francisco restaurateur Sam Gordon announced he would pay for the record-breaking ball of Maris' 61st home run. It was a ransom that had packed the right-field porch and made it appear in photographs that there was standing room only at Yankee Stadium that afternoon. But the official attendance for the historic game was only 23,154. For that, blame commissioner Ford Frick's proclamation for possibly deflating the public interest in Maris' pursuit of Ruth's record.

Still, Yankee starter Bob Turley, who was in the bullpen that day, recalled seeing fans crowded together in right field hoping to catch the historic home run.

"One guy had his coat off—he was going to try to catch the ball with his coat, Turley remembered. "We all had our gloves on. When he hit it, we ran underneath the stands toward the dugout to congratulate him. I hit my head on a beam and knocked myself down. I saw stars. I was the last to get to the dugout. All the players had him surrounded. They had to push him back out to acknowledge the crowd."

As fans in right field fought for the ball, back on the diamond Maris rounded third base, took a celebratory handshake from third base coach Frank Crosetti, and headed for home plate.

"And here is the fellow with 61," Red Barber said to his television audience. "You're seeing a lot today."

Berra congratulated Maris as he crossed home plate. A fan who sneaked onto the field and a batboy greeted Roger as he hustled into the dugout, where he was flooded by teammates. Maris went down the bench of the dugout, then emerged back on to the field and removed his cap, tried to return into the dugout but was urged back up onto the steps to acknowledge the fans one more time. When Maris tried to sit down again, his excited teammates refused to let him, pushing him back into view. Again he waved his cap at the crowd. At that moment, a message flashed on the Yankee Stadium scoreboard: MARIS 61 HOMERS BREAK RUTH'S 1927 RECORD FOR A SEASON.

"Well, you haven't seen anything like this, have you?" Barber said to his broadcasting partner, Mel Allen.

"Nobody ever has, Red," said Allen. "Nobody's ever seen anything like this."

Nobody was making a big deal about it, but that had actually been the 62nd home run he had hit in 1961. Earlier in the season Roger had lost a home run he hit in a game that was rained out before it had been played long enough to become official.

On this day, after Roger's record-breaking dinger, there were still five more innings to play in this season finale. This game would be decided by Maris' solo shot, the only run Yankee starter Bill Stafford and the bullpen needed in shutting out the Red Sox. Before the bottom of the sixth inning, Roger slipped into the clubhouse to see Sal Durante, who had been brought down to meet Maris. Durante wanted to give Roger the ball, which touched Maris. The two of them posed for photographers, holding the ball and a pinstriped Yankee uniform shirt with No. 61 on the back. Maris, though, was also fully aware of the San Francisco restaurateur's $5,000 reward for the record-breaking item and refused accept the ball, telling Durante to keep it and "make yourself some money." Eventually the restaurateur generously gave the ball over to Roger, who had told reporters in the Yankee clubhouse the obvious, that this had been "the biggest home run I ever hit."

"I thought nothing could match the thrill I got when I hit my 60th, but this beats everything," he said. "Whether I beat Ruth's record or not is for others to say, but it gives me a wonderful feeling to know that I'm the only man in history to hit 61 home runs. Nobody can take that from me."

From his room at Lenox Hill Hospital, Mantle had watched Maris slug the record breaker, feeling a bit like a man witnessing his best friend marry the woman that he was in love with. The moment soon brought tears to his eyes. How could it not? He knew better than anyone else that this was a record that had been waiting for him to break it. He had even said, after his Triple Crown season, that he thought he would eventually surpass Babe Ruth's monumental achievement. The record had his name on it, just waiting for Mickey to claim it. In 1970, I asked Mantle if what he felt was anything like those lines from a Rolling Stones song released a couple of years earlier? *You can't always get what you want/But if you try sometime/You find/You get what you need.*

"My whole life," he said, "feels like that."

Years later, Mantle would acknowledge having envied Maris for finding the strength to corner baseball's Holy Grail.

"Everyone always thought it would be me who'd do it," he said. "But it wasn't. The only regret I have about it was that I wish I'd been healthy enough to give him a better run. In my heart, I have to think I'd have been there myself, but that's not to take anything away from Roger because he's the one who broke it."

Roger Maris' feat breaking the revered, 34-year-old single-season home run record held by Babe Ruth transcended the sports world and seeped into the social fabric of America, something he realized a few days later when he received an important letter.

"My heartiest congratulations to you on hitting your 61st home run," it read. "The American people will always admire a man who overcomes great pressure to achieve an outstanding goal.

"John F. Kennedy"

18

A King Dethroned

*"As a ballplayer, I would be delighted to
do it again. As an individual, I doubt that
I could possibly go through it again."*
—ROGER MARIS

FOR THE FIRST TIME IN HIS LIFE, MICKEY MANTLE HAD TO REALIZE THAT
there was someone of his generation upon whom the baseball gods had
smiled more favorably than they ever had—and possibly ever would—
on him. Babe Ruth's majestic home run record, which for the past
decade had been reserved for Mantle, now belonged to a teammate.
Had it been only five years earlier that Mickey had celebrated the
magical year of 1956, when the Yankees had topped Mantle's Triple
Crown season by winning the team's 17th World Series championship,
made all the more memorable by Don Larsen's perfect game in Game
5? It had been a feat saved by Mantle's full-speed running catch of a
400-foot blow to deep left-center field in the fifth inning that Mickey
would call "the best catch I ever made."

"There would have been no perfect game for Larsen without what
Mantle did to catch [Gil] Hodges' line drive," the *Washington Post's*
Shirley Povich later wrote. "That ball was certain to fall in until a flying

Mantle reached the scene from nowhere and speared it backhanded. Larsen should have blown him a kiss."

Larsen might have blown him a double kiss. Not only did Mickey save the perfect game, but he also won it. Through three innings, Larsen had been matched in perfection to that point by the Dodgers' Sal Maglie, who earlier had pitched a no-hitter for Brooklyn in the home stretch of its pennant race. Then in the fourth inning, Mickey shattered Maglie's own perfect game by pulling a curveball down the right-field line, where it barely cleared the foul pole at Yankee Stadium's 296-foot sign. It was all the scoring that Larsen and the Yankees would need.

The only thing that could have topped it would have been for Mantle to have broken Babe Ruth's home run record, which he had threatened all season. Mickey, though, was looking forward to doing that. In his mind, it was inevitable for him to do so, and he was putting Babe Ruth on notice.

"I'd rather have won the Triple Crown than to have broke Babe Ruth's record," Mickey told broadcaster Len Morton at season's end, "because I doubt that I'll ever have another chance to win the Triple Crown, but I think that if I get to play another 12 to 14 years, that I'll break Babe Ruth's record."

Now, Mantle had to be wondering: Could he break Roger Maris' record? Mickey would turn 30 in a matter of days that October. How many more years would he have to hit 62 home runs? Could he stay injury free long enough in any of those seasons to mount another threat at the record? And 1961? How had it all come apart for Mantle? Not an injury but a vitamin shot in the hip gone awry? And from President Kennedy's doctor, at that? Could he have been a quack in Camelot?

John F. Kennedy had first been treated by Jacobson in September 1960, shortly before the 1960 presidential election debates. The president also had enough confidence in Dr. Jacobson to call him to Palm Beach in May of 1961 to check on first lady Jacqueline Kennedy, who had been suffering depression and headaches following the birth of John F. Kennedy, Jr., in November 1960. A month later, in June 1961, the doctor had even accompanied the president to Europe aboard Air Force One for the Vienna summit with Soviet premier Nikita Khrushchev. He treated Kennedy 45 minutes before his scheduled meeting with Khrushchev. How then could this doctor to JFK have so screwed up a simple injection to Mantle's hip so as to sideline him at the most important moment of his professional life?

But, as Mickey and the world would learn, there were serious unanswered questions about this man who was called "Doctor Feelgood" and "Miracle Max" by many in New York circles. Not much was known about him except that he had fled Nazi Germany in 1936 and established an office on the Upper East Side of Manhattan, where he treated many famous clients and other famous people, not the least being the grandmother of celebrated Yankee fan Billy Crystal. "You feel like Superman," author Truman Capote, another of his clients, said about Miracle Max. "You're flying. Ideas come back at the speed of light. You go 722 straight hours without so much as a cup of coffee." Curiously, among Dr. Jacobson's clients was President Kennedy's mistress Judith Exner, and perhaps there some of the unsavory aspects of JFK and Camelot should have raised red flags. Judith Exner was also the girlfriend of Sam Giancana, the boss of the Chicago underworld, as well as Mafia associate John Roselli—accounts supported by FBI reports, as well as Secret Service and White House phone logs and staff documentation.

What was in his secret vitamin treatments? According to a 1972 *New York Times* exposé, Dr. Jacobson was injecting patients with up to 30 to 50 milligrams of amphetamines—speed—highly addictive stimulants that made for the "Feelgood" effect. In administering injections to combat Kennedy's severe back pain, Dr. Jacobson then was pumping up JFK with amphetamines, some with potential side effects that included hyperactivity, impaired judgment, nervousness, and wild mood swings. But President Kennedy was apparently untroubled by what he might have been shooting himself up with. According to government records, by May 1962, Dr. Feelgood had visited the White House at least 34 times to treat Kennedy. Bobby Kennedy reportedly was concerned enough about the treatments that he had the president submit Jacobson's concoctions to the U.S. Food and Drug Administration. The agency's findings were that President Kennedy was shooting up with amphetamines and steroids. "I don't care if it's horse piss," Kennedy is quoted as saying in author Frederick Kempe's book *Berlin 1961*. "It works." President Kennedy's White House physicians eventually put a stop to the treatments over concerns of this inappropriate use of steroids and amphetamines. In 1975, Dr. Jacobson's medical license was revoked by New York authorities.

Had a Camelot-connected Dr. Feelgood speed quack derailed whatever remote chance Mickey Mantle might have had of beating Maris to Ruth's great record? We will never know. But who's to say that Mantle might not have ended up like another of Dr. Jacobson's clients, former Kennedy presidential photographer Mark Shaw, who, in 1969, died at the age of 47, of what the New York City chief medical examiner concluded to have been "acute and chronic intravenous amphetamine poisoning?" Mickey, after all, thought he was dying as he staggered from Jacobson's office to his home at the St. Moritz Hotel that fateful September day after receiving the injection.

Better still: How was it that two of the biggest names of the day, the popular new president of the United States and America's leading baseball hero, could become patients—if not victims—of an Upper

East Side drug pusher? And why had the injection caused so much havoc with Mantle's health in September 1961? More importantly, why hadn't Mantle just gone to see one of the Yankees' own team doctors? In *The Last Boy: Mickey Mantle and the End of America's Childhood*, biographer Jane Leavy suggests that the Mick chose to see Dr. Jacobson because he had actually contracted a venereal disease and didn't want the Yankees to know about it.

Third baseman Clete Boyer finally copped to the obvious. "I can't believe you goddamn media people are so dumb," he told me. "Nobody ever figured it out. Why would he have gone to another doctor other than the Yankee doctor? How 'bout the clap? C-L-A-P."

Boyer had a good laugh at the credulousness of sportswriters who solemnly reported the progress of a virus that had somehow "lodged in his buttock"… "The 24-hour virus, and it got infected?" Boyer said. "C'mon."

But perhaps what might have doomed Mantle most in his home run *mano a mano* with Maris may have been in not fully understanding the psyche of his opponent, a teammate he had tried to help out by rooming with him. This was a Roger Maris with a martyr complex feeding an insatiable appetite for feeling that he was abused, ignored, and otherwise disrespected. It was a monster that had hovered over him since his childhood, and Maris should have been thankful. At times, especially while in high school and later as a professional ballplayer, it seemed as if Roger sought out suffering or persecution because it fueled a psychological need that drove him to succeed. And it had been in acting out in response to feeling victimized that Roger found a catalyst for overcoming setbacks, real and imaginary, and achieving his success.

When he joined the St. Louis Cardinals in 1967, Maris confided in pal and teammate Mike Shannon the behind-the-scenes story of the motivation for breaking Babe Ruth's record. Roger's incentive, he told Shannon in a rare admission, had been spite. This actually dated back to the 1960 season, when Maris had a fabulous first half, at one point even ahead of Ruth's record pace when he first drew mention of comparisons to the Babe. "In 1960 [fans] had begun to cheer Mantle and boo him, and he decided quietly to get even by beating Mantle out for the club home run championship," David Halberstam wrote in *October 1964*. "If they wanted to boo, he would give them something to boo about…. Later when sportswriters claimed there was considerable bitterness between [Mantle and Maris] they were wrong. The bitterness was between Maris and the fans and subsequently the Yankee management. Though it should have been the easiest thing in the world to root for both men, that was not what happened."

But there had been something else more directly involved in helping Maris triumph over Mantle. When manager Ralph Houk moved Mantle from batting third to cleanup in the lineup, he had effectively given Roger a significant advantage over Mickey. In 1961, Maris had 590 at-bats, 67 more than Mantle's 514, and 698 plate appearances compared to Mickey's 646. At his rate of homering once every 9.52 at-bats, Mantle hypothetically over another 67 official times to the plate would have produced seven more home runs—tying Maris at 61 home runs.

None of this was even close to consolation for the lost opportunity. For now, Mantle could only take solace in what he had accomplished this season. Not since the days of Ruth and Gehrig had any two players or any team exhibited the kind of power that the Yankees unleashed that year. Together, Maris and Mantle's 115 combined home runs broke Ruth and Gehrig's record of 107 from 1927. In 1961, the Yankees also had four other players hit 20 or more home runs as they set a team record with 240 home runs.

In the 1961 World Series, Mantle struggled out of the hospital to play against the Cincinnati Reds in a display of courage that won him even more admirers. Backup catcher Johnny Blanchard was among those who saw Mantle's infected hip in the clubhouse dressing room and later said: "[The surgical wound] was from the bone up, not from the skin down. The way the wound was dressed was first with a coating of sulfur right down on the bone, by the hip where it was, then it was covered with gauze and then bandaged over. It was unbelievable this guy could walk, much less play."

Play Mickey did. Mantle didn't get into either of the first two games of the World Series at Yankee Stadium, which the Yankees and Reds split. Whitey Ford pitched a two-hit shutout in the opener for his third consecutive Series shutout, including the two from 1960, which made Stengel's questionable pitching decisions seem that much more ludicrous. Mickey finally got into the World Series, starting in the third game at Cincinnati's Crosley Field. He went hitless in four at-bats, though the Yankees won, taking the Series lead. "When he came to bat," Blanchard recalled, "you could see a spot of blood on his uniform by his hip. We could all see it."

Mantle started again in Game 4, but opened the wound in the first inning while making a catch in right-center field. It was especially important for Mickey to be in this game because Whitey was going after yet another of Babe Ruth's records—for consecutive scoreless innings pitched in the World Series. Mantle came up for his second at-bat of the scoreless game in the top of the fourth inning. "He could barely stand," *Los Angeles Times* columnist Jim Murray would write. "…he hit one off the center-field fence but barely made first base like a guy crawling with an arrow in his back. 'Look at his pants!' someone cried. They were covered with blood. He was hemorrhaging." With Ford having broken the Babe's pitching record, Mantle came out of the game for a pinch-runner. The Yankees would win the World Series the next day, and fly home with yet another championship.

It had been a glorious season for Mickey, surpassed only by his Triple Crown year and his largely overlooked 1957 season. Perhaps even more significantly, it had changed the public perception of Mickey Mantle. Having been tested through a decade of boos and indifference, Mickey now saw himself finally accepted by New York as its hero. For Mantle, this newfound popularity was an important crossing of a personal threshold: his undeniable acceptance by New York fans.

"After Roger beat me in the home run race in 1961, I could do no wrong," Mickey said. "Everywhere I went I got standing ovations. All I had to do was walk out on the field. Hey, what the hell? It's a lot better than having them boo you... I became the underdog. They hated him and liked me."

Ultimately, it may have been part of Maris' legacy to make Mantle finally appreciated even by his critics, who could have more easily accepted Mickey breaking Ruth's record—Stengel had said he was the next Ruth, hadn't he?—than someone they considered an "imposter," as sportswriter Frank Deford described Maris.

"Ironically, Mantle was always going to be a Hall of Famer, a great Yankee," observed broadcaster Bob Costas. "Maris needed the record, this season, to have a place in history."

The fans' resentment of Maris would build over the coming years. Part of it was over breaking Babe Ruth's home run record. Part of it, too, was over surpassing Mantle, or, at least, one of the expectations of Mantle. Mickey was the prodigal son who could abuse his gifts and great expectations, but some New Yorkers had adopted him as their native son—a Yankee, who, like DiMaggio and Berra and Gehrig, had been with the team from the start of his major league career. However, the feelings toward both Maris and Mantle were not limited to New

York. Maris had broken one of the game's most defiant records, and the next spring he was booed by hard-core Babe Ruth fans around the league and in Detroit he was even pelted with garbage from the right-field seats. In spring training in 1962, Maris stuck to his brooding, anti-press stance, and also caught barbs when he refused to pose for a picture with Rogers Hornsby, the three-time .400 hitter of another era. "He called me a bush leaguer," said Maris. It was true. Hornsby took a dim view of a player who had never hit .300 in his life now being called the new home run champion. Hornsby said bluntly, "He has no right to break Babe Ruth's record."

Mickey basked in the new acceptance. If he hadn't gotten what he wanted, maybe this is what he had needed. The 1961 season had brought out Mantle's utter unpretentiousness. Both Maris and Mantle had come to the major leagues as small-town kids. However, in his record-setting season, Maris came off in public as sullen and spoiled—Mantle as aw-shucks and unaffected. Mantle could be endearing, without even trying. On a visit to Disneyland one time, Mickey agreed to pose for Disneyland publicity photos with a menagerie of Disney characters. All smiles and cooperative, Mantle heard the photographer say, "Goofy, move a little to the right, please." Mickey gladly obliged, only to have the photographer quickly say, "No, not you, Mr. Mantle. I meant Goofy."

Understandably, in the years after 1961, Mantle would have broken the new Roger Maris home run record if it had been something sports fans could have voted on. Head-to-head, Mickey Mantle or Roger Maris, who should own what was once Babe Ruth's home run record? It would have been a landslide victory for The Mick.

...but I think that if I get to play another 12 to 14 years, that I'll break Babe Ruth's record....

When Mantle said that in 1956, who would have guessed that Mickey's best years wouldn't last as long as might have been imagined? He wouldn't go out on a streak of World Series championships like DiMaggio. He wouldn't have final seasons rivaling Ted Williams. Who would believe that after 1961, he would play only seven more years, and he would be only a shell of himself in his final four seasons? There was one more World Series championship, in 1962, and three more World Series home runs in 1964, raising his unmatched career total to 18. Mickey hit 35 home runs and drove in 111 runs, batting .303 in that 1964 season, arguably deserving of what would have been his fourth MVP Award. He finished runner-up to the Orioles, Brooks Robinson. In 1962, Mantle belted 30 home runs, drove in 89 runs, and batted .321.

But each time fans sensed what might have been a historic last hurrah—and Mickey's long-destined triumphant assault on Ruth's, er, Maris' home run record—the injury bug sidelined him.

May 18, 1962. On the final out of a game the Yankees lost to the Twins 4–3, with the tying run on second base, Mantle hit a low line drive on one hop to the shortstop, Zoilo Versalles. Versalles bobbled the ball and Mantle, seeing this, strained for more speed.

"I was watching the shortstop," said coach Wally Moses. "When I looked for Mantle he was already down."

"It looked as if he'd been shot," said Bob Fishel, the Yankee publicist. "He hit the ground that hard."

What Mantle had done was tear a muscle—the adductor muscle, the doctor said later—in his right thigh, so that he could not straighten his leg. When he fell he landed smack on his left knee, and as the weeks passed, it was this knee that bothered Mantle most. Mantle lay on the base path for five minutes before he was helped off the field. Inside the locker room he showered while leaning on crutches, then dressed slowly. His face looked gray and tortured. As he left, he managed to muster a smile for reporters. "See y'all," he said. Then, the grin gone, he went outside, where Yankees co-owner Dan Topping was waiting to take him to the hospital.

Mantle was hospitalized several days and then went home to Dallas to stay with his wife, Merlyn, and four sons. He had been there about a week, getting daily therapy from Wayne Rudy, the trainer of the Dallas Texans football team, when Yankee general manager Roy Hamey asked him to rejoin the team. "I won't say the players are brooding about him," Hamey explained at the time, "but maybe they'll feel better if he's around."

Mantle met the team in Los Angeles, where Bobby Richardson recalled: "He was sitting there in the bus by himself when I first saw him. I just walked up to him and shook his hand. It's hard to explain, but just seeing him gave me a lift." The Yankees won two out of three games from Los Angeles to tie for the league lead.

"I got you into first place," cracked Mantle as the team flew back to New York. "Now you're on your own."

Mantle's knee seemed to take forever to heal, and manager Ralph Houk cloaked his worry in forced humor. One evening before a night game, Houk was talking to Mantle and some other Yankees in the locker room.

"I don't see why you can't run stiff-legged," he told Mantle. Houk straightened his left leg and took off down the length of the room, disappearing into the showers. Mantle almost fell over laughing so hard. When Houk reappeared seconds later, he was still running with one leg stiff.

"I can go pretty good this way," he said.

When Mantle returned, he led the Yankees to their 27th pennant and a World Series victory over the Giants, winning his third MVP

Award. But he played only 123 games, many of those while still hobbling. The milestone season would have to wait.

June 5, 1963. In a game against the Orioles in Baltimore, Mantle chased a long fly ball hit by Brooks Robinson that was sailing high toward a chain-link fence. As Mickey jumped, crashing into the wall, he hooked his cleats in the chain-link fence and ricocheted back, causing the front part of his foot to bend violently up and back. He had broken a bone in his foot and was fitted with a knee-high plaster cast, sidelined and out of the lineup for 61 games. The season was a loss. Mantle played in 65 games and had a mere 213 plate appearances.

"With all of the injuries, coupled with the deteriorating legs, no doubt I could have called in sick and stayed away from the ballpark," Mickey wrote of that time in his autobiography. "Yet somehow I'd get myself up one more time, and still another, thinking that by some miracle, it would all come back. No more hurting, no more wobbly knees, no sore shoulders, no aches and pains anywhere. Foolish, but that's how it was."

19
Encore

"I guess I did something evidently that was sacred, something I wasn't supposed to do."

—ROGER MARIS

HOW DO YOU FOLLOW BREAKING THE GREATEST SPORTS RECORD OF THE 20th century? You don't. Not even Babe Ruth could. He did slug 54 homers in 1928, and the Yankees repeated as World Series champions, as did the Maris-Mantle team in 1962. But it would be four years before Ruth and Gehrig won another pennant and World Series title. What was it Roger Maris said to reporters when he arrived at spring training in 1962? "This was the first time in 34 years that someone hit 60 home runs. Anybody who expects me to do it again must have rocks in his head." The Yankees of Maris and Mantle would reel off five consecutive American League pennants, and their World Series crowns were only one fewer than what the Ruth-Gehrig teams won. Ah, what might have been, had Whitey Ford pitched three times in the 1960 series, as he should have?

It was no coincidence that the last three good years of Mantle's career were also the last three good ones of the Yankees dynasty that Mickey and Roger Maris helped sustain. In 1962, he won his third

MVP Award, even though he did not lead the league in home runs, average, or RBI. However, Yankee publicist Jackie Farrell may have summed up Mantle's impact when he said, "What did he lead the league in? He led the league in manhood, that's what." Playing in only 123 games because of various injuries, Mantle still hit 30 home runs, collected a .321 average, and drove in 89 runs. It was enough to make Mickey the team's first $100,000-a-year player since Joe DiMaggio.

The 1963 season, however, turned out to be almost a microcosm of Mickey's career, filled with great promise and dashed by injury. That spring was one in which Mantle befriended Pete Rose, a young Cincinnati Reds rookie who impressed Mickey when he saw him running to first base on a walk during an exhibition game. Mickey called Rose "Charlie Hustle"—a nickname that would stick to the future all-time hits leader throughout his career. Despite increasing pain and swelling in his legs, Mickey started off enjoying another solid season and seemed headed toward another MVP-caliber year. On May 22 that season, Mantle even hit a pitch from Bill Fischer of the Athletics that struck the façade atop the right-field upper deck and nearly became the only fair ball ever hit out of the old Yankee Stadium. Modern analytics later determined that this home run had left Mickey's bat at an angle of 27 degrees with a velocity of 124 miles an hour, making it one of the hardest-hit balls in baseball history— and would have traveled 503 feet if it had completed its flight and landed on River Avenue outside the Stadium. But then a few games later Mantle broke his foot when he caught it on a chain-link fence in Baltimore as he tried to make a leaping catch of a ball hit by the Orioles' Brooks Robinson.

One of the great laments of Mantle's career—and what might have been, if not for the injuries—is that he historically misused his rehabilitation time while he was on the disabled list, in part because his great athletic ability allowed him to get away with it. The 1963 injury was yet another example. Three and a half months after the injury, as he was completing his half-hearted rehab, Mickey and Whitey went to have dinner at a farm outside Baltimore that belonged to friends of the Mantles. They drank into the night, sleeping there, and then had to drive straight to the ballpark the next morning. In the clubhouse, Whitey put Mickey in the showers and then in the whirlpool, trying to get him presentable just to sit on the bench during the game. During batting practice, former teammate Hank Bauer, now coaching for the Orioles, couldn't help but notice that Mickey was in terrible shape. Mantle assured him he would be okay because he wouldn't be playing. Both Mickey and Whitey then made certain to stay far away from Yankee manager Ralph Houk. When the game began, Mantle hid under a pair of sunglasses and napped on the far end of the bench. But in the eighth inning, Mickey was awakened by Whitey, sitting on the bench next to him.

"Wake up, wake up," Whitey whispered to him. "Houk's coming."

Houk walked down from the other end of the bench. "Can you hit, Mick?" he asked.

"I'm not eligible," Mickey replied. "I'm on the disabled list."

"No, you're not," Houk said. "You went on the active list today."

Mickey began moving around preparing to pinch hit. He didn't want to tell his manager that he was so hungover that he couldn't see straight, and Houk hadn't picked up that Mickey was in no shape to play. At first, Mickey couldn't find his cap until Whitey realized he had been sitting on it. Mickey's cap looked as rumpled as he felt, and he found a batting helmet to put over it. Whitey was behind him when Mickey picked out one of his bats.

"Mick," Ford said, "hit the first pitch you see."

In the Orioles' dugout, Bauer walked over to Billy Hitchcock, Baltimore's manager, to confer about Mickey. Moments later, with Mickey at the plate, the Orioles called a time out so that Bauer could talk to pitcher Mike McCormick on the mound. Bauer advised McCormick that Mantle was just off the disabled list and hungover to boot. Bauer told McCormick that Mickey would never be able to get around on a fastball.

Following Whitey's advice, Mantle swung at McCormick's first pitch—a head-high fastball—and hit it out of the park. He circled the bases with Bauer looking on from the Orioles' dugout in stunned silence. In the Yankee dugout, Mickey slumped back down on the bench next to Whitey.

"Kid, great hit," said Whitey. "I dunno how you hit that."

"Hitting the ball was easy," Mickey shot back. "Running around the bases was the tough part."

In a sense, then, Mantle hadn't changed from the man and the player he had been since his rookie season. He was older, of course, and his body remained banged up and sore. Perhaps if he had been a more introspective person, dealing with the 1961 season might have been nearly impossible. Coming so close to accomplishing the goal everyone—even Mantle himself—had set for him, and then seeing someone else actually reach it, well, hell, some would say that wouldn't only be a monumental disappointment but also incomprehensible to deal with.

When Mickey returned to Dallas in late October 1961, he sank into a depression that no amount of alcohol could help. In our conversations of a decade later, he said he couldn't even get drunk enough to get the 1961 season out of his mind. He kept reliving the good, the bad, and the ridiculous. He seethed with the anger he had controlled during the season. He was no fan of Casey Stengel, but he now actually felt he would have been better off with the flexible lineup Stengel had employed in 1960. Casey had flipped Mickey and Roger from No. 3 and cleanup depending on the opposing pitcher, so that Mantle hadn't batted behind Maris most of the time in 1960. Maris batted cleanup in 288 plate appearances, with Mantle batting third in 296 plate appearances. Starting September 6, 1960, Stengel batted Mickey lower in the lineup than Roger every game and then straight through the seven-game 1960 World Series. In 1961, Mantle batted cleanup in every game he started. Mickey now wondered if he shouldn't have said something about that. He said he thought about calling Houk and raising the issue, but he didn't. However, he had called Mel Allen and complained to him about the Dr. Jacobson he sent him to. Allen was apologetic, Mickey recalled, but maintained that this doctor also treated the president of the United States.

What finally brought Mickey a sense of perspective and peace was his home in the Preston Hollow section of North Dallas, where the Mantles had lived since 1958. The Mantle home was a four-bedroom beige house on an acre of emerald green with an inviting swimming pool separating two wings wrapping around it. To a newcomer, the house with its beige upon beige décor could redefine Mickey Mantle, for it had a casual elegance about it that looked lived in, but also showed the distinctive touch of someone who loved him and knew that the home had to be as impressive as the American hero who lived there. The trophy room in the back of the house was reminiscent of those you would find in the athletics hall of any major university, filled with glass cases stuffed with shining hardware of all their teams' accomplishments. That is, until you realized these trophies weren't of one team but of one athlete. The most special of these were the American League MVP Awards, the Silver Bat Award for winning the

1956 American League batting title, the 1956 Hickok Belt, and, of course, the Triple Crown trophy signifying his greatest achievement.

In the fall of 1961, Mickey Mantle basked in remembering the glory of what had once been and could possibly be again. Ah, 1956. Mickey would always be able to look back and see 1956 as clearly as if it had been yesterday. The effect was sobering, as if memories of 1956 were an antidote to all the dashed dreams of the future.

"I was seeing the ball all season long like it was the size of a fucking grapefruit," Mickey told me years later. "And I mean all fucking season long, like I had fucking binoculars on, and I could read fucking [American League President] William Harridge's signature on the fucking ball as if it were three inches high. When I could see a pitch that well, there's no way I wasn't going to hit the shit out of it. Hell, Opening Day [Washington Senators pitcher] Camilo Pascual threw me two curveballs down and in, and I could read the writing on those balls like they were standing still on a [batting] tee. And whop! I planted each of them 500 feet. I knew then this was going to be a fucking great season like no other."

As he was talking, a man carrying his toddler daughter, while holding the small hand of his young son, approached our booth in a café in North Dallas, and Mickey straightened himself as he usually did when he met young fans.

"Mr. Mantle, excuse me for intruding on you like this," the man said, "but I wanted my son to meet you, if that would be all right with you."

"Of course," said Mantle, fixing that familiar grin on his face and holding out his right hand to the boy. "Good to meet you. My name's Mickey."

"Mine is, too, sir," said the boy.

Mickey's eyes lit up. "I like the name, son," he said.

"He's named after you, Mr. Mantle," the man said. "The greatest Yankee of them all."

Mantle appeared speechless as he signed his autograph for the boy on the back of an empty receipt stub a passing waitress gave him. He wrote: "To another Mickey. Your friend, Mickey Mantle, Triple Crown, 1956."

Mickey would come alive when he talked about 1956. Who could blame him? At the time, he was only the 12th player to win baseball's elusive Triple Crown—leading a league in batting average, home runs, and runs batted in. Only a handful have accomplished that in the true modern era, since the integration of the once all-White game in 1947, and Mantle's numbers that season are truly astounding: a .353 batting average, 130 RBI, and 52 homers, including a chase for most of the season of Babe Ruth's home run record at the time. Mickey had at last fulfilled expectations. He was the king of New York. "Mickey who?" teased a song by Teresa Brewer, who popped to the top of the 1950s hit parade with perky, relentlessly cheerful tunes. "The fella with the celebrated swing."

It seemed, in listening to him talk, that Mickey knew that 1956 season by heart. In less than a month that April, he batted .415, slugged four home runs, drove in 15 runs, and scored 10 runs. May turned into an even better month, beginning with home runs in three straight games. Then came May 5, his second multi-homer game of the season, with his second homer ricocheting high off the right-field façade. It was the first of three career home runs he hit off that façade, nearly leaving Yankee Stadium. Mickey's May onslaught didn't let up: Four more home runs in the next dozen games, followed by multiple homer outings, 4-for-4 and 5-for-5 showings, home runs from both sides of the plate, and finishing the month by belting homers in three straight games. The last of those, on May 30, came within 18 inches of clearing Yankee Stadium. While he had almost done that on May 5, this one had been an even more prodigious blast, still on an upward trajectory when it hit the façade in right field. Had it not, according to Yankee publicists at the time, it would have traveled over 600 feet.

"Mantle's got more power than any hitter I ever saw—including the Babe," Yankee coach Bill Dickey said on Opening Day and repeated again. Ah, the Babe. Always, it seemed, the Babe loomed over any discussion of Mickey, his potential, and the expectations. Even in his rookie season, Ruth's widow, Claire, wanted to meet the young rookie who was being mentioned as another Babe Ruth. She invited Mickey to her home, where she treated him to milk and cookies while she showed him all of the Babe's memorabilia. Mantle took particular interest in one of Ruth's famous bats, surprised by its extraordinarily heaviness, and holding it much of that afternoon.

Claire Ruth would make an effort to briefly visit with Mickey during each of her yearly trips to Yankee Stadium. She seemed to sense that there was something unique in Mantle for all the fuss that was made of him each spring and an anticipated new assault on Ruth's single-season home run record. The oversized expectations that Casey Stengel placed on Mickey as a rookie—and the inevitable disappointment—may have been best summed up by sportswriter Milton Gross, who wrote: "Mantle was to be the monument the old gent wanted to leave behind. Casey wanted his own name written in the record books as manager, but he also wanted a creation that was completely his own on the field every day, doing things no other ballplayer ever did, rewriting all the records."

In 1955, those following Mantle and the Yankees got a glimpse that a special season like 1956 was just waiting to explode. Mickey won the first of his four home run championships, and on May 13 he had the only three-homer game in his career and first switch-hit homer game—one righty and two lefty. He also hit the first of his only two All-Star Game home runs, tagging the Phillies' Robin Roberts for a three-run shot. By September of 1955, Mickey seemed certain to become the first Yankee to hit 40 home runs since DiMaggio in 1937. But in mid-September, while trying to bunt for a hit, Mickey tore a muscle in his right thigh. It was an injury that may have cost the Yankees the World Series championship when they met the Dodgers. Mantle missed the first two games. He homered in a Yankees loss in Game 3, but could play in only two of the final four games, appearing in one of those games as a pinch-hitter.

"I was an All-Star, but, fuck, let's face it—other than some moments here and there, I had some pretty shitty seasons on the whole," Mantle said in an interview a couple of years after his retirement. "The whole fucking world was waiting for me to do great things, to carry on the legacy of Ruth, Gehrig, and DiMaggio, and here's Mickey Mantle, the next great Yankee not even hitting 40 home runs. Fuck, not even 30 home runs in those first four seasons. Who the fuck was I kidding?"

Then came 1956. For Mantle, the Triple Crown year marked the time of his life when promise and potential would be fulfilled with a season that, in its own way, only raised expectations even higher. There were no signs, though, early in the season to suggest that this would be the year that Mantle would emerge as the Yankee superstar to finally make many fans forget the great DiMaggio. The season didn't begin easily. In spring training, Mantle reinjured the hamstring that had spoiled the homestretch of 1955. But the previous season had been a learning experience for Mantle. He hadn't understood how he could have led the Yankees in most offensive categories but yet teammate Yogi Berra ended up as the league's MVP. Mickey had outhit Yogi by 34 points, had slugged 10 more home runs than Berra, and driven in just nine fewer runs than the Yankee catcher. Mantle wasn't sure what to make of that until just weeks before the start of spring training when he asked the Yankees' assistant general manager, Bill DeWitt.

"Look, I was glad to see Yogi got the MVP Award," he told DeWitt. "There's no better guy in the world than Yogi. But I'm just wondering: What's a guy have to do to be considered most valuable?"

"Well, Mickey, I'm glad you asked me this," DeWitt said. "You may not know this, Mickey, but when the baseball writers are deciding who's been most valuable, they take other things into account. Maybe a ballplayer has to do more than have a good season on the field. Maybe he has to win a little personal popularity. Maybe he has to put out a little effort. Maybe he can't brush off every newspaperman who approaches him, or just clam up on him. Maybe he must make a real effort to be a little cooperative… You've got to come out of that shell."

It was no secret that Mantle had contentious relationships with many of the writers who covered the Yankees, and word had gotten around the league. Mickey was also shy and didn't like talking about himself. DeWitt explained that he was no longer a rookie, but a team leader who needed to make the extra effort to cooperate with the press. He could no longer be rude and unfriendly or cut off reporters with curt, one-word answers. In spring training, it quickly became obvious that Mantle had turned a page in his dealings with the press. He was also trying to be more patient and selective at the plate, which even opposing players noticed.

"I saw Mantle looked different down in St. Petersburg," said Musial. "It was the first time [since 1951] that he'd ever looked real sharp in the spring. He'd always struck out a lot before, but this year he was letting the bad pitches go by. And he hit a lot of real long homers even down there, where the background isn't good for hitting. If he hits .400 or 60 home runs this season, I can't say I'll be surprised. He has all the qualifications."

Mantle especially had the qualifications to take on Babe Ruth's legendary home run record.

In the 29 years since Ruth's record-setting season with the 1927 Yankees, several players had challenged the home run mark, but all had faded during the second half of the season. In 1932, Jimmie Foxx had 41 home runs by the end of July, but had finished with 58 home runs. Ruth himself had 30 home runs by the end of June in two other seasons but had been unable to surpass his own record. By mid-summer of 1956, Mantle's pace in the challenge of Ruth's record began to slacken, in part because of increasing pain in his chronically ailing right knee. In July, he hit only a handful of home runs but bounced back in August by hitting 13. In August, even president Dwight Eisenhower joined the Mantle frenzy. He attended a Yankees game against the Senators at Griffith Stadium, where he asked Mantle to hit a home run for him. In the seventh inning, Mantle obliged. Mickey went into September with 47 home runs, needing 14 homers to break Ruth's record.

Had he been healthy, Mickey might have made a stronger assault against the Babe. Mantle, though, pulled a groin muscle while he was running the bases during the first week of September and didn't homer in the first 10 games of the month. He had been leading in all three categories of the Triple Crown, but soon was passed by Ted Williams in the batting average race. At the age of 38, the Splendid Splinter was on the verge of ruining Mantle's chances at winning the Triple Crown. Mickey was now also pressing, swinging at bad pitches outside the strike zone. Each time he struck out or popped up weakly, he exploded with profanity-laced temper tantrums and wild attacks on the dugout water cooler. The ghost of Babe Ruth was getting to him. Mantle spiraled into an awful 5-for-37 slump, his worst of the season. Mickey Mantle added his name to those who had pursued Ruth into September and failed. He did not hit his 50th home run until

September 17, an extra-inning shot off of White Sox left-hander Billy Pierce at Comiskey Park. It was just his third homer of the month, though it clinched the pennant for the Yankees. But with the pressure of Ruth's record off his shoulders, Mickey could focus on his head-to-head batting average race with Williams. Though nursing the muscle pull, Mantle was leading Williams by four points going into the final series of the season, in which the Yankees hosted the Red Sox. It was one of the few times that Stengel wanted to keep him out of the lineup to rest him for the World Series, but Mickey insisted on playing.

"I didn't want to be sitting on the bench with the batting title at stake," Mantle said afterward.

Mickey connected for his 52nd home run in the first game and only pinch-hit in the second game, where he added an RBI when he walked with the bases loaded. Meanwhile, Williams got only one hit in the first two games and then conceded the batting title to Mantle by exiting the season finale after a first-inning walk. Mickey drove in a run on a pinch-hit ground ball. He finished the season batting .353, beating Williams by eight points. Mantle's pinch-hit run batted in was his 130th of the season, allowing him to nudge out the Tigers' Al Kaline by two RBI.

Mickey Mantle had won the Triple Crown. He was the first Triple Crown winner since Ted Williams in 1947.

When the Yankees won the World Series for their 17th championship, Mickey Mantle's greatest season was in the history books.

20
Passing the Torch

"Even I, a simple ballplayer, know that generations die, though it's reputations—it's legacies that endure, if they endure, to other generations."

—MICKEY MANTLE

QUITE SIMPLY, THERE WAS NO OTHER ROADSIDE ATTRACTION IN AMERICA quite like Mickey Mantle, even one fading in talent as he was in the 1960s. The young George W. Bush would rather have been Mickey than president of the United States. "Growing up a fan of Mickey Mantle, all I ever wanted to be was a Major League Baseball player and another Mickey Mantle," Bush told me in a 1999 interview. "Ask any of my old friends from that time, and they'll likely tell you that's all I ever talked about." That's how much Mantle meant to him. Bush remembered the most memorable experience of his freshman year at Yale being the April day in 1965 that he left the campus and boarded a flight for Houston. When his mother, Barbara, picked him up at Hobby Airport, she could barely contain her own excitement. She was treating her son to the first game to be played at the Astrodome, the world's first domed stadium billed as the "Eighth Wonder of the

World" by the Astros' original owner, former Harris County Judge Roy Hofheinz.

"I've got the best seats in the house for us," she told her son. Fittingly, some would say for the Bushes, a family with its roots in Connecticut, the Astros were playing the Yankees. The New York Yankees were the most storied team in baseball, and their aging superstar Mickey Mantle, of course, was one of George's favorite players.

"Great, Mom," said Bush, who was then 18. "I can't wait."

"They're called skyboxes."

Years later, Bush would shake his head when he recalled that day and arriving at one of the Astrodome's 53 luxurious skybox suites. "We got up in the skybox," he said. "It was the very top of the Astrodome. The players looked like ants. I said, 'Mom, these may be wonderful seats, but where are the players?'"

I can brag that my dad and I had better seats than the future governor and president, a high school graduation gift from my friends and bosses at the *Waco Tribune-Herald*, my hometown newspaper, whose sports staff I had joined that spring. We had box seats four rows behind the Yankees dugout along the third-base foul line. The day was April 9, 1965, and a visibly ailing Mickey Mantle, inserted as the Yankees' leadoff hitter for the occasion, officially became the first batter in the new Astrodome. Batting left-handed against right-hander Turk Farrell, Mantle ripped the game's second pitch into center field for the first hit in Houston's wondrous new stadium.

Then, leading off the sixth inning, Mickey came to bat again against Farrell and was tempted to do something he had rarely done since learning to be a switch-hitter as a child. In the on-deck circle, Mantle assumed a stance he would have taken in the right-handed hitter's batting box at home plate—of course, a no-no against a righty like Farrell, a lesson which had been hammered into him by his father

Mutt Mantle, who once sent him home in tears from a youth game for disobeying him on this. But Mutt Mantle had been dead since 1952, and Mick was hurting badly. He was in agonizing pain not only from his right knee, which caused him to noticeably limp when he ran the bases, but also from an aggravated injury to his right shoulder. It was the old right shoulder injury Mantle first suffered in the 1957 World Series when Milwaukee Braves second baseman Red Schoendienst had fallen on him during a botched pickoff play. It was an injury that reduced the strength in Mickey's once-powerful throwing arm over the remainder of his career and affected his hitting as well, especially when he batted left-handed. So this being merely an exhibition, Mantle momentarily thought about finishing the game batting right-handed to rest his aching shoulder. But he didn't

"I was kinda surprised no one made a big deal over me taking right-handed practice cuts while I waited for Turk to finish his warmups," Mickey later said. "I gotta admit the idea did cross my mind, but I wasn't gonna do that then. This was a game where the star really was the stadium, the Astrodome, with air-conditioning and an enclosed roof, and it was like a presidential inauguration or a Hollywood movie premiere. President Johnson and Lady Bird were there. The governor of Texas, John Connally, who had been almost killed with President Kennedy in Dallas just a couple of years earlier, was there and threw out the first pitch. This was maybe the biggest baseball event ever in Texas. Johnny Keane, who was from Houston, was our new manager and when he tells me I'm going to bat leadoff, he says, 'Mick, you have the who's who of Texas here to see you.' I said, 'Don't fuck with me, Johnny, you know goddamn well they're here to see the Astrodome.'"

Mickey Mantle himself was partly in the Astrodome that night for the same reason. There was nothing like the Astrodome anywhere else in America, or the world, for that matter. The sensation to player and fan alike was much the same. Imagine putting a full-size baseball stadium, yes, even like Yankee Stadium, inside a facility that was big enough to accommodate it. Then imagine it all enclosed, with a roof, and air-conditioning that made it feel like you were inside some gigantic modern business office. Players couldn't stop staring at the domed roof that looked like the top of a flying saucer. Late that afternoon during batting practice, Mickey and Roger Maris even tried to hit balls off the roof. They couldn't.

The capacity crowd that streamed into Astrodome were equally fascinated, spell-bound almost and gawking. But in the sixth inning, Mantle managed to turn the attention of a crowd of 47,876 on to himself as he swung at a Farrell fastball that exploded off the sweet spot of his bat with a ferocious, rifle-shot-like crack that had never been heard indoors. *KAAHH*-WHACK! The sound reverberated and echoed throughout the Astrodome—*KAAHH*-WHACK! *KAAHH*-WHACK!—showing this to be not the acoustics of old baseball stadiums with their murky, outdated public-address systems, but a state-of-the-art concert-hall quality for an indoor stadium scheduled to soon host a Broadway-like extravaganza featuring Judy Garland. So imagine the sound of a thunderous home run smacked at Carnegie Hall, with a symphony of *KAAHH*-WHACK! *KAAHH*-WHACK! *KAAHH*-WHACK! The sound of the bat-on-ball collision had tantalized fans since the days when Babe Ruth popularized the home run, and they could never quite get enough. And it was different when it was a home run concert by Mickey Mantle. "I had never heard such an explosive sound of bat on ball as a ball I heard hit by Mickey," former Detroit Tiger pitcher Johnny James said when Mantle homered off him in 1958. "It was by far the most awesome sound I'd heard before or since, nor had I ever seen a ball leave a ballpark so quickly.

It happened so fast I wasn't sure I actually saw what I thought I had seen."

That night Mantle's powerful home run off Farrell carried deep over the 406-feet sign in center field, creating a furor that might have been expected if the homer had been hit by a Houston Astros player. Almost instantly a giant electronic sign displaying the word "TILT" flashed on the Astrodome's monstrous scoreboard, and deafening applause, whooping, and hollering exploded in the crowd as Mickey rounded the bases in his familiar gait, even with the noticeable limp. There was no showboat standing at home watching the flight of the ball, no hot-dogging bat flip, no celebratory arm pump or hamming around the bases. Mickey had never shown up a pitcher off whom he'd just homered, and he wasn't starting now. As soon as he hit that ball, he ran hard out of the box with his head down and only started slowing up a little as he rounded second. Much of the Astrodome crowd was on its feet cheering. It took Mantle 17 seconds to circle the bases, the same brisk home run trot he would make if he were playing at Yankee Stadium—and, living in Dallas since the 1950s, it was almost as if he were playing at home.

Some fans at the Astrodome may have also sensed that Mickey, although only 33 years of age, was now in the twilight of his extraordinary career. His injuries had kept him out of spring training games leading up to the Astrodome opener. He was also playing left field, having given up his familiar center field to the younger, healthier Tom Tresh. Nevertheless, the looming decline, for Mantle, Maris, and the Yankee dynasty, would be remarkably sudden, given that they had been in 12 of the 14 World Series since Mickey's rookie year in 1951— and had won seven championships. In 1965, though, Mantle's home runs would drop off to 19 from the previous year's 35, and his runs batted in would dramatically fall from 111 to 46. Not to mention that his batting average that season of .255 would be the worst of his career to that point.

So steep a fall from so incredible a rise. Mickey couldn't have realized that he had seen his last hurrah in the 1964 World Series against the St. Louis Cardinals. It came in Game 3, on Saturday, October 10, in a packed Yankee Stadium. The game was tied 1–1 because of Mickey's error in right field in the fifth inning. Leading off the bottom of the ninth, Mantle turned to catcher Elston Howard, who was on deck, and said: "You might as well go in and start getting dressed. I'm going to hit his first pitch for a home run."

Cardinals manager Johnny Keane, who brought in veteran knuckleball reliever Barney Schultz to pitch the ninth, had just sat down when he heard the dreaded blast of a bat on a ball. Having called his shot, Mickey smacked Schultz's first pitch, a knuckleball, that Cardinal catcher Tim McCarver said "dangled like bait to a big fish… [and] lingered in that area that was down, and Mickey was a lethal low-ball hitter left-handed. The pitch was so slow that it allowed him to turn on it and pull it." The ball shot off Mantle's bat and towered majestically deep well into the third deck of Yankee Stadium. Mickey's only World Series walk-off homer, it broke Babe Ruth's World Series home run record. It would be one of Mantle's finest World Series: three home runs, eight runs batted in, and a magnificent OPS (on-base plus slugging percentage) of 1.258. But the Yankees lost in seven games in what would be Mickey's last World Series and the end of a dynasty. The Yankees would not be in the World Series again until 1976.

Mantle had not seen the swift demise of his career coming, nor the Yankees' unceremonious downfall, he later said. He thought he still had another three or four productive years ahead of him. His bad shoulder prevented him from playing center field effectively, but he thought he had already begun making a transition to Yankee Stadium's notoriously difficult left field. In the 1965 season, however, even his ability at the plate mysteriously abandoned him. It was also as if his troubles were a reflection of his team. Just as critical were a series of injuries that continued to beset Roger Maris, the man who had beaten Mantle in their remarkable 1961 home run duel.

Could that have been just four years earlier? All the aches and pains made it feel like that had been an eternity ago. In retrospect, the 1961 New York Yankees were one of the greatest teams in history, challenging the acclaim long accorded the Babe Ruth–Lou Gehrig Murderers' Row legends of 1927. In some minds, the Mickey Mantle–Roger Maris team was even better. Roger Maris would win the M&M Boys competition to break Ruth's near-sacred single-season home run record, but this was clearly Mantle's Yankees. New manager Ralph Houk made sure of that early in the season, asking Mantle to actively assume the leadership role that was his in his teammates' minds.

"Mickey was such an unselfish teammate," said his wife, Merlyn, "that it's what helped Roger [Maris] deal with all the distractions and break Babe Ruth's record. Do you know what it took for someone who wanted to break that record, who was expected to break that record, to watch his teammate do it? And Mickey was sincere. He was rooting for Roger. He loved Roger. I think that home run contest was a test for Mickey, a test of his character, a test that showed his character and who he was. And, you know what? I think that might have been more important than for him to break Babe's record."

The Mantle and Maris bond would deepen and last until Roger's death. They were together at this Yankee team's great moment, and they were there together as they hit its lowest. In 1965, Maris would play in only 46 games. Still, Mickey didn't know if he could point to one single defining event that changed the Yankees' fortunes, although he did wonder if the Yankees' surprise firing of first-year manager

Yogi Berra a day after losing the 1964 World Series hadn't killed an important chemistry and continuity within the Yankees dynasty. Yogi had been no ordinary manager of the Yankees. His influence on the team transcended that role. Yogi had been with the Yankees since the post–World War II 1946 season. He had won 10 World Series championships as a Yankee—more than any other player in major league history. He was also a three-time American League MVP and an 18-time All-Star. Casey Stengel, Berra's manager during most of his playing career with the Yankees, once said, "I never play a game without my man." And the Yankee front office turned its back on him, for Johnny Keane, whom they fired early in his second season?

"We were never the same team again," Mickey said. "Say what you will, Yogi's firing changed everything."

If the Astrodome that April night offered any clue to the upcoming decline in the 1965 season, it may have been that, despite Mickey's historic homer, the Yankees lost 2–1 in extra innings. They would go on to finish the season with a record of 77–85, a stunning 25 games behind the Minnesota Twins. It marked the first season since 1925, Lou Gehrig's first season as a starter, that the Yankees failed to finish either above the .500 mark or in the first division. That disappointment, though, lay somewhere in the weeks and months to come. For that one night in Houston, Texas celebrated a new stadium's opening in unparalleled Lone Star fashion, in which the Astrodome and Mickey Mantle would be forever linked in history.

George W. told me that after the Astrodome game he didn't pay much attention to the 1965 baseball season until an early September morning when he glanced at a newspaper sports page that shocked him. "I kinda had to shake my head," he said, "because my first thought was, *Man, that was some kind of party [that previous night]*. I couldn't believe what I was reading. The Yankees were well out of the pennant race, and Mickey Mantle was batting like .250. These weren't the New York Yankees and the Mickey Mantle I'd grown up with. It took a moment to sink in."

Indeed, at the end of 1964, the backbone of the Yankee dynasty may have still seemed to be in place, apparently ready to continue its winning ways. Then, almost without warning, it all fell apart. Some blamed the Yankee decline on the organization's failure to develop Black ballplayers, with Elston Howard being the notable exception. In this, the Yankees were like their American League brethren. It had been National League teams that signed Willie Mays, Hank Aaron, Ernie Banks, Frank Robinson, Roberto Clemente, and many more in order to stay competitive with Jackie Robinson's Brooklyn Dodgers. This led to an unprecedented dominance in All-Star competition for the National League.

Others attributed the Yankees' collapse on the forced retirement of George Weiss as general manager. Without Weiss' direction, it was believed that the Yankee farm system had deteriorated and not been stockpiled with the talent he had secured in years past. Moreover, Weiss' successor had been unable to make the kinds of midseason player deals that had historically benefited the Yankees. Houk would do no better as general manager. The brilliance he had shown in managing and handling players on the field did not translate into success in the front office. The Yankees losing their predatory relationship with the Kansas City Athletics when Charles O. Finley bought the club in 1960 didn't help either. However, if any one decision can be singled out as a turning point in the Yankees' fortunes, it may well have been, as Mantle insisted, the decision to fire Berra as manager the day after the end of the 1964 World Series.

By most accounts, Houk had reached the decision to fire Yogi in August, but held off because the man he wanted to hire—and eventually did hire—St. Louis manager Johnny Keane was managing the Cardinals. A day after the series ended, the Yankees fired Berra and Keane resigned. Four days later, the Yankees hired Keane. It would prove to be a disaster for both Keane and the Yankees.

"He was absolutely the wrong guy," said Yankee pitcher—and later *Ball Four* author—Jim Bouton. "The players hadn't respected Yogi, but at least they liked him. Keane they didn't like or respect. Johnny was too old for us and too much of a traditionalist, and he never could get used to our outrageous habits and lifestyle."

Keane's fatal mistake with the players may have been not getting off to a good start with their hero and leader. Mantle's stature had grown not only among his own teammates, but among opponents as well. In part this was because of his personality, but it was also because of his sportsmanship and his utter refusal to strut or show off in any way. "Baseball has an unwritten law against such behavior," George F. Will would note years later. "Etched on every fan's mental retina is the archetypal sight of Mickey Mantle in his home run trot, with his head down, so as not to show up the pitcher." Once, when Detroit's Al Kaline was taunted by a youngster who said, "You're not half as good as Mickey Mantle," he replied, "Son, nobody is half as good as Mickey Mantle."

By the spring of 1965, Mickey was set in his ways, especially his drinking and partying, which even Stengel had never seriously tried or wanted to change. Keane was a religiously devout man who wanted his teams to comply with curfews, and who took spring training games with the seriousness of a rookie. When he saw that the Yankees, which the exception of Bobby Richardson and Tony Kubek, followed Mantle's example of after-hours carousing, he decided to squelch it by making an example of Mickey. Seeing Mantle hungover after a night of partying, Keane grabbed a fungo bat and a bag of balls and sent

Mickey out to center field to shag some flies. Keane emptied the ball bag, hitting ball after ball that forced Mantle to run in all directions. "I had been playing center field in the major leagues for 15 years—I knew how to catch fly balls," Mantle recalled. "I knew he wasn't providing instruction. He was trying to make me sick, trying to set an example. And I didn't like it."

Keane continued with his personal crusade to change Mantle by punishing him with outfield drills until Mickey finally tired of it. Keane happened to hit him a short fly ball that the hustling Mantle fielded on the run, and then threw as hard as he could at the head of his manager. The startled Keane ducked just in time and figured that Mantle knew how to play center field under any condition. "I kept my distance," said Mantle. "When we did talk, there were no arguments. More often than not, we had staring contests. Eventually, the situation got so bad that if I had been financially set, I would have retired at the end of the season."

That season the Yankees were also plagued by injuries, which wasn't unusual. But what was unusual was the manner in which Houk and Keane handled the injury situation and the team. Elston Howard was kept behind the plate despite an injured arm. Tony Kubek developed chronic back problems that forced him to retire at the end of the season at the age of 29. But possibly the biggest failure of the Yankees, as a team and a business, was failing to take care of Roger Maris, who when healthy was still their most potent hitter. When Maris broke his hand during the season, management deliberately kept the extent of the injury from him so that he would continue playing.

"I slid into home plate, jammed my fingers into the umpire's shoes," Maris told Yankee historian Peter Golenbock in a 1973 interview. "He was standing a little bit too close to the plate. This was in May. I dislocated two fingers, and they pulled the fingers back out and put them back in the joint. That was all right. We left New York the following day and went to Washington. The first time I took a swing in Washington something popped in my hand and that was it. That gave me a long vacation.

"We took x-rays in Washington. We took them in Minneapolis. We took them in New York. There was never any mention of a break, and at first I started out going into the field and taking infield and throwing a baseball. The ballclub, every four or five days, they would ask me to take batting practice. I'd try a few swings, and it didn't work, and it got to the point where I couldn't even throw a baseball, because I couldn't hold a baseball in my hand. And yet they were continuously asking me to take batting practice."

"Was this to get the fans to come to the ballpark when they saw you batting?" Golenbock asked.

"This I don't know," said Maris. "I can't speak for Ralph Houk, who was the general manager, or Johnny Keane, what the reasons were behind it. I can't speak for them. It's just something I've never understood: How I can go from May to the end of the season to find out I have a broken hand? Granted it wasn't broken and showing through. But I knew it was broken, and press-wise everybody was, 'Well, once again Roger Maris is just jaking.'"

21
The Last of the Racehorses

*"After Roger beat me in the home run race
in 1961, I could do no wrong. Everywhere
I went I got standing ovations."*

—MICKEY MANTLE

A HEALTHY MARIS ALONG WITH A HEALTHY MANTLE. WHO KNOWS WHAT might have happened? Maris would recover enough to play his final two seasons with the Cardinals, to whom he was traded, helping St. Louis win the 1967 and 1968 pennants and the 1967 World Series. In the 1967 World Series, Maris batted .385, with a home run and seven RBI, in what was the best World Series performance of his career. But then, Roger was still furious at the way he was treated by the Yankees even after he broke Babe Ruth's record—or possibly because he *had* broken Ruth's record.

He had played when hurt. Then when he was so hurt that he couldn't play, the Yankees had hidden from him the medical diagnosis that he had a broken hand and had the gall to accuse him of being a prima donna unwilling to suit up over a minor injury. Roger didn't become aware of the severity of his injury until September, two weeks before the end of the season, when his friend Julie Isaacson arranged for a private examination. Extensive x-rays detected a break at the base of his hand where a small piece had detached from the main portion of the bone. It was only when Maris told the Yankees he was leaving for home in Independence that general manager Ralph Houk came clean.

"Rog, I might as well level with you," Houk finally told Maris. "You need an operation on that hand."

Maris felt himself profoundly betrayed by Houk and the Yankee organization, which quickly tried to make it appear it was the team's doctors who had discovered the extent of the injury. The Yankees' medical staff may have known the severity of the injury, but only now were they making it public. "We had hoped that nature would reunite the hamate bone, which often happens," the team told the news media. "We had hoped surgery wouldn't be necessary, but when we saw that the hook was not going to rejoin the main bone, we decided to operate." Although he underwent surgery after the season, he was never again a serious power threat. Maris played in seven World Series in the 1960s, the most of any player in the decade. He batted .217 with six homers and 18 RBI in 41 Series games.

"I've always said I'm out there because it was the best way I knew to support my family," Roger told author Peter Golenbock in 1973. "And the only way I could support my family was to make good money. The only way I could get good money was to go out there and do the job. If I'm sitting on the bench jaking or otherwise, I'm not supporting my family. It's sort of stupid to have someone come up with something like that.... It takes all kinds. I know when I ran into the wall in the 1963 World Series—I played one game and a couple of innings—I hit the wall with my left arm and injured it to where it was about a month before I could do much with it. Then I read in the paper that after Ralph reviewed the World Series films, he said he now believes something was wrong with me. It's almost as though he was saying prior to that nothing was wrong with me. These are things you don't understand."

Maris wanted to retire after the 1966 season, but when he told Ralph Houk of his decision before the end of the season, Houk convinced him to wait to make the announcement. The Yankee front office assured him it had no plans to trade him and would let him retire, but in December he was dealt to St. Louis. Couldn't those damn Yankees ever deal truthfully with Roger Maris? To his credit, he would bounce back and, as a member of two more pennant-winning teams and another World Series champion, he would enjoy the proverbial last laugh.

Who could have imagined, though, that we had seen the best of Mickey Mantle or that he would be history in three more years? He began the year with 454 career home runs, and who hadn't thought that he would soon be nearing the magic 500 numbers? But by June, Mantle himself thought his career was over. His nagging injuries had worsened, and he was batting an un-Mickey Mantle .240. By then, the Yankees also had reluctantly concluded that this might be Mantle's final season. Forget ever coming close to Babe Ruth's career 714 home runs, 659 of them as a Yankee. It looked like Mickey might not even catch up to Lou Gehrig's career mark of 493 homers. So the Yankees decided to give Mickey a special day at the Stadium, an honor that had been bestowed on only four other players—Ruth, Gehrig, DiMaggio, and Berra.

"Mantle's Misery," *LIFE* magazine called the season in its July 30, 1965, issue. What underscored the frustration of Mantle and the Yankees hitting rock bottom was photo-journalist John Dominis' memorable photograph of Mickey flinging his batting helmet away in disgust, apparently shot during the first-ever "Bat Day" at Yankee

Stadium, packed with 72,244 fans for a June 20 doubleheader. "It isn't any fun when things are like this," Mickey is quoted in the story. "I'm only 33, but I feel like 40."

Writer John R. McDermott's portrait of Mantle is sympathetic but telling:

"All season long it has been this way, or worse. There was a night, for instance, when he stood in left field at Yankee Stadium, shackled to his two luckless legs, tensing his body for the next play. The pain had already started in his thighs and was throbbing through his elaborately bandaged knees. There was no longer enough cartilage in his knees to absorb the shock of running—and the pain would be almost unbearable if he suddenly had to change direction. He glanced behind him at the four-foot fence that borders left field and circles out toward center. A ball caroming off that concrete arc could make a fool of him. Left field, a new position for him, was full of hard and soft spots, subtle depressions and holes that could catch a spike and wrench his leg. There was a crackling and a ball arching up toward him. He forced himself to run in and to his right. But a younger player rushed out from the infield, screamed, and waved him off and pocketed the ball in his glove for the third out. Mantle jerked himself to a wincing stop. Then he jogged toward the dugout, taking small steps, running like a toy whose spring has wound down, his arms and elbows flopping as if to help take the weight off those legs."

Still, to fall so low after such a great height. Did the Yankees tank the 1965 season? No, it's unlikely, though the rhetorical question begs asking. Those Yankees had seven of the same everyday players as the 1964 Yankees, except for Roger Maris, whose injury limited him to 46 games. These Yankees had four-fifths of the previous season's starting rotation and, in essence, the same team back that had won 99 games in 1964, then lost the World Series to the Cardinals in seven games. But these Yankees were also plagued by age and overconfidence. Perhaps it took someone coming in from the outside to see the Yankees for how they really were. In 1965, that role belonged to journeyman catcher Howard Rodney Edwards, known as "Doc" Edwards, who was traded by the Kansas City Athletics to the Yankees to back up the aging Elston Howard. Edwards was in for a shock when he soon realized this was no longer the World Series team of recent memory.

"They were not the Mickey Mantle and the Whitey Ford and the Roger Maris that we knew," Edwards recalled. "They had reached a point in their lives where they were all hurt. You just don't take that many thoroughbreds and replace them with ponies—and, in my case, a draft horse—and win races. You just don't do it."

Enough also can't be said of how these were different times. America was breathing heavily on the neck of the '70s, the alchemically dreamy age that American author Tom Wolfe, the stylish sage of the New Journalism literary movement, had christened the "Me Decade." The Yankees' face of this age of varnished dandyism and self-promotion, of course, was Joe Pepitone. He was a respected three-time All-Star at first base who may be remembered as much for being the first major league ballplayer to bring a hair dryer into the locker room, as well as carrying a bag of hair products to control his rapidly balding head and not one, but two toupees. He had squandered his $25,000 bonus, enjoyed acting as the team clown, and had a reputation for partying as if he were Mickey Mantle. In his 1975 autobiography, *Joe, You Coulda Made Us Proud,* Pepitone famously claimed to having smoked marijuana and gotten stoned during the season in the '60s with the proverbial last boy himself, Mickey Mantle.

"He didn't like that too much," Pepitone said in a *Rolling Stone* interview. "In front of people, he'd tell them, 'That was bullshit, that would never happen!' But it was true! He came to my room, him and

Whitey [Ford], and they could smell the shit in the room. They said, 'We heard you do that shit. What's it like?' 'Well, try it!' 'Oh, no, no, no!' 'C'mon, take a hit!' They each took a hit. Next thing I know, they're talking to me about all kinds of shit, and they're laughing at anything I said. I could have had them jumping up and down on the bed, if I'd wanted to!"

In 1965, though, a clubhouse exchange between Mantle and the then-24-year-old Pepitone cut to the heart of one of the internal problems that may have led to the demise of the Yankee dynasty that season. In that incident, Pepitone walked into the clubhouse bragging about the balls he had slugged in batting practice when Mickey turned to him.

"You think that if everyone on this club is batting .195 and you're batting .200 that's all right, huh?" Mantle asked.

"Sure," said Pepitone, "I got to think about myself—it's the only way I'm going to make my money."

"Well, you keep batting .200," said Mantle, "and you'll make a lot of money, Jody."

Pepitone immediately shut up.

By this time, the Yankees were shell-shocked in a season gone wrong. Almost every major publication had picked the Yankees to win a sixth straight pennant. It shows what they knew. When heroes fade, it isn't with the drama of Achilles being killed by an arrow destined by the gods to the only mortal weakness of an otherwise immortal. Mortals, be they athletes or teams, just whimper quietly and go away. The Yankees in their history had witnessed this and relished it. Gehrig slid from superstar to spastic. Ruth was put out to pasture with a bankrupt team in Boston. DiMaggio, barely able to hobble, bore the stings of Casey Stengel's insults, a clown's folly. And Yogi Berra was ingloriously fired. Mickey Mantle? Perhaps the Yankees didn't know what to do with him.

"I was the most honored player at the Stadium," Mantle would later tell me, "because our teams in the mid and late '60s were goddamn awful, and so was attendance. So they'd say, 'Hey Mick, can we honor you with a Mickey Mantle Day?' Sure. What they weren't saying, which was true, was, 'Hey, Mick, attendance is down. We need a sellout. How 'bout we honor you with a Mickey Mantle Day?'"

Mickey was right, of course. The Yankees honored him with four Mickey Mantle Days. Three of them came during the Yankees' worst seasons, when attendance had tumbled to near-record lows. The fourth Mickey Mantle Day was held in 1997, two years after his death. The first was held near the end of that disappointing 1965 season, commemorating Mantle's 2,000[th] game on September 18 against the Detroit Tigers. Just as Mickey knew would happen, the Yankees sold out the Stadium that day, selling more hot dogs, popcorn, and beer—especially beer—than at almost any time that season. The Yankees made a killing out of their aging star, salvaging what they could out of a horrendously disappointing season. Mantle's cut of the take was more gifts than he knew what to do with: a new car; two quarter horses; vacation trips to Rome, Nassau, and Puerto Rico; a mink coat for Merlyn; a six-foot, 100-pound Hebrew National salami; and a Winchester rifle. Yankee Stadium was dressed up in the bunting normally used for Opening Days and World Series. Fans brought large banners reading "Don't Quit, Mick" and "We Love The Mick." It was a celebration which even the archbishop of New York, Francis Cardinal Spellman, had helped promote, "an almost holy day for the believers who had crammed the grandstands early to witness the canonization of a new stadium saint," author Gay Talese wrote in his *Esquire* profile of Joe DiMaggio.

It would be DiMaggio who would give the celebration the behind-the-scenes drama that would overshadow the event in the memories of many. And it had nothing to do with his supposed feud with Mickey. Knowing the importance of the event in Yankee lore, Joe flew to New York to personally introduce Mantle on his special day. The two men had never been friends, but they were friendly with one another and not the bitter enemies that the news media and others sought to portray. They were around each other at the annual Yankee Old Timers' Day games as well as almost every spring because DiMaggio attended the Yankees' training camps as a special instructor. They were also a photographer's dream, and they were routinely photographed together.

In 1961, famed photographer Ozzie Sweet worked with the two Yankee legends in a photo session that he said dispelled any idea of feud between them. Sweet recalled that Mantle appeared "relaxed and confident" around DiMaggio, who seemed "antsy and uncomfortable." So much so that Sweet said he carefully watched his step. "With anyone else, I might say, 'Adjust your cap…'" said Sweet. "But with Joe, I didn't dare. I just wanted to quickly get some images of the two of them together." In one photograph from that session, Joe looks as if he is awkwardly straining his neck as he tried to move his head closer to Mantle's. "I didn't know what the heck he was doing there," said Sweet. "But with Joe, I didn't want to fool around for long. I didn't want to say, 'Mr. DiMaggio, could you please change the angle of your neck so you don't look like a turtle?' I think he might have walked away!"

DiMaggio was famous for brooding over even perceived insignificant slights. For instance, DiMaggio always insisted on being the last player to be introduced at Old-Timers' games, basking in the loudest applause produced when the fans' energy and enthusiasm reached a fever pitch. But there was one time when the public address announcer unintentionally introduced the great Yankee Clipper before Mantle instead of last. That meant that it was Mantle who received the biggest and loudest ovation. "I heard Joe was pissed off about it," Mickey later remarked with obvious satisfaction.

Of course, there were times when Mantle himself seethed at playing second fiddle to Joe, such as over the 1960s classic song "Mrs. Robinson." Amid the social and political upheaval of the 1960s, songwriter Paul Simon wrote the song's most memorable lyric, "Where have you gone, Joe DiMaggio? A nation turns its lonely eyes to you." Simon later told author David Halberstam that a disappointed Mickey Mantle once asked why he'd used DiMaggio in the song and not him. Simon chose not to get into the complex idea of the simpler times of DiMaggio, so he said to Mantle, "It was syllables, Mickey. The syllables were all wrong."

At that first Mickey Mantle Day, with the Yankee franchise in decline and Mickey already talking about retirement, DiMaggio's presence seemed a reminder of Yankee pride even in bad times. He was, after all, the image of quintessential New York Yankee grace, tall and regal as if a national aristocrat in his exquisitely tailored, pinstriped suit. With all eyes on him, DiMaggio waved to the fans as he walked with his customary grace from the dugout onto the field after he was introduced. It was then that he noticed Mickey's mother, Lovell, standing off alone to one side. DiMaggio was first a gentleman, so he went to Mantle's mom and, cupping her elbow in his hand, escorted her to where all the players and dignitaries were lined up along the infield grass. There, at home plate, DiMaggio glanced at Mantle, who was in the Yankee dugout with Merlyn and their boys. Then, Joe's thin smile froze and for a split second changed into a dark scowl.

Senator Robert F. Kennedy was walking back and forth in the dugout, anticipating his own introduction. DiMaggio bitterly hated both Bobby Kennedy and his brother, the late president, for their romantic involvement with Marilyn Monroe. He blamed them, among others, for her personal demise and death. The Joe DiMaggio–Marilyn Monroe romance, of course, is one of America's most famous love stories. His love and devotion to her lived long past their nine-month marriage of 1954. He also believed a reconciliation might have been possible, and was devastated when Marilyn was found dead of an overdose in 1962. Since then, DiMaggio had avoided anything having to do with the Kennedys, but now that seemed unavoidable. In November of 1964, Bobby Kennedy had been elected to the U.S. Senate from New York and now was perhaps even more important than DiMaggio to the honor being bestowed on Mickey Mantle. What was Joe intending to do? For the moment, he turned his attention to Mickey and his special day. "I'm proud," he announced to the fans at Yankee Stadium, "to introduce the man who succeeded me in center field here in 1951. He lived up to all expectations and there is no doubt in my mind that he will one day be in the Hall of Fame."

Mickey and his family walked onto the field amid a wild, thunderous standing ovation that was sustained for several minutes. Mantle waved and smiled at the adoring crowd, then posed with his wife and sons for the photographers kneeling in front of them. His speech was typically short. "I think just to have the greatest baseball player I ever saw introduce me is tribute enough for me in one day," he said. "To have any kind of success in life I think you have someone behind you to push you ahead and to share it with you… and I certainly have that," he said, acknowledging his wife, Merlyn, along with his four boys and his mother. It was especially important to Mickey to know that donations made by the fans and the Yankees would be going to the Hodgkin's Disease Fund that had been founded in memory of Mantle's father, Mutt. "I wish he could have been here today," Mickey said. "I know he would be just as proud and happy at what you all have done here as we are.

"There's been a lot written in the last few years about the pain that I've played with. But I want you to know that when one of you fans, whether it's in New York or anywhere in the country, say, 'Hi Mick! How you feeling?' or, 'How's your legs?' it certainly makes it all worth it. All the people in New York, since I've been here, have been tremendous with me. Mr. Topping, all of my teammates, the press and the radio and the TV, have just been wonderful. I just wish I had 15 more years with you."

Mickey's eyes welled with tears as he turned and shook hands with the dignitaries and officials standing nearby. The DiMaggio-Kennedy drama, what there was of it, was about to unfold.

"Among them now," wrote Talese, "was Senator Kennedy, who had been spotted in the dugout five minutes before by [Yankee broadcaster] Red Barber, and had been called out and introduced. Kennedy posed with Mantle for a photographer, then shook hands with the Mantle children, and with Toots Shor and [New York political leader] James Farley and others.

"DiMaggio saw him coming down the line and at the last second he backed away, casually, hardly anybody noticing it, and Kennedy seemed not to notice it either, and just swept past, shaking more hands...."

"Mickey Mantle Day" in September 1965: As the scheduled game got underway that day, the pitcher for the Detroit Tigers was a right hander named Joe Sparma. When Mickey came up to bat in the bottom of the first inning that day, he received another thunderous ovation from the crowd. Then, Tigers pitcher Joe Sparma did an unbelievably classy thing. Stepping off the mound, he walked to home plate and extended his hand to offer Mantle his personal congratulations.

"You know, I've never had a chance to meet you in person," said Sparma, "and I've always admired you."

Mickey was so moved that it took him a moment to settle into the left-handed batter's box. The crowd had applauded again, and Mantle once more tipped his batting helmet to acknowledge his fans. But had the mercurially unpredictable Sparma, who had quarterbacked Ohio State to a Big Ten championship in 1961 only to quit the team two years later over differences with coach Woody Hayes, just played Mickey like those street hustlers in his rookie year? He returned to the mound and wasted little time in striking out Mantle to end the inning and put an early damper on Mantle's day.

A smirk crossed Mickey's face, and he looked at Tigers catcher Bill Freehan, who later recounted the meeting in his memoir *Behind The Mask*.

"They have a day for me and your manager's got to put some hard-throwing kid out there," Mantle said. "Couldn't he have put in some soft-tossing left-hander for me to hit off of, so I could look like a hero in front of all those people?"

22

Maris & the Mick in Excelsis

*"The last six years in the American League
were mental hell for me. I was drained
of all my desire to play baseball."*

—ROGER MARIS

A PHOTOGRAPH OF ROGER MARIS IN THE FULL EXTENSION OF HIS SWING, hitting his 61st home run of the 1961 season and breaking Babe Ruth's revered record, adorned the back of the program handed out at Roger's funeral mass on December 19, 1985. He was 51 years old when he died after a long bout with lymphatic cancer. "He was sick, so sick for so long," his wife, Pat, said later. "You knew it was coming, but it was a shock and not a shock at the same time. You just go on, like anything else."

Among the 900 or so braving the snow and a temperature of two degrees above zero to pay their tribute to Maris that day at St. Mary's Cathedral in Fargo, North Dakota, was his former Yankees slugging mate Mickey Mantle. "Mantle, his blond hair graying," recalled Ira Berkow, the *New York Times* Pulitzer Prize–winning columnist, "held a white handkerchief and wiped his eyes and nose." The handkerchief wasn't for a runny nose from the cold, Mickey later told me when we caught up at a baseball card show in Southern California. "I was bawling, almost like a baby at times," he said. "You know, those dreams I used to tell you about? Now when I have them, Roger's in them, like he was back in the day."

For Mantle, as like so many others, the memory of Roger Maris is that same image of his powerful swing that Pat specially requested be used for the funeral program: the heroic Roger Maris accomplishing something that no other ballplayer—not even the incredible Mickey Mantle—could do. It was a single-season home run record that would stand longer than Babe Ruth's 34-year mark. And when Maris' record was finally broken, first by Mark McGwire in 1998 and then by Barry Bonds in 2001, the legitimacy of those new records would be forever marred because they had been produced by players using performance-enhancing drugs. In fact, Babe Ruth and Roger Maris remain the only two players in the game to hit 60 or more home runs in a season without the aid of PEDs.

There are heroes, and then there are heroes. When Roger Maris died in 1985, his acceptance among baseball fans, even among many Yankee faithful who once booed him mercilessly, had dramatically changed. The long, chilly relationships between Maris and the Yankees, Maris and the fans, and Maris and New York had at long last thawed. The Yankee organization under the ownership of George Steinbrenner finally brought him back to Yankee Stadium after more than a decade of Roger rejecting overtures. Could anyone except the Yankee diehards blame him? He had quietly retired to Florida, comfortable with a Budweiser beer distributorship awarded to him by Gussie Busch, who owned both the Cardinals and Anheuser-Busch. That deal eventually made Roger's family and heirs multi-millionaires. In 2005, Anheuser-Busch agreed to pay at least $120 million in cash to the Roger Maris family as part of a settlement that ended a defamation trial and other litigation.

For Roger, business, like baseball, wasn't about the money but the respect. He returned to Yankee Stadium when Steinbrenner convinced him that his olive branch was sincere by retiring his uniform number, honoring him on the same field where Gehrig had once said his famous farewell, and giving him a place he deserved in the pantheon of Yankees legends.

On July 21, 1984, Roger Maris was honored at Yankee Stadium as he and former teammate Elston Howard had their uniform numbers, No. 9 and No. 32 respectively, retired and added to the wall in the stadium's Monument Park. Each player was also presented with a plaque to be placed with others beyond the stadium's left-center-field wall. Already sick, Roger was emotionally overwhelmed, especially by the words on the plaque and their acknowledgement of his historic achievement, which had never before been properly recognized by Major League Baseball nor by the Yankees.

ROGER EUGENE MARIS
AGAINST ALL ODDS
IN 1961 HE BECAME THE ONLY PLAYER TO HIT
MORE THAN 60 HOME RUNS IN A SINGLE SEASON.
IN BELATED RECOGNITION OF ONE OF BASEBALL'S
GREATEST ACHIEVEMENTS EVER.
HIS 61 IN '61,
THE YANKEES SALUTE HIM AS A GREAT PLAYER
AND AS AUTHOR OF ONE OF THE MOST
REMARKABLE CHAPTERS IN THE HISTORY
OF MAJOR LEAGUE BASEBALL.
ERECTED BY
NEW YORK YANKEES
JULY 21, 1984

"Wonderful," Roger said to his longtime friend Dick Savageau, as they walked away from where the plaque had been temporarily placed. "*This* is what it should have been like. *This* is what I was waiting for."

Seventeen months after the Yankees retired his number, on December 14, 1985, Roger Maris died.

Mantle, who served as a pallbearer, insisted that Maris was a "better person" and "better family man" than he was, adding, "If anyone went early, I should have been the guy." In the Fargo cemetery, Maris' baseball-diamond-shaped headstone reads "61" and "Against All Odds."

"Roger can now rest in peace," Mantle told me over drinks in an Orange County hotel bar.

Mickey recalled how Roger, feeling beleaguered by a hostile press— "Maris Sulks in Trainer's Room" one New York tabloid headline blared—during the chase for Ruth's record in 1961, had complained near the end that: "'It's as if I'm in a trap and can't find an escape. It's really beginning to get to me now. I can't take it anymore, Mick. What can I do?' Like I had an answer. What did I tell him? We were in the trainer's room, freshly stocked with beer. I handed him a bottle and I said, 'Rog, you'll just have to suck it up and take it.'"

But then it always seemed so easy for Mickey Mantle. And it was that time, that age of the Kennedys and Camelot, when things that appeared so hard for the rest of us just came so naturally for him.

America in the 1950s, leading into the 1960s, was also not so much a stage as a set piece for television, the new national phenomenon. It was a time when how things looked—and how we looked—mattered, a decade of design. From the painting-by-numbers fad to the public fascination with the First Lady's apparel to the television sensation of Elvis Presley to the sculptural refinement of the automobile, American life in the 1950s had a distinct style in material culture and in art history at eye level. America in the 20th century, to be sure, seemed to have a need for sports heroes such as Mickey Mantle, Roger Maris, and others to transform from largely conventional baseball figures into pop-culture deities of entertainment, which is what the game ultimately became in Mantle's time and thereafter. Mantle would be the cultural equivalent of Elvis, Marilyn, and James Dean. He was young, he was handsome, and he came to be seen on television in millions of homes in ways DiMaggio, for instance, never was.

It should be no surprise that popular biography has reflected this conversion, or that the change parallels the way baseball has come to be viewed in the years since Mantle arrived on the American scene. In a sense, the image of all popular figures is a reflection of the public that follows them. But with a dead figure that reflective process grows exponentially—like the compounding effect of a series of mirrors. As a cultural symbol whose life can now be made into anything with impunity, sports heroes like Mantle, Maris, and others became, in Elvis biographer Greil Marcus' words, "an anarchy of possibilities"—a reflection of the public's mass fears and aspirations and also a constant vehicle for discussing those sentiments. They evolved into a collection of cultural deities—modern-day equivalents of the Greek gods, who were immortal while sharing the characteristics of the human beings who worshipped them.

"We didn't just root for him," recalled broadcaster Bob Costas in his eulogy of the Yankees' switch-hitting slugger. "We felt for him. Long before many of us ever cracked a serious book, we knew something about mythology as we watched Mickey Mantle run out a home run through the lengthening shadows of a late Sunday afternoon at Yankee Stadium."

A decade after Maris died, Mickey Mantle, too, was gone. As with almost anything involving Mantle, the final two years of his life were a panoply of spectacle and celebrity. That period also seemed to underscore the contrast in the personal lives of Mantle and Roger Maris, the man Mickey said was the man he most admired and wished he could have been like.

In late December 1993, as Mickey prepared for a knee replacement operation on his left knee, and possibly on his right knee as well, he was distracted while talking to doctors who were fellow members of the Preston Trail Golf Club with its exclusive membership of Dallas' elite. Members knew Mantle as a fun-loving guy who sometimes gave them some unexpected awkward moments. Mickey, for instance, had a tendency to walk into the club's restaurant to order a drink completely naked. Mantle had also on occasion shocked members of a nearby country club by going skinny-dipping in the club's pool. At Preston Trail, the members committee reached a point where it even instituted "The Mickey Mantle Rule," prohibiting anyone nude from entering or lounging in the club's restaurant.

Otherwise, Mickey was one of the most popular members and often would solicit free advice from the doctors he played with. A doctor who happened to be one of Mickey's golf partners at Preston Trail that December day in 1993 noticed something that concerned him behind Mantle's bloodshot eyes and jaundiced-looking skin. The next day Mickey had a complete physical examination that alarmed his doctor. Mantle's red blood cell count was at a dangerously low level, and preliminary tests showed that he had done serious damage to his liver. The doctor was concerned enough to order an MRI scan that would provide a thorough examination of the condition of Mickey's liver. The experience would prove cathartic, as Mantle would later explain to Jill Lieber of *Sports Illustrated*:

"For an hour and 15 minutes, I lay in that MRI tube, and I thought, 'What am I doing here? This must really be serious.' It was hard to keep from crying, thinking about the bad shape I was in, how I had abused myself with alcohol for 42 years, all the people I'd let down. I was worried that fans would remember Mickey Mantle as a drunk rather than for my baseball accomplishments. I had always thought I could quit drinking by myself, and I'd do it for several days or a couple of weeks, but when I got to feeling good again, I'd go back to getting loaded. I was physically and emotionally worn out from all the drinking. I'd hit rock bottom."

Three days after Christmas, Mickey checked into the Betty Ford Center in Rancho Mirage, California, where he was assigned Room 202. In the 1980s, the Betty Ford Center had become the most high-profile substance addiction rehabilitation program in the country, largely because of its clientele of Hollywood stars and celebrities. The treatment program at Betty Ford is based on Alcoholics Anonymous and its fabled 12-step program that includes regular meetings in which you are forced to confront your problems by talking openly about them. For Mickey, it was a 32-day period that forced him to talk tearfully about his failure as a father and husband, his drinking addiction and his behavior while drunk, his bouts with depression and thoughts of suicide.

"I thought I might pass out the first time I stood up in a meeting at the Betty Ford Center and said, 'I'm Mick and I'm an alcoholic,'" he later recalled.

In an interview several months after his Betty Ford Center stay, Mantle elaborated:

"It took me a couple of times before I could talk without crying. You're supposed to say why you're there, and I said because I had a bad liver and I was depressed. Whenever I tried to talk about my family, I got all choked up. One of the things I really screwed up, besides baseball, was being a father. I wasn't a good family man. I was always out, running around with the guys. Mickey Jr. could have been a helluva athlete. If he'd had my dad, he could have been a Major League Baseball player. My kids have never blamed me for not being there. They don't have to. I blame myself."

Suddenly sober, Mantle's guilt about how he had neglected his family intensified. He felt so guilty that he chose not to have them come visit him during family week. He spent that time, instead, with Greer Johnson, his girlfriend and the woman with whom he had lived the last decade of his life. Then, in March, only just weeks after Mantle left the Betty Ford Center, his son Billy died of a heart attack at age 36. Billy had complicated his ongoing fight with Hodgkin's disease with drug and alcohol problems. He had been in addiction rehab treatment four times in four years, and he had undergone heart bypass surgery in 1993. Danny Mantle brought the news to his father at the locker room at Preston Trail, where Mickey had just finished his daily round of golf. "We were worried," said Danny, "that the news might send him back [to drinking]."

Mantle, however, was finally ready to be the head of his family. He insisted on being the one to break the news to Merlyn, knowing that of all the family members she had been the closest to Billy. Mickey called it "the most agonizing thing I've ever had to do." Merlyn had checked into a rehab center in Wilmer, Texas, and had to deal with news of her son's death while she was struggling to regain control of her own life. Mickey, meanwhile, maintained his sobriety while mourning his son and through the death of his mother at the age of 92 a year later. If his son's premature death hadn't broken him to drink again, he knew nothing would.

Mickey now was determined to rededicate himself to his family, to his fans, to his image and reputation, and to baseball. In perhaps the most moving interview of his life, Mantle discussed his career and his addiction on national television with Bob Costas. Few watching the interview could not have been touched by the sight of tears streaming down Mickey's cheeks as he talked about his life. Costas may have been one of the few who had seen behind the Mantle façade. He'd seen a man who was never really at peace with himself and he brought it up.

"I've always had the sense that there was a sadness about you," Costas said "Was that true?"

"Yeah," Mantle answered sadly. "I think that when I did drink a little too much or something, it kind of relieved the tension that I felt within myself maybe because I hadn't been what I should have been."

"Because you hadn't been the ballplayer you thought you should have been?"

"Or the daddy."

"Did you ever say to yourself, 'Wait a minute. I'm one of the best ballplayers of all time. I've made a significant amount of change doing this. I'm financially secure. People seem to love me. Why don't I feel better?'"

"Maybe I do, in the back of my mind, feel like I've let everybody down some way or other. I know there is something in there that's not fulfilled or something. I don't know what it is… I can't explain it."

Mantle's emotional confession reinforced his following among his fans and connected him with a new loyal following. He was, if the imperfect man, indeed the perfect hero for a nation now accustomed to forgiving the contrite and welcoming back the repentant. But it was to be a short-lived comeback

In the spring of 1995, Mickey began suffering from stomach pains that he thought were from acid indigestion. He had always had a high tolerance for pain and put off being alarmed at first. But on May 28, a Sunday, Mickey was admitted to the Baylor University

Medical Center for tests. Nine days later, Mickey was still in the hospital, feeling worse than when he had been admitted. The tests confirmed how sick he felt. That day, Dr. Daniel DeMarco, Mickey's gastroenterologist, and other specialists from Baylor Medical Center informed Mickey that his liver was beyond healing. The tests, they told him, had revealed that he had cancer of the liver, cirrhosis, and hepatitis C. The latter, which was dormant, probably stemmed from a blood transfusion in one of the operations during his baseball career. The immediate threat on his life was the cancer, and only a liver transplant would save his life.

Doctors ultimately announced that Mickey had liver cancer and needed a transplant to live. Out of respect for his privacy, Mickey's doctors still did not reveal how close Mickey already was to death. He was sinking into a coma and might not live another 48 hours without a new liver. Ironically, it was probably the family's reluctance to fully disclose the gravity of Mickey's condition that would largely be responsible for the public outcry over how quickly he received the transplant. There was also a measure of concern over whether giving a liver to an old alcoholic was appropriate.

On June 8, Mickey received his new liver on the second day after being placed on the transplant waiting list. The public criticism and allegations of favoritism were almost immediate. Dr. Goran Klintmalm, the head of the Baylor Transplant Institute, later would say that Mickey probably would have died had he not received the new liver when he did. "Mick was extraordinarily sick," said Klintmalm. "He was the only one here in North Texas waiting for a liver who was that sick. The donor liver was the right blood group. You cannot ethically deny a patient what may be the only chance he has. You don't know if or when you will get another one. So obviously we did the transplant."

Almost immediately after the transplant operation, the Mantle family and the hospital were deluged with an outpouring of calls and telegrams wishing Mickey a speedy recovery. Months later, the United Network for Organ Sharing issued a report on its review of Mickey's case and concluded that he had been fairly given a liver transplant and that no selection procedures had been waived to give him preferential treatment. Only when he was released from the hospital on June 28, a month after being admitted, did Mickey begin to fully understand the accusations of favoritism in his liver transplant. He himself may have stated the argument in his own defense best. "People think I got that liver because of who I am," he said in an interview, "but they have rules they go by. They told me I had one day to live. If I hadn't got this one, I wouldn't have made it."

Mantle's sense of humor had been unaffected. At a press conference a month after the transplant, Mantle spotted noted memorabilia collector Barry Halper and said, "Hey Barry, want to buy my liver?" Halper declined. He told Mickey he was just there to see how he was doing. Mantle and Halper had become friends over the years, and Mickey had been a visitor to his home, where he showed him a collection that eventually would be sold for close to $22 million in 1999.

Later, when Halper spoke to Mantle's doctor, he was offered Mantle's liver again. Halper again declined. After some prodding from the doctor to take something for his collection, Halper asked for the scalpel used to operate on Mickey. The doctor no longer had the scalpel, but said he would come up with something. Halper left his business card and Federal Express account number, and a week later a package arrived at Halper's house. Inside was a pair of stained surgical gloves. "Mickey had complained of hemorrhoids in the last week of his life," recalled Halper. After a doctor examined him, Mantle insisted that the gloves be sent to Halper. "I didn't ask him for that," said Halper. "But he sent it to me." Halper did not include the gloves in the auction of his collection but kept them, along with a statement of authenticity from the doctor and the Federal Express label. "I keep it in the garage because my wife said, 'If you even think of bringing that in the house….'"

Unfortunately, there were complications, chemotherapy treatments, and blood transfusions. Losing almost 40 pounds from the 208 pounds he weighed when admitted, Mickey now looked skeletal, gaunt, and weak. Even an adjustable commemorative baseball cap from the 1995 All-Star Game, played at nearby Arlington that month, looked several sizes too big for him.

"I owe so much to God and to the American people," he told reporters. "I'm going to spend the rest of my life trying to make it up. It seems to me like all I've done is take. Have fun and take. I'm going to start giving something back. I'd like to say to kids out there, if you're looking for a role model, this is a role model…" Mickey pointed at his chest with his thumb. "Don't be like me. God gave me a body and an ability to play baseball. God gave me everything, and I just…" Mickey gave off a "pfffttt!" He had kissed off his talents, as he had much of his life.

"It's dangerous to make cardboard figures out of people," Bob Costas would later say in assessing Mantle's life. "You're always going to be wrong. He was neither entirely this or entirely that. But there's always the possibility for redemption. There's always the possibility that the better angels of your nature will take over in the end."

Mickey Mantle died on August 13, 1995. He was two months shy of 64. He was interred in a crypt next to his son Billy inside a huge concrete mausoleum, at the Sparkman-Hillcrest Memorial Park in Dallas. The inscription underneath Mickey's name on the outside of the crypt reads simply "A Great Teammate." His oldest son, Mickey Jr., who died of non-Hodgkin's lymphoma five years later at the age of 47, would also be laid to rest there next to his father. Merlyn, who never remarried, was also interred there after her death in 2009 at the age of 77.

Mantle's sons David and Danny are in their sixties and live in Dallas. They occasionally go to their father's old stomping ground in New York City, where one day a few years ago David was walking in Manhattan when a passer-by did a double-take.

"I thought you were dead," said the stranger.

"No, I'm still alive," David responded. His resemblance to his father is haunting.

"People come up to me and ask if I know who I look like. I always wait and see. Then I tell them I'm his son."

Yes, the city still belongs to Mickey Mantle.

Epilogue

IN THE FIRST YEARS OF HER WIDOWHOOD, PATRICIA MARIS HAD TO endure baseball's continued slighting of her husband's memory. She didn't like it any more with Roger gone than when he was still alive: the belittling of his home run record by an asterisk status that had been put in place in 1961 to placate what sportswriter Shirley Povich had called "the millions of members of the Babe Ruth cult who considered their hero's 60-homer year sacred and inviolate."

To be accurate, there never was an asterisk on Roger Maris' 1961 home run record that stood for 34 years. The notion of an asterisk was a myth created by the country's sportswriters looking for the simplest explanation of then–baseball commissioner Ford Frick's midseason ruling that Ruth's record would have to be broken in the same number of games, 154, that existed in the Babe's season in 1927. Never mind that those same sportswriters were tripping over themselves in the frenzied reporting that continued on Roger's chase of the record even after that season's game 154 came and went. Baseball's record books, what there was of them, never placed anything remotely resembling an asterisk on what Maris ultimately accomplished in 162 games. The asterisk, though, became part of the game's mythology, unfortunately misleading many to look upon Roger Maris as some kind of second-class home run record holder. He was not.

In the years after 1961, that asterisk—again, an asterisk that never existed—haunted Maris and his legacy. When Maris died, the invisible asterisk was a centerpiece of his story and how his legacy was weighed and measured. The fact of the matter is that Ruth and Maris were recognized separately. But with no asterisk anywhere. Just acknowledgment by the Elias Sports Bureau, official record keeper for Major League Baseball, of the Babe as the home run record holder for the 154-game season and Roger as the home run record-holder for the 162-game season. That designation remained in place for three decades. Then in 1991, nearing the 30th anniversary of Maris' 61-homer season, baseball commissioner Fay Vincent declared that Roger deserved to be recognized as the single-season home run king irrespective of the number of games in a season. The ruling was based on Vincent's recommendation and adopted by an eight-man major league committee for statistical accuracy. The Maris "decision does not diminish or demean the contributions of Babe Ruth to the game of baseball," Vincent said in a statement. "He is, among other things, responsible with Judge Landis for saving our game after the Black Sox scandal of 1919. He is also surely the most famous player in the history of the game and will remain so for generations to come.

"This change allows Roger Maris to receive the recognition he deserves for setting one of the game's most important records."

But had Vincent's ruling even been necessary? Technically, no. Actually a decision in the 1960s making Maris the official single-season record holder had gone overlooked and possibly not even known by some baseball officials. According to the official Baseball Encyclopedia, Maris already had been listed as the single-season home run leader without an asterisk or any annotation. Bill Rosen of Macmillan, publisher of *The Baseball Encyclopedia: The Complete and Official Record of Major League Baseball,* said the statistical committee in 1991 had simply confirmed what a special records committee had done in 1968. That earlier committee had ruled, according to the encyclopedia, "For all-time single-season records, no asterisk or official sign shall be used to indicate the number of games scheduled."

No one in baseball, though, had been looking out for Roger Maris' interests, certainly not the Yankees, either while he was chasing Babe Ruth' record in 1961, and especially not after he had hit his 60th home run when his team's organization stood by and allowed his achievement to be diminished by the game. It was almost as if the New York Yankees were satisfied keeping the Babe's name on the record. For reasons known only to the team's front office, in taking sides, the Yankees had chosen one of its own. If Mantle couldn't be the one to break the record, then at least keep it in the real family. In Roger Maris, author Roger Angell wrote in *The New Yorker* in early 1991, baseball had "a player who had been a Yankee for only two seasons. If Mickey Mantle, a Yankee hero almost from his first days as a pinstriped rookie, had swatted the magic blow, many old-timers still believe, the New York front office would have raised an ungodly fuss over any diminishment of the new record, and it would have stood unsmirched, as it deserved."

By 1991, though, Maris' record-breaking achievement had taken on new appreciation. In those 30 years, no player had come close to challenging baseball's home run record—not anywhere near. No player even hit 50 homers until Albert Belle in 1995, the same year Mickey Mantle passed away. Then in the coming decade, the way baseball players and all athletes trained changed dramatically. No one really talked about it. You didn't have to. You could see it. Players had bulked up in almost cartoonish fashion. So lampoonish—including gigantic Popeye arms and bulging necks—that, in retrospect, it's a wonder it didn't set off an immediate alarm about steroids, though perhaps no one wanted to believe it. The denial was widespread in a game that had lost its place as the national pastime and a sport struggling to overcome the eighth work stoppage in its history after the 1994–95 Major League Baseball strike. So the game accepted the steroid era with blind eyes and open arms, financially thriving again in the home run explosion that was as extraordinary as it was unbelievable, made possible by performance-enhancing drugs. The silver lining of that fraudulent era was the revival of the Maris and Mantle home run record chase of 1961, as seen through the lens of almost four decades of sentimentality and perspective. But then, nostalgia has always been baseball's best friend.

"It's funny, over the years I've had a lot of letters from people who said they respected Roger and the way he played and the way he handled himself, and it always made me feel good," said Patricia Maris, who was given a flashback to the days of Roger's glory year. "When [Mark McGwire and Sammy Sosa in 1998] started in on the record bit, we all knew it would be broken someday, but the way it was done was kind of sad."

The 1998 McGwire-Sosa home run spectacle proved to be too personal for Patricia Maris, who had to be hospitalized by the end of that summer. When McGwire was about to break the record in early September, Patricia flew to St. Louis from Gainesville, Florida, with her four sons and two daughters to be present for the passing of the torch. But after arriving on Sunday she had to be admitted to Barnes-Jewish Hospital, where she was treated for an irregular heartbeat. Two days later, she returned to the hospital for treatment of the same condition. This happened several hours before the Cubs-Cardinals game at Busch Stadium in which McGwire broke Roger's single-season home run record. McGwire, who had invited the Maris family to be present, had begun the afternoon by holding the bat

Maris used to hit his 61st home run. Later, he cried as he talked about what that moment had meant.

"I touched it with my heart," McGwire said. "When I did that, I knew tonight was going to be the night. I can say my bat will lie next to his, and I'm damn proud of it."

After McGwire broke the record that night, the Cardinals had an 11-minute delirious celebration of what *New York Times* columnist Selena Roberts called "Bulk Fiction": McGwire "almost hop-scotching to first base on his joy ride to history," scooping up his son at home plate and climbing the box seat railing to embrace the Maris family. "You look back at it all now and say, 'Was that real?'" wondered Roger's longtime buddy Dick Savageau. "You don't want to take anything away from them, particularly a good guy like Mark McGwire, but you wonder if some of them are getting an extra edge. With everything that you read and see, I sometimes think, *My goodness, did anyone really break Roger's record?*"

Exactly. *Roger's record.* It has increasingly come to be known as that.

"That home run chase in '98 brought Dad's name and his accomplishments back into the public eye," said Roger Maris Jr. "A whole new generation of fans got a chance to know my dad. That's why I don't look back on it as a negative at all. Mark was great about honoring dad's memory. . . .

"I had suspicions even back in '98 when Mark broke the record. But what was I going to do?"

The graciousness of Patricia Maris and her family cannot be applauded enough, and perhaps the baseball gods were mindful. Having saved baseball in 1998 with his epic home run duel with the Chicago Cubs' Sammy Sosa, McGwire's claim on the record was tarnished by admissions and revelations about the use of performance-enhancing drugs. Sosa hit 66 home runs in 1998, 63 homers a year later, and 64 in 2001. Barry Bonds of the San Francisco Giants broke McGwire's record with his 73 home runs in 2001. All were too good to be true, and all those achievements are tainted by evidence and/or accusations that those players used performance-enhancing drugs.

"I wish I had never touched steroids," McGwire said in his public mea culpa, which came five years after his embarrassing refusal to discuss his steroid use during a televised Congressional hearing. "It was foolish and it was a mistake. I truly apologize. Looking back, I wish I had never played during the steroid era."

"The only thing Dad was on was unfiltered Camel cigarettes," said Maris' son Richard, "and I'm pretty sure those didn't help him hit any more home runs. In fact, they're probably what drove him to his grave.

"We still consider Mark a friend. It's not like we want him condemned to hell or anything."

In his heart, McGwire must have known that he owed the Marises a personal apology. Somehow, through the shame he tried to wipe away in interviews, he continued holding the belief that, despite his performance-enhancing drug use, he could have still broken the home run record because of his God-given talents. Critics didn't buy it. As more than a few of them put it: God-given gifts may have turned Mark McGwire into a good home run hitter, but man-made drugs made him a mythic one.

On the day he finally came clean about his sin against baseball and its records, he classily called Patricia Maris and apologized before he went public with his steroids confession. "I think she was shocked that I called her," McGwire told the *New York Times*. "I felt that I needed to do that. They've been great supporters of mine. She was disappointed, and she has every right to be. I couldn't tell her how so sorry I was." Told by broadcaster Bob Costas during another interview that certain Maris family members have said that they now consider Roger Maris'

61 home runs in 1961 to be the authentic home run record, McGwire responded: "They have every right to."

"My mom was very touched by his call," said Richard Maris. "She felt sorry for Mark—that he's going through this. She conveyed that we all make mistakes and move on from there."

Patricia Maris appreciated the gesture, but she also believes historians may have a renewed appreciation for her husband. A portrait of Pat from her later years shows a woman with a strong but kindly face and a firm, determined mouth. Her silver hair was parted on the left, and her sparkling eyes were as large and girlishly bright as when Roger first saw her. A devout woman, Pat never lost her faith that she and Roger would be gloriously united through old age. They still are. She is the loving overseer and keeper of his legacy. Roger Maris lives, not just in her memories but also in the game he played on his own terms and whose fame is kept alive by the record he still holds in the minds of many and continues to be chased as surely as each season begins. Roger Maris is having redemption, and his feat is more impressive with time. Roger Maris' record—and it is his record—has become a cause célèbre at a time when baseball desperately needs one.

"It fell to Roger Maris to break the sexiest record in professional sports," said Steve Hirdt of the Elias Sports Bureau in perhaps putting the feat in its simplest context. "That will always be the line on Maris' baseball epitaph." Each year, too, more people jump on the Maris-in-the-Hall-of-Fame bandwagon. Sadly, it's a long shot. He may never be enshrined in Cooperstown, but that will be its loss. Roger's baseball immortality doesn't need a group of sportswriters' endorsement. He might have liked that line, though a better one is a *New York Times* story lead that could be republished every summer or when the talk turns to heroes who are few and far between.

"Roger Maris is having one heck of a year."

He hasn't hit a home run since 1968, and he's been gone since 1985, but he grows in stature every day.

Author's Note

BIOGRAPHERS AMBITIOUSLY FOOLISH ENOUGH TO UNDERTAKE A DUAL biography of two baseball legends who at times seemed to thrive in long, combative love-hate relationships with other writers must, by definition, be willing to endure an unending amount of that emotional chaos seeping into the research for such a book. Otherwise there is no understanding them. It is also suggested to assume that the subjects, if not as crazy as the world they lived in, were even madder than the world of fans who cheered, admired, envied, booed, or heckled them. My old history professor at Baylor, Ralph Lynn, used to say that to understand Napoleon Bonaparte, one had to understand France: half of France despised Napoleon; the other half thought they *were* Napoleon. So, too, with Roger Maris and Mickey Mantle.

Roger and Mickey ultimately became the yin and yang of American baseball in the mid-20th century, when the game was on its last leg as the national pastime. It was as if the two teammates reflected a universe governed by a cosmic duality, sets of two opposing and complementing principles or cosmic energies. Among Yankee fans and New Yorkers, these powers tilted heavily toward Mantle. But outside New York, in the non-Yankee world, *there* Roger Maris came to have a significant following because of who he was, and the fact that he wasn't Mickey Mantle, the Yankees, and New York City.

It took me an adult lifetime to understand that, not to mention an uncomfortable long study of Roger and his world as the child of

Eastern European immigrants as opposed to America's immigrants from Western Europe. We are all immigrants of different levels from different places, and all Americans—but the distinction of being from Eastern as opposed to Western Europe is one that can't be taken for granted. I was strongly influenced in this by the late philosopher and writer Michael Novak, whom I first met in the mid-1970s at a Harvard University panel group that had nothing to do with baseball but everything to do with immigrants and ethnicity in America.

We had each recently authored controversial books on the subject. Mine was *Chicano Power,* about the civil rights uprising in the Southwest among young Mexican American student activists. Novak's book was *The Rise of the Unmeltable Ethnics.* Both of our books took on the White power political establishment, but his was causing unexpected waves because it was an attack from within. Novak, who was White, not Chicano or Black in the racially awakening post-60s age, proposed that the White ethnic was a distinct race of Whites—primarily Eastern European immigrants—different from WASPs, who had attempted to erase their cultural heritage and assimilate.

Baseball and Roger Maris didn't come into the picture of Novak's thesis until a couple of nights later. I had recently befriended a Harvard paleontologist called Stephen Jay Gould, a Yankees fan and baseball nerd like myself. Journalist and author David Halberstam, a mutual friend, had introduced us, knowing that both of us had longstanding interests in DiMaggio and Mantle. I was a Nieman Fellow at Harvard in the mid-70s, and we had spent many long hours talking baseball at the Faculty Club where we dined with Michael Novak a couple of nights after our panel group. I knew that Gould's grandfather had emigrated from Hungary, and I thought the Slovak-American Novak might want to meet another Harvard-educated unmeltable ethnic. It was a night of surprises all around. When he learned Gould and I were big Mantle fans, Novak launched into the greatness of the Croatian-American Roger Maris having triumphed over the "prince of WASP America" Mickey Mantle in breaking Babe Ruth's single-season home run record 15 years earlier.

I was dumbfounded. In my entire young life of cheering for Mickey Mantle, I'd not once thought of him as White Anglo-Saxon Protestant, which he was, though hardly religious. It was not something I had focused on then, nor later in writing my books about Mickey. Nor had I given much concern to Maris' ancestry in writing about Roger, not seriously, until this book. How much did Roger Maris' Eastern European background play into how he was treated as a ballplayer by fans and teammates? Not close to as much, I believe, as it played in his personal development as a child and into manhood. I am not alone, as I came to learn. In their wonderful biography, *Roger Maris: Baseball's Reluctant Hero,* authors Tom Clavin and Danny Peary went out of their way to showcase a quotation obviously meant to suggest Maris' alienation.

The mockery made him feel an outsider; and, feeling an outsider he behaved like one, which increased the prejudice against him... Which in turn increased his sense of being alien and alone. A chronic fear of being slighted made him avoid his equals, made him stand, where his inferiors were concerned, self-consciously on his dignity.

—Alduous Huxley, *Brave New World*

WHEN ROGER MARIS DIED IN 1985, his acceptance among baseball fans, even among many Yankee followers, had dramatically changed. The Yankee organization under the ownership of George Steinbrenner had brought him back into the fold. But that was just baseball, which can be a confluence of cultures all its own. But on the personal side, did Roger himself ever get past the ethnic isolation of his youth, any more than early generation immigrant Americans today? Especially those who grow up having their own ethnic identity and the worth of it dictated by immigrants fortunate to have arrived in America first? That was the America Roger Maris grew up in, and it is vital in understanding who he was.

Mickey Mantle is another story, one that I have been privileged to write about in other books. I also had the good fortune of having known Mantle, having first met him in Dallas when I was a young newspaper reporter and Mickey was still struggling to find his footing in retirement. I spent time with and around Mantle in the 1970s and again in the 1980s when he was often in Southern California during the early big days of baseball card shows and the sports memorabilia circuit. I never met Roger Maris. I spoke to him a few times in the mid-1980s. He wasn't in good health, and *Sports Illustrated*, where I was a writer at the time, had assigned me to hang out with him for a cover piece. Yeah, good luck. Roger was living in Florida at the time but having treatments at the M.D. Anderson Hospital and Tumor Institute in Houston. It was not to be.

As fate would have it, one of the best interviews Roger gave after his retirement—and there weren't many—was with my friend and fellow Yankees historian and author Peter Golenbock in 1973. When Peter learned I was working on this book, he immediately sent me a copy of the previously unpublished interview to use. Thank you, Peter!

Altogether, counting my previous three Mantle books and now this dual biography, I have interviewed more than 400 ex-teammates, players, coaches, friends, classmates, and family of the two players. I was most fortunate in having had dozen of hours of conversations and interviews with Mickey in the 1970s—as well as a treasure trove of conversations with two of the women in Mickey's life: Merlyn in the

1970s and Mantle's longtime New York girlfriend, Holly Brooke, from 2006 until her death in 2018.

When we last spoke in late 2006, Merlyn Mantle and I reminisced about the conversations she and I had years ago. She appreciated that I had honored my promise not to use the material until after she and Mickey had passed away. The notes from those conversations and interviews were packed away with all my reporting and research material from the 1970s.

It has been only in recent years that I was able to locate those boxes in storage for inclusion in my journalism and book archives being donated to the Texas Collection at my alma mater, Baylor University. In recovering that material, I also hit the mother lode. In addition to notes from my conversations with Merlyn, I found additional notes I'd forgotten about, including many of the conversations and interviews with Mickey Mantle during that time. These were notes that were not among the material I had used on Mantle for other books.

In early 1974, we had relocated from Dallas to Houston, packing up books and research material in shipping boxes, some of which remained sealed through that move as well as through subsequent moves over the years to Cambridge, Massachusetts, and then to storage in Southern California. Those notes provided the bulk of the previously unpublished interviews used in *Mantle: The Best There Ever Was* and this book.

Those included interviews with Mickey, Merlyn, and Billy Martin, who was manager of the Detroit Tiger during that time and whom I met through Mantle when Billy visited them in Dallas.

I also relied on the recollections of Holly Brooke, Mickey's girlfriend during his 1951 rookie season and on-and-off-again lover over the years. She is a source many biographers, myself included, wanted to interview in the time since. However, none of us could locate her, and some off us concluded that perhaps she had passed way. Then in 2006, just weeks before Merlyn Mantle called my then-agent Mike Hamilburg wishing to talk to me, I received an email from someone whose correspondence would prove equally fortuitous. A relative of Holly Brooke eventually put me in contact with her and it began a decade-long friendship until her death in 2018.

I was extremely fortunate because, as I said, journalists and authors had been looking for her since the 1950s. She was an important missing link to Mantle from his rookie year. But she was more. It turned out she stayed in touch with Mickey even after he married Merlyn in December 1951, resuming her affair with him at various times through the mid-1960s. She was blessed with an incredible memory and a seemingly encyclopedic knowledge of New York in that golden age, as well as of Mantle's life and his friendship and relationship with Roger Maris. Brooke—aka Marie Huylebroeck and Lady Holly Blaney—died at her home off Central Park in Manhattan on April 9, 2018. She was 94.

Roger Maris' 61 Home Runs In 1961

RESEARCH BY BASEBALL ALMANAC

HR #	GM #	Date	Pitcher	Throws	Team	Where	Inning
1	11	04/26/1961	Paul Foytack	Right	Detroit	Away	5th
2	17	05/03/1961	Pedro Ramos	Right	Minnesota	Away	7th
3	20	05/06/1961	Eli Grba	Right	Los Angeles	Away	5th
4	29	05/17/1961	Pete Burnside	Left	Washington	Home	8th
5	30	05/19/1961	Jim Perry	Right	Cleveland	Away	1st
6	31	05/20/1961	Gary Bell	Right	Cleveland	Away	3rd
7	32	05/21/1961	Chuck Estrada	Right	Baltimore	Home	1st
8	35	05/24/1961	Gene Conley	Right	Boston	Home	4th
9	38	05/28/1961	Cal McLish	Right	Chicago	Home	2nd
10	40	05/30/1961	Gene Conley	Right	Boston	Away	3rd
11	40	05/30/1961	Mike Fornieles	Right	Boston	Away	8th
12	41	05/31/1961	Billy Muffett	Right	Boston	Away	3rd
13	43	06/02/1961	Cal McLish	Right	Chicago	Away	3rd
14	44	06/03/1961	Bob Shaw	Right	Chicago	Away	8th
15	45	06/04/1961	Russ Kemmerer	Right	Chicago	Away	3rd
16	48	06/06/1961	Ed Palmquist	Right	Minnesota	Home	6th
17	49	06/07/1961	Pedro Ramos	Right	Minnesota	Home	3rd
18	52	06/09/1961	Ray Herbert	Right	Kansas City	Home	7th
19	55	06/11/1961	Eli Grba	Right	Los Angeles	Home	3rd
20	55	06/11/1961	Johnny James	Right	Los Angeles	Home	7th

HR #	GM #	Date	Pitcher	Throws	Team	Where	Inning
21	57	06/13/1961	Jim Perry	Right	Cleveland	Away	6th
22	58	06/14/1961	Gary Bell	Right	Cleveland	Away	4th
23	61	06/17/1961	Don Mossi	Left	Detroit	Away	4th
24	62	06/18/1961	Jerry Casale	Right	Detroit	Away	8th
25	63	06/19/1961	Jim Archer	Left	Kansas City	Away	9th
26	64	06/20/1961	Joe Nuxhall	Left	Kansas City	Away	1st
27	66	06/22/1961	Norm Bass	Right	Kansas City	Away	2nd
28	74	07/01/1961	Dave Sisler	Right	Washington	Home	9th
29	75	07/02/1961	Pete Burnside	Left	Washington	Home	3rd
30	75	07/02/1961	Johnny Klippstein	Right	Washington	Home	7th
31	77	07/04/1961	Frank Lary	Right	Detroit	Home	8th
32	78	07/05/1961	Frank Funk	Right	Cleveland	Home	7th
33	82	07/09/1961	Bill Monbouquette	Right	Boston	Home	7th
34	84	07/13/1961	Early Wynn	Right	Chicago	Away	1st
35	86	07/15/1961	Ray Herbert	Right	Chicago	Away	3rd
36	92	07/21/1961	Bill Monbouquette	Right	Boston	Away	1st
37	95	07/25/1961	Frank Baumann	Left	Chicago	Home	4th
38	95	07/25/1961	Don Larsen	Right	Chicago	Home	8th
39	96	07/25/1961	Russ Kemmerer	Right	Chicago	Home	4th
40	96	07/25/1961	Warren Hacker	Right	Chicago	Home	6th
41	106	08/04/1961	Camilo Pascual	Right	Minnesota	Home	1st
42	114	08/11/1961	Pete Burnside	Left	Washington	Away	5th
43	115	08/12/1961	Dick Donovan	Right	Washington	Away	4th
44	116	08/13/1961	Bennie Daniels	Right	Washington	Away	4th
45	117	08/13/1961	Marty Kutyna	Right	Washington	Away	1st
46	118	08/15/1961	Juan Pizarro	Left	Chicago	Home	4th
47	119	08/16/1961	Billy Pierce	Left	Chicago	Home	1st
48	119	08/16/1961	Billy Pierce	Left	Chicago	Home	3rd
49	124	08/20/1961	Jim Perry	Right	Cleveland	Away	3rd

HR #	GM #	Date	Pitcher	Throws	Team	Where	Inning
50	125	08/22/1961	Ken McBride	Right	Los Angeles	Away	6th
51	129	08/26/1961	Jerry Walker	Right	Kansas City	Away	6th
52	135	09/02/1961	Frank Lary	Right	Detroit	Home	6th
53	135	09/02/1961	Hank Aguirre	Left	Detroit	Home	8th
54	140	09/06/1961	Tom Cheney	Right	Washington	Home	4th
55	141	09/07/1961	Dick Stigman	Left	Cleveland	Home	3rd
56	143	09/09/1961	Mudcat Grant	Right	Cleveland	Home	7th
57	151	09/16/1961	Frank Lary	Right	Detroit	Away	3rd
58	152	09/17/1961	Terry Fox	Right	Detroit	Away	12th
59	155	09/20/1961	Milt Pappas	Right	Baltimore	Away	3rd
60	159	09/26/1961	Jack Fisher	Right	Baltimore	Home	3rd
61	163	10/01/1961	Tracy Stallard	Right	Boston	Home	4th

Acknowledgments

Maris & Mantle would not have been possible without the assistance of many individuals.

The most important of those sources may have been my late literary agent Mike Hamilburg. He died January 1, 2016, at the age of 82. Mike was a teenager during the 1961 season when Roger Maris and Mickey Mantle made their dramatic season-long chase of Babe Ruth's home run record. But at the time Mike's father, Mitchell, was one of the biggest agents in America, as well as a baseball fan, and he knew there was a buck to be made in Hollywood on Maris and Mantle.

After the 1961 World Series, Hamilburg signed Maris and Mantle to star in a kids sports comedy—*Safe at Home!*—for Columbia Pictures that was shot quickly in the off-season. Maris and Mantle played themselves, with William Frawley in his final film role playing a coach of the New York Yankees. Along the way, Hamilburg also got the M&M boys into the Doris Day–Cary Grant film *That Touch of Mink*. Mantle allegedly even had a brief fling with Doris, if his bragging is to be believed. Still, Roger and Mickey pocketed $25,000 apiece off roles in *Safe at Home!* and another $10,000 from *That Touch of Mink*.

Much of the time Maris and Mantle spent making those movies in Hollywood and Florida, they were housed by Hamilburg. The person waiting on them hand and foot? Young Mike Hamilburg, the producer's fastidious assistant who kept a detailed diary and copious notes of all his time with the two sluggers soaking in the off-season sun. Years later, Mike was always ready with Mickey Mantle stories. He had many. He represented my 2002 Mantle biography and left me a ton of memories and countless personal files about Mantle and Maris, as well as the notes and memos his father made during that time.

My heartfelt appreciation and gratitude goes out to Mike, whose contribution helped deepen my understanding of the Maris-Mantle friendship and dynamics back in that day. As David Halberstam himself loved to say in talking about writing books: the context of people behaving behind the scenes—how they act and interact when they are the most vulnerable—in anecdotes, dialog, and quotes reveals far more about the subjects than interviews alone.

Thank you, too, to Holly Brooke, a good friend and source whose recollections of her life with Mickey Mantle in New York in 1951 and later were critical to the development and writing of the book, as they were for *DiMag & Mick: Sibling Rivals, Yankee Blood Brothers* and *Mantle: The Best There Ever Was.* She is missed beyond words.

My profound thanks to those with whom I have the great luxury of working: my editor at Triumph Books, Jesse Jordan, who also edited my *Gehrig & the Babe* book; Bill Ames, the acquisition editor who helped baby both the book and me to another nice landing at Triumph; and my *consigliere,* the late Alex Jacinto, who guided me through the best of *Taquitos Jacintos* in Hollywood, East Los Angeles, and Pasadena, as well as through the most difficult of times. Alex died too young in 2019 from complications of knee replacement surgery.

A special tribute goes out to fellow Mantle biographer, Yankee historian, and friend Peter Golenbock. Talk about unselfish class and grace.

Pete Rose has always been magnanimous in sharing his memories and recollections of his time with Mantle and Maris in the 1960s and in helping me understand the unique culture and dynamics of the major league clubhouse.

Andrew Vilacky and Tom Catal of the Mickey Mantle Museum in Cooperstown have always been extraordinarily gracious and generous in their hospitality and friendship with me and my family, as well as in sharing their library for use in this and other books.

Greer Johnson, Mantle's "soul mate" the last 10 years of his life, was extremely kind in reminiscing about Mickey and graciously trusting me with her memories and remembering Mickey's conversations with her about his time battling and playing with Roger Maris, and many of the other important people in his life. This book, like *Mickey Mantle: America's Prodigal Son,* would not be as complete in its assessment of Mantle without her assistance.

The late Ray Mantle, one of Mickey's brothers, was charitable and good-hearted in sharing memories of growing up with Mickey, especially in clearing up discrepancies in other accounts of Mantle's early life. Ray also was extremely forthcoming in his own personal insight into Mickey's relationship with their father and Mickey's friendship with Roger Maris.

A tip of the cap goes out to author Michael Novak, of course, and his fellow "unmeltable White ethnic" Stephen Jay Gould, who had all these theories as early as the 1970s about how and why Mantle had been the greatest ballplayer ever and became even more convinced with the advent of sabermetrics late in his shortened life.

Special thanks to these individuals for their support or assistance in tangible and intangible ways: Hank Aaron, Marty Appel, Jim Bacon, Penni Barnett, Ed Attanasio, Jim Bellows, Keven Bellows, Yogi Berra, Hollis Biddle, Jim Bouton, Jennifer Boyd, Jimmy Breslin, Jerry Brown, Jeff Brynan, Jim Bunning, Ken Burns, George W. Bush, Cathy Byrd, Claudia Caballero, Elissa Walker Campbell, Al Campanis, Dave

Campbell, Ruben Castaneda, Paul Cohen, John B. Connally, Dino Costa, Bob Costas, Kevin Costner, Warren Cowan, Billy Crystal, Francis Dale, Teo Davis, Cody Decker, Carl Dias, Joe DiMaggio, James Duarte, Ryan Duren, Mel Durslag, Tom Eggebeen, Carl Erskine, Roy Firestone, Robert Fitzgerald, Randy Flowers, Whitey Ford, Don Forst, Dudley Freeman, Arthur Fuentes, Carlos Fuentes, Randy Galloway, Peter Gammons, Cathie Flahive Gilmore, Mikal Gilmore, Carole Player Golden, Johnny Grant, Kathy Griffin, Carlos Guerra, Chris Gwynn, David Halberstam, Denis Hamill, Mike Hamilburg, Arnold Hano, Thomas Harris, Jickey Harwell, Timothy Hays, Don Henley, Mickey Herskowitz, Tom Hoffarth, Joe Holley, Ken Holley, Elston Howard, Derek Jeter, Chipper Jones, David Justice, Ron Kaye, Ray Kelly, Jennifer Kemp, Liudmila Konovalova, Dennis King, Steve Kraly, Doug Krikorian, Sandy Koufax, Tony Kubek, Ring Lardner Jr., Don Larsen, Chris LaSalle, Jean LaSalle, Lisa LaSalle, Frances LaSalle Castro, Tommy Lasorda, Tim Layana, Timothy Leary, Jane Leavy, Jill Lieber, Carole Lieberman, Jerry Lumpe, Mike Lupica, Ralph Lynn, Michael Moldovan, Sara Moldovan, Willie Mays, Barbara McBride-Smith, Dick McCall, Julie McCullough, Mark McGwire, David McHam, Frank Messer, Lidia Montemayor, Jim Montgomery, Louis F. Moret, Dennis Mukai, Bridget Mulcahy, Mark Mulvoy, John Murphy, Stan Musial, Joe Namath, Jack Nelson, Don Newcombe, Peter O'Malley, Edward James Olmos, Bill Orozco, Robert Patrick, Dick Patyrak, Octavio Paz, Thomas Pettigrew, Robert Redford, Jimmie Reese, Pee Wee Reese, John Reilly, Liz Reilly, Rick Reilly, Bobby Richardson, Wanda Rickerby, Phil Rizzuto, Tim Robbins, Phil Alden Robinson, Gregory Rodriguez, Jim Rome, Carol Rose, Chris Russo, Emilio Sanchez, Richard Sandomir, Susan Sarandon, Dick Schaap, Jeremy Schaap, Dutch Schroeder, Vin Scully, Bud Selig, Diane K. Shah, Gail Sheehy, Pete Sheehy, Charlie Sheen, Ron Shelton, Bob Sheppard,

Blackie Sherrod, Ivan Shouse, Buck Showalter, Norm Siebern, T.J. Simers, Paul Simon, Marty Singer, Bill Skowron, George Solotaire, Lee Strasberg, Susan Strasberg, Ben Stein, George Steinbrenner, Sallie Taggart, Gay Talese, Don Tanner, J. Randy Taraborrelli, Joe Torre, John Tuthill, Peter Ueberroth, Keith Urban, George Vecsey, Sander Vanocur, Robert Vickrey, Fay Vincent, Don Wanlass, Tommy West, Ted Williams, Tom Wolfe, Clare Wood, Gene Woodling, Steve Wulf, Don Zimmer.

My appreciation to the entire staff of the Baseball Hall of Fame Museum Library in Cooperstown, New York, for their cooperation on so many levels. Thanks also to the library staffs of *TIME* and *Sports Illustrated, Newsweek, The Sporting News,* The Associated Press, the *Los Angeles Times, The New York Times,* the *New York Post,* the *New York Daily News, Newsday, The Washington Post,* the *Boston Globe,* the *Dallas Morning News,* the *Houston Chronicle,* the *Detroit Free Press,* the *Kansas City Star, The Oklahoman,* and the *Tulsa World;* ESPN Archives, MLB.com, the New York Yankees, the National Archives and Records Administration, the reference departments at the New York Public Library, the Beverly Hills Public Library, the Santa Monica Public Library, the Dallas Public Library, and the Library of Congress; and the administration of the Commerce [Oklahoma] Unified School District.

Special gratitude again goes out to my loyal noble muse, Jeter, the prince of all Labrador retrievers who has been at my side while I've written all six of my books published in the past decade. He is as much the "author" of those books as I am. Jeter passed away May 19, 2020. He was 10.

This book might never have been written without the inspiration and sacrifice of my wife, Renee. She knows my scribbling and ad-libbed shorthand so well that she is better than I in deciphering my notes. Her love and devotion make me a very lucky man.

Finally, my sons, Trey and Ryan, are always supportive of their old man when he disappears to write, even though it's not about their Dodgers. My thank you too, to their respective, loving spouses, Frances and Claudia. And now there is my grandson, Oliver, apparently either a pitcher or a quarterback, who has left his mark on my MacBook Air, if not on this book.

Bibliography

Allen, Maury. *Roger Maris: A Man for All Seasons.* New York: Donald J. Fine, 1986.

Appel, Marty. *Pinstripe Empire: The New York Yankees from Before the Babe to After the Boss.* New York: Bloomsbury USA, 2012.

Barra, Allen. *Yogi Berra: Eternal Yankee.* New York: W.W. Norton, 2009.

Berger, Phil. *Mickey Mantle.* New York: Park Lane Press, 1998.

Berkow, Ira. *Beyond the Dream: Occasional Heroes of Sports.* New York: Atheneum, 1968.

Yogi Berra, with Dave Kaplan. *Ten Rings: My Championship Seasons.* New York: William Morrow, 2003.

Bouton, Jim. *Ball Four.* New York: World Publishing, 1970.

Canale, Larry. *Mickey Mantle: The Classic Photography of Ozzie Sweet.* Richmond, Va.: Tuff Stuff Books, 1998.

Cannon, Jimmy. *Nobody Asked Me, But... The World of Jimmy Cannon.* Eds. Jack Cannon and Tom Cannon, New York: Holt, Rinehart and Winston, 1978.

Castro, Tony. *DiMag & Mick: Sibling Rivals, Yankee Blood Brothers.* Guilford, Ct.: Lyons Press, 2016.

———. *Gehrig & the Babe: The Friendship and The Feud.* Chicago: Triumph Books, 2018.

———. *Mantle: The Best There Ever Was.* Guilford, Ct.: Rowman & Littlefield, 2019.

_____. *Mickey Mantle: America's Prodigal Son.* Dulles, Va.: Brassey's Books, 2002.

Cataneo, David. *I Remember Joe DiMaggio: Personal Memories of the Yankee Clipper by the People Who Knew Him Best.* Nashville: Cumberland House Publishing, 2001.

Clavin, Tom. *The DiMaggios: Three Brothers, Their Passion for Baseball, Their Pursuit of the American Dream.* New York: Ecco, 2013.

Clavin, Tom and Peary, Danny. *Roger Maris: Baseball's Reluctant Hero.* New York: Touchstone, 2010.

Cramer, Richard Ben. *Joe DiMaggio: The Hero's Life.* New York: Simon & Schuster, 2000.

Creamer, Robert W. *Babe: The Legend Comes to Life.* Evanston, Ill.: Holtzman Press, 1984.

_____ & Sports Illustrated. *Mantle Remembered* (SI Presents). New York: Warner Books, 1995.

_____. *Stengel: His Life and Times.* New York: Simon and Schuster, 1984.

Daley, Arthur. *Kings of the Home Run.* New York: G. P. Putnam's Sons, 1962.

Durso, Joseph. *Casey: The Life and Legend of Charles Dillon Stengel.* Englewood Cliffs, NJ: Prentice-Hall, 1967.

Engelberg, Morris and Schneider, Marv. *DiMaggio: Setting the Record Straight. St. Paul, MN:* Motorbooks International, 2003.

Falkner, David. *The Last Hero: The Life of Mickey Mantle.* New York: Simon & Schuster, 1995.

Flynn, George. *Lewis B. Hershey, Mr. Selective Service.* Chapel Hill and London: University of North Carolina Press, 1985.

Ford, Whitey and Mantle, Mickey. *Whitey and Mickey: a Joint Autobiography of the Yankee Years.* New York: Viking Press, 1987.

Golenbock, Peter. *Dynasty: The New York Yankees, 1949–1964.* Chicago: Contemporary Books. 2000.

_____. *Wild, High and Tight: The Life and Death of Billy Martin.* New York: St. Martin's Press, 1994.

Gould, Stephen Jay. *Triumph and Tragedy in Mudville: A Lifelong Passion for Baseball.* New York: W. W. Norton & Co., 2003.

Greenberg, Hank. *Greenberg, Hank: The Story of My Life.* Ed. Ira Berkow. New York: Times Books, 1989.

Halberstam, David. *October, 1964.* New York: Villard Books, 1994.

Hart, Jeffrey. *When the Going Was Good: American Life in the Fifties.* New York: Crown Publishers, 1982.

Hines, Rick; Larson, Mark; & Platta, Dave. *Mickey Mantle Memorabilia,* Iola, WI: Krause, 1993.

Houk, Ralph, and Charles Dexter. *Ballplayers Are Human, Too.* New York: G.P. Putnam's Sons, 1962.

Kahn, Roger. *Beyond the Boys of Summer: The Very Best of Roger Kahn.* Ed. Rod Miraldi. New York: McGraw-Hill, 2005.

Kennedy, Kostya. *56: Joe DiMaggio and the Last Magic Number in Sports.* New York: Sports Illustrated, 2011.

Kubek, Tony, and Terry Pluto. *Sixty-One: The Team, The Record, The Men.* New York: Macmillan, 1987.

Lansky, Sandra and Stadiem, William. *Daughter of the King: Growing up in Gangland.* New York: Weinstein Books, 2014.

Leavy, Jane. *The Last Boy: Mickey Mantle and the End of America's Childhood.* New York: Harper, 2010.

Leinwand, Gerald. *Heroism in America.* New York: Franklin Watts, 1996.

Linn, Ed. *Hitter: The Life and Turmoils of Ted Williams,* New York: Harcourt Brace & Co., 1993.

Mann, Jack. *The Decline and Fall of The New York Yankees.* New York, Simon & Schuster, 1968.

Mantle, Merlyn, Mickey Jr., David and Dan. *A Hero All His Life,* New York: Harper Collins, 1996.

_____ with Gluck, Herb. *The Mick,* New York: Doubleday, 1985.

_____ and Herskowitz, Mickey. *All My Octobers,* New York: Harper Collins, 1994.

_____ and Pepe, Phil. *My Favorite Summer,* 1956, New York: Doubleday, 1991.

Maris, Roger, and Jim Ogle. *Roger Maris At Bat.* Des Moines and New York: Meredith Press, 1962.

McCarver, Tim, with Phil Pepe. *Few and Chosen: Defining Cardinal Greatness Across the Eras.* Chicago: Triumph Books, 2003.

McCarver, Tim, with Danny Peary. *The Perfect Season: Why 1998 Was Baseball's Greatest Year.* New York: Villard Books, 1998.

Murcer, Bobby, with Glen Waggoner. *Yankee for Life: My 40-Year Journey in Pinstripes.* New York: HarperCollins Publishers, 2008.

Pepitone, Joe, with Barry Stainback. *Joe, You Coulda Made Us Proud.* Chicago: Playboy Press, 1975.

Richardson, Bobby. *The Bobby Richardson Story.* Westwood, NJ: Fleming H. Revell, 1965.

Roberts, Randy and Smith, Johnny. *A Season in the Sun: The Rise of Mickey Mantle.* New York: Basic Books, 2018.

Robinson, Ray. *Iron Horse: Lou Gehrig in His Time.* New York: W.W. Norton & Co., 1990.

Rosenfeld, Harvey. *Roger Maris*: A Title to Fame.* Fargo, ND: Prairie House, 1991.

Schoor, Gene. *The Illustrated History of Mickey Mantle.* New York: Carroll & Graf, 1996.

Shecter, Leonard. *Roger Maris: Home Run Hero*. New York: Bartholomew House, 1961.

Smith, Marshall and Rohde, John. *Memories of Mickey Mantle: My Very Best Friend*. Bronxville: Adventure Quest, 1996.

Smith, Ron. *61*: The Story of Roger Maris, Mickey Mantle, and One Magical Summer*. St. Louis: Sporting News, 2001.

Stout, Glenn, ed. *Top of the Heap: A Yankee Collection*. Boston: Houghton Mifflin, 2003.

Vincent, Fay. *The Last Commissioner: A Baseball Valentine*. New York: Simon & Schuster, 2002.